THE
Homeschooling
Handbook

Revised 2nd Edition

MARY GRIFFITH

THE
Homeschooling
Handbook

Revised 2nd Edition

From Preschool

to High School,

a Parent s Guide

PRIMA PUBLISHING

Published by Prima Publishing, Roseville, California. Member of the Crown Publishing Group, a division of Random House, Inc., New York.

PRIMA HOME LEARNING LIBRARY and seal and PRIMA PUBLISHING and colophon are trademarks of Random House, Inc., registered with the United States Patent and Trademark Office.

Interior illustrations by Lisa Cooper

Library of Congress Cataloging-in-Publication Data

Griffith, Mary.
     Homeschooling handbook : from preschool to high school : a parent's guide / Mary Griffith. — Rev. 2nd ed.
          p. cm.
     Includes bibliographical references and index.
     ISBN 0-7615-1727-8
     1. Homeschooling—United States—Handbooks, manuals, etc.
     I. Title.   II. Title: Home schooling handbook.
     LC40.G75   1999
     371.04 ' 2—dc21   99-15075
                                                                          CIP

02 03 04 05 DD 10 9 8 7 6
Printed in the United States of America
Second Edition

Visit us online at www.primapublishing.com

CONTENTS

ACKNOWLEDGMENTS

One of the real pleasures of writing and eventually revising this book was working with the homeschooling parents who so willingly and articulately shared with me how their families homeschool: Karin Boosman, Lisa Medlen Bugg, Tammy Cardwell, Carolyn Clark, Deborah A. Cunefare, Laura Derrick, Alisanne Fleitman, Peggy Flints, Pam Hartley, Shari Henry, Linda Inouye, Beverly S. Krueger, Ava Miller, Cindy Sulaiman, and Grace Sylvan. Contributing additional material for the revised edition were Carol Burris, Tammy Glaser, Elizabeth Kanna, Monica Molinar, Barb Simonds, and Jennifer Tompkins. All were unfailingly helpful, eager to explain their own versions of homeschooling, and terrific reminders of why I so much appreciate and enjoy the homeschooling community.

Once again, thanks are due to the friends and colleagues from whom I've learned and continue to learn much of what I know about homeschooling (and many of whom also shared details of their homeschooling lives): Helen and Mark Hegener, Patrick Farenga, Micki and David Colfax, Donna E. Nichols, Ann Zeise, Linda Dobson, Janie Levine, Dianna Broughton, Sandra Dodd, Edith Touchstone, Anne Wasserman (known to homeschoolers on the Internet as "anne in chicago"), and Karl Bunday (who graciously allows me to include his ever-growing list of colleges friendly to homeschoolers); my dedicated fellow activists (and dear friends) from the Homeschool Association of California: Barbara David, Melissa Hatheway, Kim and Julie Stuffelbeam, Steve Greenberg, Diane Kallas, Lanis LeBaron, Carol Edson, Jill Boone, Lillian Jones, and Margaret Arighi; and the stimulating crowd of regular posters on the Home Ed and Unschooling Internet mailing lists and in the America Online homeschooling forums.

The folks at Prima Publishing continue to make the process of getting books ready for publication seem almost easy, especially Jamie Miller, Michelle McCormack, Laura Larson, and Leslie Ayers.

And still to thank are all those homeschooled kids—including my own daughters—who continue to provoke and exhaust and astonish and energize and amaze their parents. I am privileged to watch them learn and grow.

TERMS

Several terms are commonly used to refer to parents taking direct responsibility for their children's education by teaching them at home, and debate within the homeschooling community over which term is most appropriate is surprisingly lively.

Consider the basic choices: *unschooling; deschooling; home education;* and *home schooling, home-schooling,* or *homeschooling.* The choice is not as simple or as meaningless as it first appears.

Unschooling and *deschooling* are a bit confusing. *Unschooling* can mean the actual process of educating one's child outside the confines of a conventional school, and it can also be a specific approach to learning that emphasizes following the child's interests. Though all unschoolers are homeschoolers, not all homeschoolers are necessarily unschoolers. *Deschooling* can also mean the process of educating children outside the conventional classroom, but most often today it refers to the process of getting used to homeschooling. Many children and parents who are accustomed to learning taking place in a formal classroom setting need several weeks or months of "deschooling" to settle comfortably into a homeschooling routine.

Home education is not a bad choice. It's fairly inclusive, covering all kinds of homeschooling styles without seeming to imply that any one is more proper than others. It's a bit awkward, though, to adapt when you need to use a different part of speech, as with *home educators, home educated,* or *home educating.*

Home schooling, home-schooling, and *homeschooling* are actually all the same term, demonstrating differing levels of acceptance. The same thing happened with computer terminology a few years back. First there was *micro computer,* which gradually turned into *micro-computer* and, finally, *microcomputer.* (Of course, nobody talks about microcomputers much anymore, but that's a different story.) Academic articles about homeschooling still frequently use the two-word version, although the compound is making headway. The hyphenated version is becoming rarer, although it's still often seen in newspaper articles about homeschooling, often side by side with the other versions while copy editors waffle on the decision of which to use.

I adopted the compound version—*homeschooling*—years ago because it seemed less awkward than the others and was flexible enough to take on all the noun and verb and adjectival forms without too much trauma. Homeschoolers could homeschool their homeschooled children without an overabundance of hyphens or other confusion. As you can see, the meaning of the term varies: It can refer to the educational process itself, to the children who are the objects of that process, to the parents who choose that process for their children, and to the entire population of families who homeschool.

I also like the inference I can take from the compound version: *Homeschooling* somehow seems less formal and institutional a term than *home schooling*. It sounds more like its own meaning and less like a borrowed term than the others do.

Some homeschoolers, though, dislike the word and prefer something such as *home learning* or *homelearning* as more in line with their understanding of the concept. I've even heard of those who feel that *home* is too limiting and opt instead for *world learning* or some similar variant. Although such terms may be more in keeping with their users' views, they tend to keep those users constantly explaining what on earth they are talking about.

As David Guterson explains in his book *Family Matters*, *homeschooling* is an odd word for what it describes, but it does have the distinct advantage of being readily understood by the general public. That's a hard advantage to beat, and I won't even try.

INTRODUCTION

Announcement: "We're homeschooling our kids."
Response ten years ago: "You're doing what? What's that?"
Response today: "Oh, yeah? I know someone who does that. But
I could never do it myself—it would be so much work!"

Homeschooling has definitely arrived. From a few decades ago, when the practice was so rare that the word hadn't entered the language, homeschooling has become one of the fastest-growing educational movements in the country. Accurate estimates are hard to come by (some states make no counts of homeschoolers), but most experts agree that, as of 1995, at least half a million school-age children were getting their education from their parents, outside of schools. Some authorities put the number as high as a million and a half to two million. However they may dispute the total number of homeschoolers, those authorities agree that the homeschooling is growing rapidly, by as much as 20 percent annually in some regions.

On first encountering the idea of homeschooling, most parents find the whole concept peculiar at best and likely view it as something only a demented person would even consider. I know that I certainly thought homeschooling was a crazy idea when I first heard of it, before my children were even born. How could a parent possibly handle teaching all the things kids need to know by the time they graduate from high school? I certainly wasn't going to be interested in teaching precalculus or chemistry—they were hard enough for me to handle when I was in school. History and English would be easier, but still, the idea of coming up with all those lesson plans and keeping my kids focused on their work was daunting, to say the least. And wouldn't they suffer socially, without the give-and-take of school life, all the friends, all the school events and activities we take for granted?

Somehow, though, the idea stuck with me. I found myself fascinated by the ways my daughters found to constantly learn new things and astonished by the enthusiasm and tenacity they brought to everything they did. As they approached school age, I began to wonder what would happen to that eagerness and energy in school—it was not an attitude I connected with much of what I remembered of my own school days. Homeschooling began to sound like a very sensible idea, and I began seriously looking into homeschooling as an educational option for my daughters.

Where Did Schools and Homeschooling Come From?

Homeschooling is actually nothing new. Minus the name, it's been a commonplace part of rearing children for all but the last 150 years. Until well into the nineteenth century (and in some areas, even into the twentieth century), the family was the basis of social life. In a mainly agrarian society, the home was where children learned what was necessary to function in their community. This learning included everything from basic chores to enough reading and arithmetic to keep themselves from being cheated, how to grow and store their food, how to make a living, and even how to make their own dwellings and tools. Often, the local community supported a school for its children, but attendance was seldom mandatory. Family work—planting and harvesting on the farm, business and trade needs in urban areas—always took priority.

In the larger cities, schools were common enough that a majority of children attended some type of school, most often a private school that charged tuition (although many public schools also charged tuition). Such schools varied greatly, from the "dame schools" in which a few children were tutored in the teacher's parlor, to the small "academies" with classical pretensions, to larger, more formal private schools intended to prepare students (usually male) for serious college education.

With immigration and industrialization came the "common school" movement. Reformers such as Horace Mann in Massachusetts and Henry Barnard in Connecticut lamented that those who were most in need of education did not attend schools of any kind. They attributed the widespread poverty of the period not to the massive dislocations caused by the move from an agricultural to an industrial economy but, rather, to character flaws in the poor. With strong support from manufacturers and merchants, the reformers promised new public schools to produce workers who would be, as Mann said, "more orderly and respectful in their deportment, and more ready to comply with the wholesome and necessary regulations of an establishment." In 1852, Massachusetts established the first state compulsory school law, under which children who were not either working in factories or attending school could be convicted of the new crime of truancy. The school movement spread rapidly, despite protests from those who were unwilling to pay the new school taxes and those who found the heavily Protestant flavor of the new schools distasteful. (This period also saw the creation and rapid growth of the parochial school system, as Irish Catholic immigrants sought alternatives to the public schools whose overtly Protestant learnings clashed with their own beliefs.) By the end of the nineteenth century, compulsory school attendance was a given for most Americans.

The model for most of the public school systems created during the late nineteenth century was one we would easily recognize today. All students, rich or poor, attended the same schools, segregated into age-level groups to study a prescribed curriculum presented by an instructor specially trained for the job. Implicit in the curriculum, and an important part of it, were moral development and good work habits, through which the students would become capable workers and responsible citizens. Alternative approaches to education, such as those of Rudolf Steiner and his Waldorf schools or Maria Montessori, seldom made their way into public schools.

By the middle of this century, the idea that schools were a necessary condition for getting an education was firmly embedded in American society. Successive waves of school reformers questioned the content of the curriculum and whether schools should be educating for "good citizens" or "good workers" or even for outstanding intellectual accomplishment. New instructional techniques were explored, but the premise that schools were required for children to become competent adults was never seriously questioned.

There were always a few people who avoided compulsory schooling, however. Sometimes they were rural families, who lived too far from the nearest school to make regular attendance practical, or families whose livelihood required constant travel, or simply eccentrics who chose to teach their children themselves, despite whatever the local laws said. Somehow they managed to raise children who survived their lack of schooling, and some, such as Margaret Mead and Thomas Edison, did far better than merely survive.

In the 1950s and 1960s, a few of the then-current wave of reformers began to ask different questions. Ivan Illich questioned whether schools make us less competent by training us to depend on an outside authority to tell us what and how to learn. He asked how we could realistically expect authoritarian institutions such as schools to effectively teach democratic principles. Jonathan Kozol looked at both the structure and content of schools and argued that they effectively maintain racial and economic segregation. John Holt argued that children learn quite differently from the ways they are taught in school and that too much instruction actually hinders learning. Raymond Moore criticized the ever-earlier ages at which children begin school, arguing that formal academic work should not start until children are at least eight or ten years old.

Holt, after thinking and writing for years about ways to reform schools and teaching to make them more effective, ultimately decided that the task was impossible and began to advocate homeschooling as a solution. In 1977, he began publishing a magazine, *Growing Without Schooling,* to explain his ideas and found that he'd struck a nerve: By the tenth issue, he'd received more than ten thousand letters from parents looking for better ways to help their children learn.

During the 1980s, the homeschooling movement expanded in another direction with the closure (because of changes in tax regulations) of hundreds of small Christian schools. Parents who had turned to private church schools as refuge from the worldly orientation of public schools suddenly found homeschooling their only acceptable option (and dozens of curriculum companies who had served the Christian school market suddenly found they needed homeschool customers they'd previously scorned). This new wave of Christian homeschoolers was so large that the popular public image of homeschoolers became the caricature of the intensely religious family isolating their children from the world to protect them from the evils of evolution and sex education.

Over the last fifteen years, the number of homeschoolers has continued to grow rapidly. Homeschooling support groups report their memberships growing by 20 or 30 percent annually; some have actually doubled or tripled their membership from one year to the next. Once a rare and slightly oddball approach to education, homeschooling has become a widely known and accepted alternative.

Why Families Choose Homeschooling

Many families come to homeschooling the way I did, chancing on the idea from a book or a news article and finding it appealing enough that their kids never make it to school in the first place. Others choose homeschooling as the least awful available alternative: Their children have problems in school, they're worried about violence or drugs, a private school is too expensive or doesn't solve the problem. Or, more and more often today, parents know families who homeschool and find the example worth emulating. Most of us, though, find that our reasons become more complex the longer we keep at it. For whatever single reason we may have started, we soon discover that, beyond all the tangible advantages we expected, homeschooling becomes a way of life, an approach to living with our kids that is rewarding in itself.

Ask homeschooling parents why they homeschool, and you'll get lots of answers:

· · ·

We homeschool because we love it, but that is an answer that can only come from having done it. . . . I knew that the kids would get a better education, and it was really important to me that they keep their joyful interest in life and learning, that they know that they could accomplish anything they wanted to. . . . Years later, I would have to say that I homeschool because it is a way of life that I can support and that the kids are so much better prepared to deal with life, careers, families, friends, and higher education because of the time that they have spent with a variety of people of different ages. The old socialization question that we are always asked—well, now I say that is exactly why I homeschool. —*Jill*, California

· · ·

My husband always wanted to homeschool but I did not. When it came down to it, I decided to homeschool because God told me to (no, not in an audible voice, but I couldn't mistake it anyway). We would continue to homeschool for that reason if no other, but I have found far too many more reasons through the years to be willing to stop now. . . . It is important to me that my children learn to enjoy learning, and, quite frankly, I believe that is a difficult thing to achieve in a classroom situation. It is also important to me that they gain the skills they need to live in the real world, which I also see as a somewhat difficult goal to attain while locked away in a classroom. I desire curriculum and activities that are geared to their particular ability levels, interests, and aspirations, and these things can only be produced when all teaching/learning is done one on one. —*Tammy*, Texas

· · ·

We first considered homeschooling because my husband's job requires him to travel extensively and for long periods of time. It seemed like the only way for our family to stay together. As we have learned more and settled into homeschooling, it has become more and more an issue of personal freedom. . . . My children get the individual attention and the privacy they need, as well as the time to grow up unhurried. I have the great pleasure of seeing them learn and grow and of learning right alongside them. Sending them off every day to learn somewhere else would seem to me to be giving up one of the most joyful aspects of parenting.
—*Laura*, Texas

. . .

My primary reason for homeschooling is socialization. I want to let each of my children live, grow, and decide for herself who she is and what her beliefs are. I believe that the structure of school effectively prevents this, pure and simple. . . . I have many other reasons, some selfish. I love my kids, didn't come by them easily in either case, and enjoy their company. I want our family to decide the schedule we use—if we want one at all. I want to respect that Shauna is in a coma at 8 A.M. but fresh and alert at 10 P.M. I want Rosalie, who fatigues easily when reading (because of her corneal scarring), to read in short bits, when it fits for her. I want to plant two hundred flower bulbs in the front yard, get muddy, have a great time, and do it all in the middle of a Friday morning, right in front of God, the attendance officer, and anyone else who happens by. I want to see Shauna blooming as a writer, because no one is telling her how to do it. I love seeing my kids find amazing, inventive answers to real-life needs. To solve problems, both create things that they wouldn't have thought of if someone had rushed in with "the way everyone else does it."
—*Carol*, California

. . .

We homeschool because we honestly believe that schools are pointless and potentially dangerous, that they are a waste of time. We believe that schools cannot be "improved" to the point that we would think that they were a good place for our children to get an education. We believe that children, adults, anyone learns best by following their own interests and that human beings learn by immersion, from the time they are born. If I become interested in, say, harps, I immerse myself in it. I go to concerts; I buy harp music; I check out books from the library. I do not "study" a subject determined by some other person for one hour, then move on to another subject determined by some other person for another hour. I follow my own interests; I learn what I want to, when I want to, in the way I want to. While learning about harps, I will incidentally learn many other things. I will learn, perhaps, to read music. Or about the curing of wood to make harp frames. I might learn about another country and a period of time in which they made harps. Now I might not have had, at another time, an interest in learning to read music, for example. But if I become interested in playing beautifully on a harp, learning to read music will probably become necessary to reach that goal. In the same way, if children want to start a lawn-mowing business so that they can afford summer camp, they're going to want to learn something about math and finances to make that goal a reality. To me this is the essence of homeschooling; and it is the very thing that no school could possibly duplicate, even if it desperately wanted to. —_Pam_, California

. . .

It's a whole way of life that allows us to be together as a family and live our lives in a more meaningful way. Before, when our son was in school, he saw very little of his dad—that alone is reason enough. Once in a while, I'll tell (spout off to) people what I really think about the way kids are being raised by their peers in schools, but I try not to get into negatives too much, because it makes people uncomfortable. I think all those kids of the same age being together day in and day out is weird! And I think their behavior is weird! I think parents giving their kids away to strangers to raise is weird! —_Lillian_, California

. . .

When our oldest was five, I knew that she wasn't ready to be away from me, and I simply started telling people that we were

homeschooling, although I am sure that I didn't know anything about it at the time. When she was six, I just liked being around her so much that she continued to stay home. When she was seven, I thought that I really knew what homeschooling was all about, and because we were having fun, we kept doing it. I would say that my top two reasons for homeschooling are that I like to be around my two kids. After that, my reasons go way back to my own school experiences, which were not positive, and to my youngest brother, who graduated from our "model" school district an angry, violent, and illiterate young man. Once out of the institution, he learned how to read, operate computers, and run successful businesses. When he died, he was a successful man in every way, and none of it can be credited to his "education."
—*Barbara,* California

* * *

Our number one reason is that our educational philosophy is inconsistent with learning in a school setting. . . . Other important elements are the family environment, a less hectic pace of daily living, and flexible scheduling, so even if a learner-directed approach were somehow miraculously available in a school setting, we would not want to send our children there eight hours a day (maybe a few hours a week, though). . . . Amazingly, for a couple that used to agonize over every major decision and many minor ones, Brad and I had a lot of clarity on this one issue. As soon as we heard about it, it just made a lot of sense to both of us, and we have always felt it was the right decision for us. —*Linda,* Hawaii

* * *

Taking the Plunge

So, how do you decide whether you want to homeschool? Obviously, if you've picked up this book, you're at least intrigued by the idea. Equally obviously, you need a lot of information to help you decide. The rest of this book will tell you how homeschooling works for families who've been at it for years and for families who've just started. We'll talk about the academic research into its effectiveness, about the legal rules governing it, and about the variety of possible approaches to learning at home. We'll cover some practical aspects of homeschooling: where to look for materials, how much it can cost, and how to evaluate what you're doing. Most of all, we'll try to give you some idea of what homeschooling can be like from day to day and what you can typically expect at various stages of the process.

While you're reading this book, try to think about what you want for your children, what abilities and knowledge you'd like them to have as adults, and how homeschooling might help to achieve those goals. Think also about how your family works and what methods you would be comfortable with. It might help to consider the following questions and to reread them occasionally as you go through the book. These aren't questions you need to answer definitively or specifically before you ultimately decide, but thinking about how you might answer them will help you as you gather information and determine whether you want to take the plunge into homeschooling.

- Why are you considering homeschooling? Are your reasons educational, social, political, religious, or some combination of these? How will your reasons affect your family's approach to homeschooling? Your methods? Your choice of materials?

- Who will make the decisions about homeschooling? Can everyone in the family live with the consequences of those decisions?

- How would your children feel about the idea? How do their expectations compare with yours? Do they have friends and activities outside of school? Would homeschooling be a major adjustment for them?

- How do your friends and relatives feel about homeschooling? Will the feelings or opinions of others (friends, family, officials, "experts") cause problems for you? How will you deal with them?

- How much planning do you want to do? Can you trust yourself and your children to learn, or would some kind of packaged curriculum better suit your style?

- How will teaching your kids at home affect your life? What trade-offs will you have to make? Will the benefits be worth the sacrifices? Will money be a problem?

- And the absolutely determining question that you must consider seriously: Do you genuinely enjoy spending time with your children? This is not "Do you love your children?" or even "Do you like your children?" The question is whether you enjoy spending large amounts of time with your children every single day. No matter what your reasons for homeschooling are, homeschooling will not work if, aside from the normal, everyday squabbles and upsets we all go through, you do not enjoy each other's company most of the time.

CHAPTER ONE

Does Homeschooling Really Work, or What Do We Tell the Grandparents?

EXPERIENCED HOMESCHOOLERS—those who've been at it for at least a couple of years—often forget how scary the first year can be. New homeschoolers have so many new ideas to think about and so many possible options to consider, all while they're trying to make themselves comfortable with the idea of dispensing with such a traditional part of American childhood. No matter how attractive and plausible the idea of homeschooling sounds, it's hard to avoid that underlying worry about whether it's really a reasonable and effective means of education.

New homeschoolers may alternate between two extreme fantasies about the long-term results of choosing homeschooling for their families. The first may be prompted by some lovely late autumn afternoon spent watching your daughter patiently working with her younger brother to organize a collection of fallen leaves by shape and color. Maybe they'll grow up to be respected scientists, you think. Your daughter will go to medical school and eventually do research resulting in a cure for Alzheimer's. In her spare time, she will work as a volunteer with the Special Olympics and compose chamber music as a hobby. Your son will become a theoretical physicist and win the Nobel Prize for his work on tachyons and multidimensional, nonlinear time streams. In his spare time, he will work as a tutor in an adult literacy program and write critically acclaimed poetry. Both will marry and have equally brilliant and well-adjusted children. On your fiftieth birthday, your children will throw you a party, at which they announce that everything they are and have done they owe to you and to the fact that they were homeschooled.

The second fantasy is a bit different. This one is a natural for the cold, rainy morning when neither child can concentrate on anything, except for bickering with each other and complaining to you how boring their lives are. You realize that they will grow up to be nasty, mean individuals, illiterate and innumerate. They will each be fired from a succession of menial jobs. Your daughter will enlist in the Army but wash out of basic training. She will go on general assistance and write you frequent letters asking for money. Your son will join a bizarre survivalist cult living in Palo Alto and be under long-term FBI surveillance because of the frequent threatening letters he writes to savings and loan mortgage officers. On your fiftieth birthday, you will get letters from both of them complaining that everything they are and have done they owe to you and to the fact that they were homeschooled.

You realize intellectually that both fantasies are completely unrealistic, but your mother keeps asking you whether you're really sure about what you're doing to her grandchildren, and some of your friends tell you stories they've heard from other friends about people they've heard of who tried homeschooling and discovered that it just doesn't work. How do you know that you're doing the right thing, that you're not dooming your children to lives of poverty and ignorance? What is known about how well homeschooling works, anyway? And even if it works for most families who try it, how do you know it will work for your own family?

In this chapter, we'll try to answer some of these questions. We'll look at some of the formal research into homeschooling and its effectiveness and some of the reasons the research may not give us much useful information. We'll also talk about how homeschoolers view the effectiveness of homeschooling and what all this means for new or prospective homeschoolers trying to decide whether homeschooling will work for them.

Academic Research into Homeschooling

Numerous studies—master's theses, doctoral dissertations, and professional journal articles—have been done on homeschooling. I can't begin to cover all of them (and after the first few, they all start to sound the same, anyway), but in this section I'll give you a sample of the results they typically find. First, let's take a look at some research into the academic effectiveness of homeschooling:

- In a 1990 master's thesis, Mark Tipton compared the scores of eighty-one West Virginia homeschoolers on the Comprehensive Test of Basic Skills (CTBS) with those of conventionally schooled children. He found that the homeschooled third graders scored significantly higher on vocabulary, reading comprehension, mathematics concepts, science, and total mathematics; lower in spelling; and about the same in other areas. Homeschooled sixth graders scored higher in composite scores, vocabulary, reading comprehension, and total language and similarly in other areas. Homeschooled

> Numerous studies—master's theses, doctoral dissertations, and professional journal articles—have been done on homeschooling.

ninth graders scored higher in reading, lower in mathematics, and similarly in other areas. Homeschooled eleventh graders scored higher in reading and similarly otherwise. Tipton also found that the longer the period that families planned to continue homeschooling, the better their children's scores were.

- In 1992, Robert Calvery and others compared standardized test scores of 428 Arkansas homeschoolers with those of nearly 90,000 conventionally schooled students. They found that fourth- and seventh-grade homeschoolers scored higher than their schooled peers in math, reading, language, science, and social studies; tenth-grade homeschoolers scored higher in reading, math, science, and social studies, but lower in language.

- In a 1993 article, Maralee Mayberry looked at some of the variables known to correlate with successful learner outcomes, such as "an atmosphere of cooperation and interdependence" and "an orderly but warm and concerned learning environment," and found that many were common in homeschool settings.

- J. F. Rakestraw, looking at Alabama homeschoolers in 1987, and Jon Wartes, looking at homeschoolers in the state of Washington in 1990, both found that the possession or lack of a teacher credential by homeschool parents had no effect on educational outcomes for the homeschooled students.

- In the same study of Washington homeschoolers, Wartes also found no differences in educational outcomes between homeschooling families using a school-like teaching style and those with a less formal style of learning.

- Florida researcher Richard Medlin administered a battery of aptitude, achievement, and attitude tests to thirty-six homeschooled children. Comparing the scores on the different types of tests, he found that achievement test scores were higher than aptitude scores, and he concluded that the higher achievement test scores could not be credited solely to ability. Oddly, he also found that although a shorter school year and less formal teaching style correlated with higher scores, parents felt a greater degree of satisfaction with more formal programs.

Affective outcomes, or the social development of homeschooled students, is also a major topic of homeschooling research:

- April D. Chatham looked at the social contacts of Oklahoma twelve- to eighteen-year-olds in 1991. For a month, twenty-one homeschooled and twenty public school teens kept records of the number of people they talked with for at least two minutes. According to Chatham, the homeschooled students were not much different in the number of social contacts they had, but they did not feel as much support or closeness from their peers as the school students did.

- For his 1992 doctoral dissertation, L. Edward Shyers studied the social behavior and beliefs of eight- to ten-year-olds. He found that the children had similar views of themselves, whether schooled or homeschooled, but that children who had always been homeschooled showed significantly fewer behavior problems.

- In a review of existing homeschooling research published in 1991, Wartes and Brian Ray found that homeschoolers generally score as well or better than their schooled peers on tests of academic achievement and that homeschooled students are confident and well adjusted emotionally and socially.

And what about the long-term effects? How do homeschoolers fare in their adult lives? (This area of research is only starting to be explored because only recently have there begun to be large enough numbers of homeschooled adults to study.)

- J. Gary Knowles, in 1993, studied fifty-three adults who had been homeschooled. He found that none was unemployed or on public assistance and that, typical of the age group, two-thirds were married. A higher-than-average proportion were self-employed. More than 75 percent felt that homeschooling had enhanced their social skills, and 96 percent said they would choose to be homeschooled again if given a second chance at childhood.

Evaluating the Research

All that research sounds pretty good, doesn't it? The closest thing to a negative finding in that whole list is the Oklahoma study in which homeschoolers' peer friendships were less intense than schooled kids', and that could be easily explained by homeschoolers' normally close family relationships and their wider assortment of friends of all ages. But what about all the negatives of homeschooling? Where's the research that shows all the problems homeschooling can cause?

In fact, negative research on homeschooling is virtually non-existent. Subscribers to Internet mailing lists on homeschooling are occasionally greeted with frantic messages from graduate students doing literature searches or parents looking into homeschooling. "Where's the other side of the story?" they ask. Now and then, we'll hear of a family for whom homeschooling did not work, whose children returned to school. But the children simply returned to school; they did not continue struggling with an unsuccessful option to the point that the children became horrible object lessons for the dangers of home education. Homeschoolers are a self-selecting bunch—they don't continue homeschooling for years if it doesn't work for them.

So this lack of negative research means that homeschooling is an undisputedly successful and effective form of education, right? Not exactly. There are a number of problems with even the positive homeschooling studies—specifically, with the biases of the researchers, the population of homeschoolers available for study, and the tools researchers use to determine successful academic and affective outcomes.

First, let's look at how test populations for homeschooling studies are found. One obvious route for a researcher interested in homeschoolers would be to contact a state department of education to get a nice large random sample. Unfortunately, many states don't keep records of homeschoolers. Or, perhaps the state maintains records, but a sizable chunk of the state's homeschooling population doesn't bother to register with the state, thus skewing the available sample. Perhaps the researcher could find a suitable sample through a homeschooling support group or a magazine aimed at homeschoolers. Good idea, but homeschoolers often are not the least bit interested in cooperating with such studies.

Why not help with homeschooling research? Wouldn't most homeschooling families love to help prove the effectiveness of their educational choice? Part of their reluctance comes from some of the early studies attempted in the late 1970s and 1980s. All too often researchers showed up in homeschoolers' homes, armed with clipboards and stopwatches, prepared to observe the number of "on-task minutes" children spent in each academic subject area. They looked for classroom behaviors rarely found in home education settings and failed to notice the other kinds of learning taking place right in front of them. Naturally enough, the subjects of such studies developed an aversion to such intrusions.

Other homeschoolers of the period, which also saw many legal challenges to homeschooling, simply preferred to stay out of view for fear that their participation in research might somehow put them at risk for visits from local truant officers or social workers. Most homeschool support groups still decline to sell or rent their membership lists because of such fears, which are still common among some of their members.

In recent years, even when most researchers have a better idea of what to expect, it's common for homeschoolers to decline to participate in studies simply because of the increased interest in homeschooling. It's become practically a trendy topic for dissertations and theses, and homeschoolers quickly tire of hearing the same basic questions again and again. For them, researchers are a distraction and an interruption whose work is unlikely to be of enough interest to make it worth the disruption.

All right, now let's suppose our researcher has found a study sample of some kind, and he gets results similar to those of the studies described earlier. More evidence proving homeschooling works? Not yet. How does he know his sample is representative of the general homeschooling population? Maybe its members are all of the same socioeconomic level, all have graduate degrees, or all belong to the same church. Maybe it's not the homeschooling that accounts for those successful outcomes, but all that money and education the parents have or the values instilled by their religious beliefs. Or maybe the kind of homeschoolers who comply with state laws requiring testing or who volunteer for testing are just the kind of people who naturally do well on standardized tests.

Let's be kind and give our researcher the good, representative sample population he needs. Can we now rely on his results? Nope, we've still got problems. What about all the different styles of homeschooling? Families use dozens, even hundreds, of different texts and curricula, and those are bound to affect the test results. And those families with children who are late readers will skew the results for younger children, even though there may be no differences in skill levels and general outcomes once such children are older. Because of the variety of homeschooling approaches, different children attain skills and knowledge at widely varying ages, and one child's lack of knowledge in a particular area may mean very little in the long run. Because of such anomalies, evaluating test results can be very difficult.

> Because of the variety of homeschooling approaches, different children attain skills and knowledge at widely varying ages, and one child's lack of knowledge in a particular area may mean very little in the long run.

Finally, there is one huge obstacle researchers are unlikely ever to overcome. Learning is an incredibly individual and complex process; numerous variables—age, natural ability, instructional methods, determination, teacher rapport, parental support, sibling order, diet and exercise, humidity, and who knows what else—contribute to the mix. How do we know that the factor determining successful test scores is the homeschooling and not one of the other variables?

The only way to answer that question, to prove once and for all that homeschooling works, is to run a controlled experiment. Get a representative sample homeschooling population, carefully match for all those variables, if you can even figure out what they all are, and randomly assign families to either the homeschool group or the control group that attends school. Let everybody go about their learning for several years, and see which group performs better. It's not likely to happen, of course, even if all the variables could be controlled—few, if any, homeschooling families would be willing to take the chance of being picked for the control group.

Besides, even if such an experiment were possible, we could still argue for years about the tests and other tools used to measure "success" and whether those tools truly give us any meaningful information. But debating the virtues and pitfalls of standardized testing and other forms of evaluation is far beyond the scope of this book.

Despite all that positive research on homeschooling, we simply can't prove that it really works. We know that most homeschoolers are proficient learners, that they are good with people and grow up to lead normal and successful lives as adults. Many homeschoolers firmly believe that withdrawing their children from school was the only way to save them from tremendous difficulties in school and in later life. But there's no way to prove that any homeschooled students wouldn't have been just as successful and turned out just as well if they'd gone to school.

The research is handy for bragging and for giving to skeptical in-laws, curious reporters, or dubious school officials when they question our judgment in choosing homeschooling. All those mean average scores and standard deviations sound terribly impressive and definitive, and homeschoolers are not above citing them in situations in which that's the sort of information people want to hear. But homeschooling research has a long way to go before it tells us anything very meaningful. Aggregates cannot tell us about individuals. For homeschoolers, the question to answer is not "Does homeschooling work?" The real question is "Can homeschooling work in our family?"

The Homeschoolers' Version

How do you figure out whether homeschooling will work for your family? You might try the anecdotal approach. The first step is to find out as much as you can about it. Read general books, such as this one, about homeschooling, and some personal accounts of how particular families have gone about it. Take a look at homeschool resource guides and catalogs and magazines to see the kinds of materials that are available. Talk to homeschoolers about what they do. Ask them why they think it works for them. See which approaches appeal to you and how the homeschoolers put those approaches into practice.

Academics

Strangely enough, academics are often the least worrisome aspect of homeschooling, and even homeschooling skeptics won't much argue the point. When you spend time with your children, as homeschoolers do, you quickly get a feel for how well they learn. In many cases, their learning seems an almost spontaneous process, occurring independently of, or even despite, whatever formal instruction you provide. You may find that some materials won't be right for your kids or that they'll want a different teaching style from the one you want to use, and you'll need to devote some trial and error to finding the right mix for all of you. You may also find that your perfect set of materials, which was so wonderful for your first child, is vehemently rejected by the next and viewed with complete indifference by the third.

You'll find, though, that you don't need to be an expert in every subject your children learn, nor will you need special training to help them learn. What you'll need is patience, a willingness to answer questions, and the energy to show them how to learn for themselves. It's rather like the old "Teach a man to fish . . ." line. Show your children how to learn what they need to know, and you'll not be able to stop them. Give them the tools and resources with which to learn, and with practice and a bit of concentration, they can handle the rest.

The "S" Word

Homeschooling skeptics will often concede that academics are seldom a problem for homeschoolers, but they'll always come through with "But what about socialization?" This question is so common that many experienced homeschoolers can hardly restrain themselves from spluttering or giggling whenever they hear someone start to ask it, and they'll often finish the question and be halfway through a detailed response before the questioner can take a breath.

• • •

The homeschool setting is ideal for socialization. In classroom settings, children are locked away for eight hours a day with thirty or so of their peers and, as a result, are deprived of the chance to interact with those outside their own age group. The homeschooling setting, on the other hand, provides the child with opportunities to interact with people of all ages, occupations, and interests, which tends to result in well-rounded, sociable, confident individuals.
—*Tammy,* Texas

> Show your children how to learn what they need to know, and you'll not be able to stop them.

• • •

Shauna has a number of adult friends, based on shared interests. Rosie has several groups of girls that she is the ringleader of, at church, dance, and singing group. They are comfortable and polite in most situations and can hold up their end of conversations. —*Carol,* California

• • •

Socialization is, really and truly, a complete nonissue. People worry about it and they shouldn't. Not even a little bit. Unless you lock your children in the basement, they will get "socialized."

There are so many opportunities that I cannot even fathom considering school as one of them: Scouts, church groups, 4-H, various classes, neighborhood kids—the list is endless. And, as I always say, "Oh, socialization? Yes, we're very concerned about that—that's why our kids won't go to school!" —*Pam*, California

. . .

We're very well socialized, thank you. I think kids, generally speaking, are bad for other kids. They may like each other, but they like chocolate, and I wouldn't let them eat all they wanted. Between swimming, neighbors, dance, Sunday school—well, they've got enough of what the world calls socialization. —*Shari*, Alabama

. . .

I have to put the answering machine on during the weekend so Ethan can play in peace with whichever friend is over visiting! I do wish he had more homeschooling friends he really enjoyed, though—most of his favorite friends go to school. —*Lillian*, California

. . .

I am strongly opposed to peer segregation. My kids are known for their ability to talk with adults, all except for the four-year-old, who's the strong, silent type. When my kids are grown up, they will have to deal with people of varying ages. Can you imagine having to work only with those people who were your own age? "I'm sorry, ma'am, we only have positions open for forty-two-year-olds. You might try the XYZ Company—they employ thirty-seven-year-olds." My kids also relate well to children of all ages. The oldest will play dolls with the younger girls. The older kids read books to the younger ones. They all play Oregon Trail together on the computer.

One of the big changes in our family that has come from homeschooling is the way our children treat each other. We were beginning to have problems with the older two girls. The younger wanted to be with the older, who would tell her to leave her alone. The older treated the younger as a burden on her life. When we began homeschooling in Indiana, they only had each other to play with. You can't continue treating your only playmate like dirt. When we made our decision to allow our oldest daughter to return to school, I told her that if the way she treated her family reverted back, she would be pulled out of school faster than she could blink her eyes. One thing I was not willing to sacrifice to her desire to be in school was our family unity. Thankfully, this has not happened. All of the kids do fight occasionally, but they get along well for the most part. They are learning to accept that each of us has strengths and weaknesses. As a family we encourage each other in our strengths and help each other in our weaknesses. —*Beverly,* Nebraska

. . .

My wife is outgoing and I'm very reserved. Emily seems to have combined both of these qualities into a safe, workable approach to life. When she encounters a new experience, she carefully checks it out, and then, when she feels safe, she dives into it. She has plenty of friends and opportunities to be out in the world. She is healthy and happy. —*Doug,* California

. . .

When my friends began to send their kids to nursery school, I began to get an inkling of what school socialization was about. They had various problems—bringing home rude new behaviors, bad attitudes, etc. One friend was focused on academics and sent her daughter to a slightly academic preschool. Well, her daughter began to fall behind my daughter academically; up to that point, they'd been neck and neck, only two weeks apart in age, and good friends.

My daughter is friendly, plays well with kids of all ages, plays well with her little brother. They have at times been almost inseparable, which I worried about for a second or two before realizing that it wouldn't be that way by the time they were grown. They keep each other company, share willingly, and work together on projects. I'm thankful they've been able to have that experience and continue to share that bond. They are both polite (because we parents treat them politely) and are usually willing to speak clearly to anyone, adult or child.

In a way, I'd say that we don't just have them home to shelter them from some bad experiences, but to have good experiences.

If I took a seedling, put it in a greenhouse, and then slowly acclimated it to the outdoors, it would thrive well—better than one started outside in the "real" world—and better than one that was sheltered so much that the outside world was shocking. I feel we've got a good balance of our outside activities and friends, and lots of time to be together and do things as our interests dictate. —*Grace,* California

• • •

Will Homeschooling Work for You?

One of the most profound lessons schools teach us, perhaps unintentionally, is to rely on other people's judgment of our accomplishments. Few of us get through twelve or sixteen years of schooling without being thoroughly trained to seek other people's approval for our work. Partly this is simply human nature, the desire to have people we respect value and respect us. But all too often, after years of seeking teachers' approval for hundreds of school assignments and validation of our accomplishments by high achievement test scores and admission to prestigious universities, we become dependent on the judgment of experts and authority figures. Those of us who do not achieve those high academic goals that schools encourage us to pursue often end up feeling like second-place finishers, even when we lead perfectly happy and useful lives in other arenas. We begin our adult lives somewhat at a loss, hesitant or even unable to determine our own interests and goals. Sometimes it takes us years to discover what competent and capable people we are and to learn to trust our own judgment of our skills and accomplishments.

For many parents, this is the most difficult aspect of homeschooling. Myriad resources are available for homeschooling families to learn with: commercially prepared curricula, textbooks, community institutions such as libraries and museums, homeschooling organizations, magazines, and lots of self-proclaimed homeschooling authorities who will feel free to tell you their version of the best, most effective way to homeschool. And there will be the traditional educators who try to persuade you that the only effective homeschooling program will be one that duplicates the school experience as closely as possible. Despite all that advice and opinion, though, the burden ultimately falls on you to decide how homeschooling can work for you.

You are the person who knows your children best, who is best equipped to recognize their interests and abilities, who cares most about their well-being, their happiness, and their ultimate success in finding a place for themselves in our society. Your main concern is not maintaining high average test scores or covering a certain number of chapters in a certain number of textbooks within a certain period of time. Your concern is that your children end up as the kind of people you'd like to see them become, with the kind of education you'd like them to have.

> Your concern is that your children end up as the kind of people you'd like to see them become, with the kind of education you'd like them to have.

To decide whether homeschooling works for you, you'll have to figure out what that means. Do you have specific academic goals for your children? Should they learn specific mathematical concepts, read certain books, and develop particular skills to be educated? Are your goals focused more on skills—that your children should be able to devise a household budget or a market plan, write coherently and persuasively, and analyze facts and ideas at a certain level of complexity? Or perhaps your goals are less concrete, and you want your children to be able to set their own goals and be able to work toward them effectively.

Whether your goals are some combination of these or something else entirely, you'll need a fairly clearly defined idea of what they are to decide whether homeschooling works for you. Without any idea of where you are going, or trying to go, you will be vulnerable to each and every expert and authority who comes along to tell you what you and your family ought to be doing, or to any story homeschoolers tell you of what worked or didn't work for their families.

One thing that surprised me when I started speaking at homeschooling conferences and workshops, usually to new and prospective homeschoolers, was the hunger for specific advice on what to do. How much television should I let my children watch? Which books should I allow (or require, or forbid) them to read? How many arithmetic problems should my six-year-old daughter do each day? What science experiments should my children be doing? It was strange and sad and a bit unnerving to be asked those questions, as though my answers, because my name was printed in a conference program, would naturally be better than their own.

> You can ask for as much advice and as many opinions as you want, but it's your job to sort these out and decide what your family needs.

It's scary, though, learning to trust your own judgment and instincts. If you rely on experts—listen carefully to every detail of their instructions and follow them to the letter—and don't like the results, you can always blame them for the problems. It's not your fault that their advice was so terrible. And after all, they were experts. How could you have been expected to know it wouldn't work?

Homeschooling requires you to take on the responsibility yourself. You become your own expert, your own authority. You can ask for as much advice and as many opinions as you want, but it's your job to sort these out and decide what your family needs. After a few months' practice, you'll laugh at how scary it seemed when you were starting out, and you'll wonder why you thought homeschooling sounded like such a heavy responsibility. It's a serious responsibility, certainly, but it's also a liberating one to realize that no one but you can decide whether homeschooling can work for you and that you'll enjoy the process of figuring it all out.

CHAPTER TWO

Legal Stuff, or Can We Really Do This?

NO SINGLE ASPECT of homeschooling worries new homeschoolers more than its legality. You might be concerned that you won't be able to handle the burden of responsibility for directing your children's education. You might question your ability to choose appropriate materials for your kids or wonder whether homeschooling might turn them into eccentrics or oddballs. But nothing else prompts quite the same level of outright fear—that dreadful vision that one day a truant officer or social worker will show up at your door with the news that your homeschooling is against the law and you are in big trouble.

For most of us, homeschooling is such a big step, so foreign to our own educational experience, that even when we have read the applicable laws and understand how they work in our state, we still harbor a nagging, irrational fear that someone will, somehow, for some reason, force us to send our children to school or even remove them from our custody. In almost every case, this fear is unwarranted. Intellectually, new homeschoolers usually understand this. Grasping the concept emotionally is another matter entirely. But as your first year of homeschooling proceeds without those menacing officials appearing at your doorstep, that anxiety will begin to dissipate. When the beginning of the next year rolls around, you probably won't even remember that undercurrent of dread that used to nag at you.

Is homeschooling a legal educational option? The short answer, of course, is yes. But the complete answer is considerably more complex. Some states are undeniably easier places than others for homeschoolers to comply with the law, and there are sometimes variations in how laws are applied from county to county and district to district. It's not uncommon to find considerable differences between what the law says and how it is applied and enforced. And legislatures and education departments make changes in the statutes and regulations governing homeschooling often enough to prompt homeschooling organizations and individuals to pay close and regular attention to their state's legal situation for homeschooling.

In this chapter we'll take a good look at the rules that govern homeschooling and try to give you enough information to make the legal aspects of homeschooling less daunting. We'll look at the legal roles of government and of parents in children's education, and at a few examples of homeschooling laws and how they work. Then we'll talk about how to learn about the legal situation in your state and what resources are available for the rare cases when legal help becomes necessary. Finally, we'll take a peek at the sometimes volatile mixture of homeschooling and politics and the possible consequences for homeschooling families.

The State's Interest in Education

Until the wide success of the common school movement in the latter half of the nineteenth century, education was primarily a matter of parental discretion. Parents decided what their children needed to learn to become competent adults. They decided what to teach at home, whether children should be apprenticed for vocational training, and if and when their children should attend some sort of formal school. With the advent of universal free public education came compulsory attendance statutes and truancy regulations. By the beginning of this century, every northern state had its own compulsory school attendance statute, and the southern states were rapidly following the trend. By the 1920s, the shift from the family to the state as the dominant authority on the education of children was so complete as to escape much notice or comment.

In 1923 came the first of three major court cases limiting the power of government to control education. A Nebraska statute forbade teaching any modern foreign language to any student who had not completed eighth grade, and a private school instructor appealed his conviction for teaching German. In *Meyer v. Nebraska,* the U.S. Supreme Court overturned the conviction, citing the instructor's right to teach, the student's right to learn, and the parents' right, within limits, to determine what their children should be taught. Although formally recognizing the "power of the State to compel attendance at some school and to make reasonable regulations for all schools," the Court ruled that Nebraska's statute was an unreasonable and arbitrary restriction of due process rights under the Fourteenth Amendment.

The Court further acknowledged the rights of parents regarding their children's education in the landmark *Pierce v. Society of Sisters* in 1925. Invalidating an Oregon statute requiring all children to attend public schools, with no private education options whatsoever, the Court said:

> The fundamental theory of liberty upon which all governments in this Union repose excludes any general power of the State to standardize its children by forcing them to accept instruction from public teachers only. The child is not the mere creature of the State; those who nurture him and direct his destiny have the right, coupled with the high duty, to recognize and prepare him for additional obligations.

In *Farrington v. Tokushige,* in 1927, the Court ruled against Hawaii in its attempts to enforce assimilation and "Americanization" of its diverse population by stringent private school regulations. Where such regulations effectively eliminate the distinctions between public and private schools, the Court said, "they deny both owners and patrons [of private schools] reasonable choice and discretion in respect to teachers, curriculum, and textbooks" and constitute a violation of parents' fundamental right under the Due Process Clause to direct their children's education.

In 1972, the Supreme Court gave further support to parental rights with its decision in *Wisconsin v. Yoder,* reversing the conviction of Amish parents who refused on religious grounds to send their teenage children to school. The Court ruled as follows:

> Government interest in universal education is not totally free from a balancing process when it impinges on fundamental rights and interests, such as those specifically protected by the Free Exercise Clause of the First Amendment, and the traditional interest of parents with respect to the religious upbringing of their children. . . .

So what do all these cases mean for homeschooling families? Basically, any government regulations affecting "fundamental" rights are subject to what is known as the "strict scrutiny" test, in which the rights of the affected individuals are balanced against the interests of the government. The government must demonstrate that it has a "compelling interest" in any action it takes that affects fundamental rights, that the action is necessary to promote that interest, and, finally, that it is the "least restrictive means" of doing so. For rights that are less than fundamental, courts use the "rational basis" test: Does the government have a "reasonable" interest in its action, and is its action "reasonably related" to that interest?

Because parents have a fundamental right to direct their children's education, statutes concerning education must pass the strict scrutiny test: The government must demonstrate that a disputed statute furthers its legitimate interest in promoting the education of children; furthermore, it must prove that there are no less burdensome ways to promote that interest. Hence, although private education in general is clearly protected as a fundamental due process right, home education specifically is not. Though at least two lower courts have ruled that home education is a fundamental right, the U.S. Supreme Court has not yet been faced with that specific question, and homeschooling statutes are, for the most part, still subject to review under the less stringent reasonable basis test.

State Homeschooling Laws

Although the federal government definitely plays a role in American education today, particularly in the strings attached to the funds it distributes to states and to local school districts, the specific rules regulating school attendance are the province of each individual state. States generally require students to attend public school between the ages of seven and sixteen, unless they fall into one of several exempt categories. The upper and lower ages vary somewhat from state to state and are often tinkered with by legislatures, although no state requires school attendance beyond the age of eighteen. The exempt categories typically include private school attendance, private tutoring by a credentialed teacher, and sometimes physical or mental disabilities that make attendance impossible. Successful completion of high school usually also exempts students from school attendance, although some states require children younger than fourteen or fifteen to continue some sort of school attendance or regular instruction.

State education statutes also regulate details of public school operations such as the number of days of instruction, the qualifications of teachers, and the course of study that must be provided. Some states apply some of these regulations to private school programs as well; other states leave private

schools relatively free from state oversight. What the rules are and how they affect homeschoolers varies considerably across the country, and we'll look at those next.

Although homeschooling is legal in one form or another in every state, not all states have statutes specifically covering situations in which parents directly provide their children's education. Some states consider homeschooling to be a form of private education, subject to the same rules and regulations governing conventional private schools. Some states regulate homeschooling directly, requiring anything from a simple registration form to lengthy descriptions of the curriculum, complete with lesson plans and texts used. Some states just want to know when families are homeschooling; others want families to get permission to homeschool from local school officials. Some states require periodic evaluation of homeschooled students by achievement tests or other means, just for statistical purposes or to determine whether students should be allowed to continue homeschooling.

Originally, I had planned to include an appendix giving basic information about the homeschooling laws of each state, but I quickly realized that such summaries would be more misleading than helpful. Many states' laws are quite complex, with several options to choose from. Often living with a particular law is much different from what a common sense reading of the applicable statutes would lead you to expect, and how laws are enforced can depend on who is doing the enforcing in any given year. Rather than risk giving you misleading or incomplete information about the homeschooling laws of your state, I'll describe some typical statutes and how they work. Later on, I'll tell you where to find information for your state and how to determine its accuracy.

Homeschooling Statutes

Most individuals new to homeschooling assume that living in a state that explicitly recognizes homeschooling as a permissible educational option would be preferable to living in a state that does not.

This is not necessarily the case. One basic lesson to be learned in looking at home education statutes is that when words such as *homeschooling* or *home education* are defined in legislation, somebody in the government suddenly has the power to regulate. Once homeschooling is recognized in the law, the state can define, evaluate, restrict, and otherwise involve itself in determining what homeschoolers are and aren't permitted to do. Whether a homeschooling statute is more or less restrictive has a lot to do with the relative strengths of the mainstream education lobbies and homeschooling organizations, the numbers of homeschoolers, and the general social traditions of the state in question.

Let's start our look at some examples of homeschooling statutes with a relatively bureaucratic one, and then move on to some of the less intimidating statutes.

Pennsylvania

Pennsylvania's homeschool statute, enacted in 1986, is one of the more complicated and detailed sets of homeschooling regulations in the United States. Unless a parent holds a valid Pennsylvania teacher credential, in which case she need only file a copy of her teaching certificate and a criminal history record with the local school district, she's in for a great deal of paperwork. Specifically, the supervisor of a home education program (the child's parent or guardian) must file an affidavit annually with the local school superintendent at the beginning of the program and every August 1 thereafter. The affidavit must provide the name of the supervisor, the names and ages of the children, and the address and phone number where the program takes place. In addition, the supervisor must attach evidence of required immunizations (or medical or religious exemptions) and an

> Whether a homeschooling statute is more or less restrictive has a lot to do with the relative strengths of the mainstream education lobbies and homeschooling organizations, the numbers of homeschoolers, and the general social traditions of the state in question.

outline of education objectives by subject matter. The statute also specifies the content of a home education program:

> At the elementary school level, the following courses shall be taught: English, to include spelling, reading, and writing; arithmetic; science; geography; history of the United States and Pennsylvania; civics; safety education, including regular and continuous instruction in the dangers and prevention of fires; health and physiology; physical education; music; and art.
>
> At the secondary school level, the following courses shall be taught: English, to include language, literature, speech and composition; science; geography; social studies, to include civics, world history, history of the United States and Pennsylvania; mathematics, to include general mathematics, algebra and geometry; art and music; physical education; health and safety education, including regular and continuous instruction in the dangers and prevention of fires. Such courses of study may include, at the discretion of the supervisor of the home education program, economics; biology; chemistry; foreign languages; trigonometry; or other age-appropriate courses.

This much gets a family started with homeschooling in Pennsylvania. The program supervisor must also maintain a portfolio of records and materials for each student, the details of which are also outlined in the statute:

> The portfolio shall consist of a log, made contemporaneously with the instruction, which designates by title the reading materials used, samples of any writings, worksheets, workbooks or creative materials used or developed by the student; and in grades three, five, and eight, results of nationally normed standardized achievement tests in reading/language arts and mathematics or the results of Statewide tests administered in these grade levels.

Furthermore, the portfolio must be reviewed annually by a licensed clinical or school psychologist, a Pennsylvania-certified teacher with evaluation experience, or a private school teacher or administrator with evaluation experience. The evaluator must provide a written report that certifies that "an appropriate education is occurring," which is turned in to the school superintendent along with the portfolio at the end of each public school year. (The superintendent can also ask for this material at any time during the school year on fifteen days' notice for the portfolio and thirty days' notice for the evaluation.) If the superintendent decides the program is inadequate, he can ask for deficiencies to be corrected within twenty days, after which a hearing by an impartial examiner can be held to evaluate the program. If the home education program is found to be inadequate, the children are enrolled in a public or private school, and the parents are barred from supervising a home education program for one year.

Depending on the local school district and the psychologist or teacher who serves as evaluator, complying with the Pennsylvania requirements can be much less painful than it sounds. Even under the best conditions, though, Pennsylvania's homeschooling rules are some of the most burdensome in the country.

South Carolina
South Carolina's compulsory attendance statute requires all students between six and seventeen (or high school graduation) to attend a public school; a state-accredited private school; a parochial, denominational, or church-related school; or some other state board–approved program. Some South Carolina homeschoolers charter as private schools, although some school districts do not regard this as a legal alternative to the specific homeschool statute.

Homeschooling programs are defined and allowed under two sections of the South Carolina education code. Under the first option, parents can teach their children at home with the approval of the school district board of trustees. The school board "shall approve" programs in which the following criteria are met:

- The parent holds at least a high school diploma or GED certificate.

- Instruction occurs at least four and a half hours per day for at least 180 days.

- The curriculum includes, but is not limited to, reading, writing, mathematics, science, and social studies, and in grades seven to twelve, composition and literature.

- Records, including a lesson plan or record book, student work samples, and records of student progress evaluations, are maintained for school district inspection on reasonable notice, and semiannual reports of student attendance and progress are submitted to the school district.

- Students have access to library facilities.

- Students participate in the state's annual assessment tests.

- Parents sign a waiver releasing the school district from liability for any educational deficiencies that might result from home instruction.

If homeschool students do not meet the promotion standards for their grade (determined by the state test scores), the school district can place the child in a public school or in a special education program or provide instructional support for the home education program. In such cases, the parent still has the option to enroll in a private or religious school instead.

The second homeschooling option under South Carolina law is to homeschool as a member and under the auspices of the South Carolina Association of Independent Home Schools (SCAIHS). The statute requirements for parent qualifications, instructional days, and areas of instruction are the same as for the district-approved option, but

SCAIHS adds a few requirements of its own, in a quest for what it calls "voluntary accountability." Specifically, SCAIHS requires that its staff review the curriculum, that parents attend a SCAIHS orientation in September; that a daily or weekly record book be kept along with a student work portfolio; that quarterly, midyear, and year-end attendance and progress reports be submitted; that students take annual achievement tests; that an annual tuition fee be paid; and so on. Failure to comply can result in the revocation of membership and loss of this option as a legal alternative.

In mid-1996, as a result of lobbying efforts by homeschoolers dissatisfied with the restrictive policies of SCAIHS, the South Carolina legislature authorized additional homeschool organizations to supervise homeschoolers under this provision of the statute. According to one active South Carolina homeschooling parent:

. . .

There's a much better climate for homeschooling here now. Many new associations have started, and the relationship between these smaller regional associations and the local school districts, for the most part, is very good. School personnel and truancy officers appreciate being able to deal with local folks when problems come up, and more school personnel are referring parents to the associations in their area. I'd describe the climate as much more welcoming. —*Dianna,* South Carolina

. . .

Washington

The homeschooling statute of the state of Washington is considerably friendlier than those of Pennsylvania and South Carolina. The compulsory attendance statute, covering children from eight to eighteen, includes a specific exemption for "home-based instruction":

Instruction shall be home-based if it consists of planned and supervised instructional and related educational activities, including a curriculum and instruction in the basic skills of occupational education, science, mathematics, language, social studies, history, health, reading, writing, spelling, and the development of an appreciation of art and music, provided for a number of hours equivalent to the total annual program hours per grade level established for approved private schools.

The statute also lists the four different ways parents can qualify to teach their children at home:

1. Possess forty-five college quarter credit hours or the equivalent in postsecondary education.
2. Work under the supervision of a certified teacher who has at least one contact hour per week with the children being instructed.
3. Be "deemed qualified" by the local school superintendent.
4. Take a class in home-based instruction at a postsecondary institution or vocational/technical school.

Parents must file an annual declaration of their intent to homeschool; ensure that records of test scores, immunizations, annual progress reports, and so forth, are kept to be forwarded to any school the child may transfer to; and ensure that annual evaluations of student progress are made, by means of either a standardized achievement test or a written assessment by a certified teacher. Students must demonstrate "reasonable progress," but the law does not explain either what reasonable progress is or who should determine whether it is being made. The final paragraph of the statute explaining home-based education confirms the law's relatively friendly intent:

The legislature recognizes that home-based instruction is less structured and more experiential than the instruction normally provided in a classroom setting. Therefore, the provisions . . . of this section relating to the nature and quantity of instructional and related educational activities shall be liberally construed.

Local school districts have no power to regulate the content or style of a home-based education program; only the letter of intent is filed with the district, mainly as a matter of record in case someone reports a homeschooled child as possibly truant. School districts do, however, provide homeschoolers with such services as special education, occupational and physical therapy, speech therapy, and so on. Participation in school sports is allowed, as is part-time classroom attendance.

Private School Statutes

Private school statutes take several forms. Some states explicitly recognize homeschooling as a category of private education; others define private schools vaguely or generally enough so that homeschooling is encompassed within that definition. Beyond that, states may regulate private schools fairly closely (at least within the limits of the constitutional principles covered earlier) or hardly at all. In the more regulatory states, homeschooling under a private school statute is not much different from doing so under an explicit homeschooling statute. In the less restrictive states, homeschooling under a private school statute is almost completely free of government oversight.

> Some states explicitly recognize homeschooling as a category of private education; others define private schools vaguely or generally enough so that homeschooling is encompassed within that definition.

California

California provides homeschoolers with several options. Quite a few public school home study programs and charter schools cater to homeschoolers. These vary in popularity depending on current state restrictions for such independent study programs, although they have the indisputable advantage of being clearly a legal option for homeschoolers.

The compulsory attendance statute requires school attendance for children from six to eighteen, with the usual exceptions for private school students and students tutored by a certified teacher. California homeschoolers who are not enrolled in public school programs must fit into these categories.

The tutoring option requires that the tutor hold a current state teaching credential for the grades being taught. "Instruction and recitation in the several branches of study required to be taught in the public schools," in English, must occur at least three hours a day, between 8 A.M. and 4 P.M., for 175 days each year. No notice of intent, registration, or evaluation with either the state (except for that required for the teaching credential) or the local school district is required.

Private schools in California are required to file an annual affidavit with the state department of education, giving the name and address of the school and its directors and administrators, and the number of teachers and students in the school. The statute requires that private schools keep records of the courses offered; faculty names, addresses, and qualifications to teach; and student attendance. Private schools must also provide instruction in the general subject areas taught in the public schools: English, mathematics, social sciences, science, fine arts, health, and physical education at the elementary level, plus they should offer courses in foreign languages, applied arts, vocational and technical education, and drivers' education at the secondary level.

Although numerous provisions of the state code specify minimum standards for school buildings, such as those for lighting, fire and earthquake safety, and so on, most apply only to schools with fifty students or more. There are no requirements for the type of building smaller private schools must use, and there is in fact a state court ruling that applies:

The word "school" has varying connotations . . . it may mean, among other things, the building in which instruction is given, or the assemblage within a building set aside for the purpose of instruction, or the combination of teacher and pupils for the purpose of giving and receiving instruction; it may be on the mountaintop, or in a school yard, or may be held together by communication through the mails, or the radio or television.

Private school teachers are not required to hold teaching credentials, the state does not regulate or approve curriculum, nor must private school students participate in any annual achievement testing or other assessment program.

California parents choosing to homeschool under the private school option must simply file the private school affidavit and keep records of their own teaching qualifications, their course of study (which is not defined beyond the general course requirements), and their children's school attendance, which by definition for homeschoolers is nearly always perfect.

California homeschoolers have had occasional problems with school officials who are hostile toward home education. In the late 1980s and throughout the 1990s, a few state education officials tried to promote various theories by which homeschooling under the private school statute would be illegal: that private schools had to be businesses that solicited enrollment from the public and were paid a fee for their services, that all private schools must use credentialed teachers, and that only private schools with fewer than six students must use credentialed teachers. Between the complete lack of a legal foundation for those opinions and the vocal opposition of several active homeschooling organizations, those theories gained little credence. Although one or two state education bureaucrats still occasionally issue opinions questioning the legality of the private school option (and even of the tutoring option) for homeschoolers, the enforcement power (mainly to verify the filing of the affidavit) that exists is clearly at the local level, and almost all counties and school districts are fairly cordial toward homeschoolers. Even in the rare cases in which local officials frown on homeschooling, they can do little to prevent it, except by distributing intimidating or discouraging memos.

Wisconsin

Like California's compulsory attendance statute, Wisconsin's requires school attendance for children between the ages of six and eighteen. Unlike California's statute, however, Wisconsin's education code is explicit that homeschooling is a form of private education: A "home-based private educational program" is a "program of educational instruction provided to a child by the child's parent or guardian or by a person designated by the parent or guardian." Further, the criteria for determining whether a home-based educational program meets the requirements of the law are exactly the same as those for all Wisconsin private schools:

1. The primary purpose of the program is to provide private or religious-based education.
2. The program is privately controlled.
3. The program provides at least 875 hours of instruction each school year.
4. The program provides a sequentially progressive curriculum of fundamental instruction in reading, language arts, mathematics, social studies, science, and health. This subsection does not require the program to include in its curriculum any concept, topic, or practice in conflict with the program's religious doctrines or to exclude from its curriculum any concept, topic, or practice consistent with the program's religious doctrines.
5. The program is not operated or instituted for the purpose of avoiding or circumventing the compulsory attendance requirement. . . .
6. The pupils in the institution's educational program, in the ordinary course of events, return annually to the homes of their parents or guardians for not less than two months of summer vacation, or the institution is licensed as a child caring institution. . . .

According to homeschoolers involved in the legislative process at the time the Wisconsin statute was enacted, the main reason for distinguishing homeschooling from private schools at all was to make clear that home education programs were not eligible for federal and state funds for school lunch programs, transportation subsidies, and so on, as conventional private schools sometimes are. The explicit homeschooling category also makes it possible for the state to take a more accurate census of school-age children and the educational programs in which they are enrolled.

Home-based educational programs are simply required to file with the state department of public instruction a form that gives the number and grade level of children in the program and certifies that the program meets the criteria listed earlier. The state does not require keeping records to verify the instructional hours, although some homeschoolers choose to do so. Wisconsin's law puts the burden of proof on the state to demonstrate that a home-based educational program is inadequate and fails to comply with the law, in which case the parents would be subject to prosecution for truancy violations. As in California, state education officials sometimes attempt more regulation of homeschoolers than the law allows, and Wisconsin homeschooling organizations actively monitor and limit such attempts.

Texas

The Texas Compulsory School Law states that "any child in attendance upon a private or parochial school which shall include in its course a study of good citizenship" is exempt from public school attendance. Until 1981, homeschooling families fit easily into this definition of private education. In that year, without any change in the law itself, the Texas Education Agency (TEA) declared as a matter of policy that "educating a child at home is not the same as private school instruction, and, therefore, not an acceptable substitute," and it began prosecuting homeschooling families. In its prosecutions, the TEA maintained that the quality or success of any homeschooling program was irrelevant as a defense because no home, by definition, could qualify as a private school.

In May 1985, Gary and Cheryl Leeper, along with five other homeschooling families, filed a class action suit against the Arlington, Texas, school district and all other Texas school districts, seeking a declaratory judgment that homeschooling did in fact meet the statutory definition of a private school. When the trial court judge found in favor of the families, ruled that homeschools are to be considered private schools, and granted a permanent injunction against further prosecutions, the state appealed. The Texas Court of Appeals agreed with the trial court, going on to state that the action of the TEA against homeschoolers "amounts to bad faith, arbitrary, capricious and unreasonable conduct and is harassment." The state appealed again.

Finally, in June 1994, the Texas Supreme Court affirmed the lower court rulings, agreeing that the TEA had no legal basis for prosecuting homeschooling families, who are indeed exempt from the compulsory attendance law. The Supreme Court lifted the injunction against prosecutions, because the ruling rendered it unnecessary, and, in an 8–1 decision, ordered the TEA to pay $360,000 in attorneys' fees for the plaintiff families.

As a result of the Leeper case, complying with Texas legal requirements is quite easy. A homeschool program must be run in a "bona fide" manner, from a written curriculum from any source, and must cover the basics of reading, spelling, grammar, math, and citizenship. Parents must reasonably cooperate with any reasonable request from an attendance officer, but there are no registration or testing requirements.

Learning about Your State Law

One of the first steps new homeschoolers should take is to learn exactly what the legal rules are for homeschooling in their states. The first impulse will probably be to call the local school district for information. This is usually a mistake. Although school administrators are normally quite familiar with the laws affecting public schools, they are often uninformed, or even misinformed, about those regarding private schools and homeschooling. A few will not hesitate to tell you what the applicable rules are, even when they actually know nothing about them. School officials today, like the public in general, are far better informed about homeschooling than they were a decade ago, but many still take homeschooling inquiries as a personal and professional affront and will not go out of their way to be helpful. (There are, of course, many exceptions, but there is no guarantee that you will get your response from an administrator friendly to homeschoolers.)

> The first impulse will probably be to call the local school district for information. This is usually a mistake.

Where, then, should you look for accurate and complete information about homeschooling? Unfortunately, there is probably no good single source. Your best bet for reliable information is a combination of sources:

- Read the law for yourself. Check with your local public or college library for a copy of the state education code. This will usually consist of several volumes, with subject indexes, annotations of court decisions affecting their interpretation and implementation, and pocket parts to keep everything current. You may have to hunt a bit to find the applicable sections, and the legal language will not necessarily be clear and easy to understand, although it will occasionally bear a vague, distant resemblance to normal English.

- Talk to any friends or acquaintances who are homeschoolers. Ask about them what they know of the legal requirements for homeschooling and where they got their information.

- Contact state and local homeschooling groups for legal information. Most groups produce some sort of "beginner packet" that outlines the basic rules for your state and gives suggestions for getting along with the law. Most will say they do not give legal advice and recommend that you contact a lawyer if you have doubts or questions, but support group information tends to be fairly reliable, because it is based on members' personal experiences. In general, because they are directly affected by regulations, homeschoolers are far more motivated to become knowledgeable about applicable regulations than are school officials. Homeschoolers have a vested interest in getting it right, and even in making sure other homeschoolers get it right, because when families have legal trouble it can adversely affect the local climate for homeschooling. If there are several homeschooling organizations in your state, it might even be worthwhile to get information from all of them, to see how closely they agree about the legal situation. Some groups may promote a particular method as the only means of complying with the law, even when there are several options to choose from, or may suggest a particularly fear-based approach, even recommending that you avoid letting your children outside during school hours or refrain from telling people you are homeschooling.

• Ask your local or state education agency what the rules for homeschooling are. Even though this is not usually the best first choice for homeschooling information, it's worth knowing the official public educators' perspective. The kind of response you get will depend on the laws of your state and the views of the officials charged with answering such inquiries. States friendlier to homeschooling, such as Washington, may provide perfectly good information; others may provide their opinion of what the law ought to be instead of what it actually is. Without contact with other homeschoolers in your state, evaluating the "official" version of the facts can be difficult.

You probably won't get a black-and-white "this is what the rules are" answer to your homeschooling legal questions. But you will get a good idea of your state's homeschooling climate and how other homeschoolers live within those rules. In many states, the rules are ambiguous at best, but by gathering as much information as you can from a variety of sources, you'll get as close as any of us can to learning "exactly" what the laws are in your state.

Living with the Law

Whatever your state's requirements—a simple filing of a form once a year, keeping a learning log, getting your kids tested every year or two, or even getting advance approval of your curriculum plans— you'll probably find that complying with them is not too complicated. For the first year or two you'll probably worry about getting it right, but the novelty of homeschooling, of doing something different from most of your neighbors, wears off quickly, and complying with even the more burdensome regulations becomes pretty routine.

. . .

We file as a private school every year, and Rosie gets some help from the public school independent study program she's enrolled in. I know the law, and therefore I don't worry about the legality. I also interact with, on average, one to five new or potential homeschoolers each week, reassuring them of the legality of homeschooling as well. I appreciate having our state homeschool association as a resource. —*Carol*, California

. . .

I worry to a certain degree about the legal stuff, meaning I intend to start getting to work at a very basic level to change the law. Our state doesn't recognize homeschooling as such, so the only way we can qualify as a private tutor, aside from having a teaching certificate, is to be under the umbrella of a private Christian school— "church school," I think the law says. So, we have to meet with them, pay out our noses, and go along, merrily or not. —*Shari*, Alabama

. . .

We file as a private school. I don't worry about legalities. I feel I could drag any school officials who'd show up into our "office/ library" and knock their socks off with all the educational stuff we've got around here and all the outside activities he's been

involved in. Ethan presents himself well, too. —*Lillian,*
California

· · ·

We file as a private school. I don't worry about legal problems
because I don't feel like a good test case—I'm not poor, single, or
on welfare. California rules are gray—not too hard, no real record
keeping is involved. No evaluations, either. —*Melissa,* California

· · ·

Illinois is easy. We are considered a nonregistered private
school. This means no lesson or curriculum plans have to be submitted, we don't need to be certified, no attendance records need
to be kept, no home visits are allowed, and testing is not a requirement. On the other hand, it's kind of scary not being ac-
countable to anyone but yourself. Having only a public school
background, it is hard not to wonder if our child is measuring up
to some standard. —*Anne,* Illinois

· · ·

We comply with Hawaii's requirements, which basically are to
submit a notice of intent to the local public school, along with annual progress reports. Any parent can homeschool their own children; we don't have to ask for permission or submit curriculums
for approval at all. The rule says parents shall keep a written
record of the planned curriculum, but we don't have to share it
with the school unless progress is inadequate, and even then, only
under certain conditions. Progress reports can take the form of
standardized tests, a written evaluation by a Hawaii-certified
teacher, or a narrative report with student samples.

From what I know, the requirements are less onerous than in
most states, except for places where homeschoolers don't have to
report to school officials at all. The statewide public school system

publicly recognizes homeschooling as
a viable educational alternative. Top
administrators have stated in the
media that parents who choose to home-
school are "very committed and doing a good job of it." On the
other hand, they have a policy of not allowing part-time enroll-

ment or participation in extracurricular activities, no use of school libraries or resources, no homeschoolers allowed to attend GED classes, and so on. And no high school credit for time spent homeschooling under any conditions.

How does all this affect my homeschooling? Personally, it's been time-consuming to write the reports. This probably reflects my conflicting thoughts on doing the report—part of me wanting to make a personal statement about our educational philosophy and brag about our wonderful learning experiences, another part feeling the school should not be given more than the minimum required to comply with the rules. On the bright side, the writing has helped us clarify our views on learning and has been an opportunity to reflect on how things are going. I've tried not to let school or societal expectations drive what we do. I think it is much easier to do this by writing my own reports than submitting to testing. —*Linda,* Hawaii

. . .

We currently live in California and intend to move to Washington state. Both states have pretty livable requirements at this time. The worst I'd have to do is make a portfolio of each child's work each year, and I can bear that if I must. Brittany is not yet of school age in California, nor in Washington. I waffle on whether I will let the authorities know that we're homeschooling. On the one hand I don't think it's any of their business—I really don't. On the other hand, bureaucrats tend to get all huffy and difficult if they discover you've broken their silly rules. So I haven't decided. —*Pam,* California

. . .

Our state has a long form to fill out, including information on the children, the course of study they are being taught, and the credentials of the teacher. We have to fill out notarized forms stating that we agree to allow ourselves to teach our children. These forms are filled out by all unaccredited schools. Home schools here are considered unaccredited schools. It's a very silly thing to make homeschoolers fill out. If the state requests it, we are also required to test our children. Currently they are not doing this. —*Beverly,* Nebraska

. . .

No matter what the law in your state is like, most homeschoolers have no legal problems connected with homeschooling. Homeschooling is now a widely known educational choice; it's not necessary to keep the fact that your family homeschools a secret from anyone or to make special rules (such as staying inside during school hours) for your children. Most homeschooling organizations and individual homeschoolers believe that homeschooling publicly and openly helps keep homeschooling legal and accepted by the public. As homeschoolers become more visible members of the community, they become more familiar as well and are likely to face fewer problems as that familiarity grows.

Getting Legal Help

In the late 1970s and through the 1980s, the legal status of homeschooling was much less firmly established, and many families had trouble convincing local school officials that homeschooling was either effective or legal. Early issues of *Growing Without Schooling* contained numerous articles discussing statutes of various states and giving updates on the latest court cases. In some areas parents were justifiably concerned that their curriculum might not be approved by a local school board or that they could be successfully prosecuted for truancy violations.

> No matter what the law in your state is like, most homeschoolers have no legal problems connected with homeschooling.

Such cases are rare today, for a number of reasons. Far more states have laws explicitly allowing homeschooling, and homeschooling cases more often involve the details of compliance with legal requirements than with the fact of homeschooling itself. In addition, public support for homeschooling is greater: Most people—even those who would never choose it as an option for their own families—find nothing objectionable about homeschooling and seriously question officials who would spend increasingly limited public resources on fixing a nonexistent homeschooling "problem."

But what if you do need legal help? What if you become one of those increasingly rare cases where your homeschooling becomes a legal problem? Where do you find the assistance you need?

Just as with finding homeschooling legal information in the first place, you should try a variety of approaches. Before you ever get to the point of needing legal help, you can do a few things to prepare for potential problems. First, make sure you are familiar with your state's law and requirements and that you have some way of keeping up-to-date on any changes. In most cases, this means joining a state homeschooling organization that monitors your state's legal system and keeps its membership informed of possible changes: legislation, court rulings, education department regulations, and so forth. Be familiar with the types of problems that could arise and consider possible ways of handling them.

Most good state groups will provide this sort of help. They will collect information on "hostile contacts" from school officials and suggest tactics for dealing with them. Such tactics should include general advice, such as staying polite and making sure you keep records of any conversations and correspondence with officials. Other advice should be specific to your local situation and include information on what materials or cooperation officials are legally entitled to from you and what your recourse under the law may be. The aim of a state group in providing such information will be to equip you to handle the situation yourself. In at least 90 percent of the cases in which local officials question a family's homeschooling, a polite but firm letter or phone call clarifying local homeschooling regulations for those officials is usually enough to clear up the problem. In any case, you can take a few steps that are nearly always effective in dealing with doubtful or hostile officials:

- Always get the name and official title of anyone who calls you.

- If an official tells you that homeschooling, or some aspect of it, is illegal, ask for the legal citation. If the official cannot give you a specific education code section or regulation to support his actions, ask him to contact you again when he can cite the legal authority for his views.

- If an official is adamant in opposing your homeschooling, try going over her head to the school board or other elected officials. Try asking a few questions about how the money used dealing with you could otherwise have been spent on, say, materials for classroom students.

- If you get no help from officials at any level, consider generating a little publicity. Reporters usually love "David and Goliath" stories, and a tale of independent homeschoolers, who don't want government money and just want to be left alone to teach their children, fighting an unsympathetic and unfeeling education bureaucracy, usually fills the bill. If you can focus some attention on the finances here, too, so much the better—everyone loves a good government waste story.

A few situations will require more than just an assertive homeschooling parent, though, and you may find you need professional legal help. Again, a state organization should be able to give you advice. Generally, state groups simply do not have the resources to provide their members with professional legal help, but most groups should be able to recommend lawyers who are informed about homeschooling issues and willing to take on homeschooling clients.

Your family lawyer, if you have one, may also be willing to help you, but may not know much about the applicable laws. Again, the state homeschooling organizations should be able to provide enough information to save your lawyer a lot of time (and you the fees for the legal research time!) learning about the field. Or, you might be able to work out an arrangement to do some of the legal research on your case in exchange for a reduced fee, if money is a problem.

Another possible alternative is a homeschooling defense organization, although there are potential problems. Two organizations actively work to defend homeschoolers in court cases throughout the country; both emphasize defending religious rights. One is the Rutherford Institute, which describes itself as "a nonprofit civil liberties legal and educational organization, specializing in the defense of religious liberty, which includes the protection of the rights of home educators." Like the American Civil Liberties Union (ACLU), Rutherford takes on cases that it feels address important legal issues in the hope of setting a favorable legal precedent. Rutherford lawyers have also on occasion assisted homeschoolers in dealing with local officials, or offered other advice.

More systematic in its approach is the Home School Legal Defense Association (HSLDA), also a religious-based nonprofit organization. Incorporated in Washington, D.C., and operating in Virginia, HSLDA offers legal representation, through appellate levels if necessary, for homeschooling families who join by paying its membership fee (usually $100, although group discounts are usually available). HSLDA also operates the National Center for Home Education, which distributes information about homeschooling and general parenting issues, and issues frequent alerts on federal and state bills it feels threaten homeschooling and general parental rights. Although HSLDA welcomes any homeschoolers as members, it calls itself "a Christian organization with a Christian board and staff" and has more experience with religious defenses to homeschooling than with other possible defenses. HSLDA also is more comfortable working with families who use a formal curriculum with a fairly structured schedule as the basis for their homeschool program.

One real risk in working with a homeschool legal defense organization is that your case can become a tool for defending the rights of homeschoolers in general rather than your case in particular. For instance, in its membership application, HSLDA states explicitly that one duty of members is to cooperate fully with the HSLDA defense team. In practice, this can mean that if you do not agree to a particular line of defense for your homeschooling program, HSLDA may withdraw from your case.

Another problem with legal defense organizations is that they are often active on issues that you may not consider related to homeschooling, and you may not be happy with part of your membership fee being used to support political positions you personally oppose. It's probably worth asking for sample copies of any newsletters or for other organization literature to see what issues such groups are involved with.

Some questions to consider when looking into any homeschool legal defense organization:

- What services will the organization provide for you? Are such services guaranteed or at the option of the organization?

- If you need to use the services of an organization lawyer, who controls your case? Will the attorney explain your legal options with the attendant risks of each and let you decide which you prefer, or will you simply be told what the defense will be?

- What kind of track record does the group have? How many cases has it handled at the trial level? At the appellate level? What kind of success has it had?

- What percentage of the organization's income is spent on direct legal services to its members? What other services or activities is the group involved in?

- Does the organization have any particular political or religious agenda? Does it get involved with lobbying or legislative efforts at either the national or state level? To what ends?

- Does the group cooperate with other homeschooling organizations? Does your state homeschooling organization recommend or approve of the legal organization?

Check with homeschooling friends and acquaintances to see what they think about legal defense groups. What experiences have they had? Do they even think such services are necessary? As with any homeschooling decision, get as much information as you can to help you decide the best option for your family.

The Politics of Homeschooling

I mentioned earlier that, despite the initial worry and panic of the first year or so, complying with state legal requirements usually becomes a routine matter pretty quickly. To the extent that legal matters are relatively easy to deal with, this is true. But it's not really the whole story. Those legal matters may become routine, but they also tend to become more irritating as we begin to realize that, in addition to being an attractive educational option for our kids, homeschooling is a political act. And because we homeschoolers tend to be independent, ornery, and opinionated individuals, we usually start asking more questions about homeschooling and education in general.

For instance, why in many states are homeschoolers held to a higher standard than the public schools? In states where homeschoolers have to achieve a certain level on standardized tests to be allowed to continue homeschooling, why aren't school students made to homeschool if their scores aren't up to par? Why are the officials who have the power to decide whether to approve a homeschooling program so often the same officials whose schools get more money if our children are enrolled in them? Why must homeschoolers work so hard to demonstrate that they are doing right by their children when public schools are not held responsible for the competence of their graduates? Why, when longer school days and years and more assessment testing haven't improved educational outcomes, do so many educators and political figures call for more of the same?

Is it any wonder homeschoolers sometimes get a bit testy documenting instructional hours? Eventually, homeschoolers in enough numbers to have an impact may decide that the time has come to try

to improve their legal situation by working with their legislature and state education officials.

We've all got opinions on how things could be better, and a good portion of us get actively involved in trying to change things. Like the rest of our society, though, we don't come close to agreeing on how things should be changed. There are the moderates, who just want a nice, workable homeschooling statute everyone can live with, and there are the perfectionists, who want the ideal homeschooling law (which they usually haven't quite figured out all the details of yet) and will settle for nothing less. There are the mild libertarians who think compulsory education laws should be abolished, so that everyone can freely choose which schools to attend or whether to attend at all. And there are the extreme libertarians who go further and demand that all government schools be shut down and the entire education establishment be privatized. There are religious homeschoolers who want their values imposed on everyone, and there are religious homeschoolers who want everyone to choose for themselves the values they live by. There are homeschoolers who run businesses serving homeschoolers, and there are those who believe "making money off homeschoolers" is immoral and unethical.

It all makes for a rather lively mix when we start trying to work together on some specific homeschooling issue, such as amending a homeschooling statute or changing the way a law is implemented. Some groups will work toward a law that allows a variety of options for evaluation and assessment, whereas others will want to "prove" homeschooling works as well or better than classroom education and demand homeschoolers be included in statewide assessment programs. At the opposite pole, some groups will question the need for any kind of assessment or evaluation of homeschoolers at all.

Such divergent views can make improving a homeschool statute difficult. Legislators often won't want to choose among competing factions to create a bill; they often prefer to have a complete bill presented that "all homeschoolers" can agree on. Occasionally one homeschooling organization manages to get a bill introduced and passed before other state organizations are aware of it, with the result that large numbers of homeschoolers get left out of the process entirely.

Homeschoolers are also not the only people with an interest in homeschooling legislation. State education bureaucrats, teachers' unions, school board associations, and other groups interested in education also have opinions about appropriate regulations for homeschoolers. Once a bill is introduced in the legislature, it is subject to amendment from all sides. Homeschoolers hoping for an improvement in their legal position can end up with regulations much more burdensome than what they started with and should approach legislative remedies with great caution.

One angle not often considered by legislators and other officials is the degree to which many homeschoolers are committed to their educational choice. Such officials are often surprised that strict regulation of homeschoolers can be counterproductive. In general, the more restrictive a homeschooling law is, the more likely it is that homeschoolers will simply choose to ignore the law. Even in states friendly to homeschooling, some homeschoolers will refuse to comply for political or philosophical reasons: They do not accept the government involving itself in any way with private education; they oppose the use of standardized tests for assessing learning; they consider the education of children purely a parental matter. A highly restrictive law is as likely to create many "underground" homeschoolers as it is to bring homeschoolers under closer state or local supervision, and some families who are uncomfortable with ignoring the law will simply move to another state where the homeschooling laws are easier to live with.

> Homeschoolers hoping for an improvement in their legal position can end up with regulations much more burdensome than what they started with and should approach legislative remedies with great caution.

. . .

My children are younger than compulsory school age, so technically I don't have to worry about state laws yet. I am leaning more and more toward the conviction that I have a very fundamental and inalienable right, as well as a responsibility, to raise and educate my children according to my sincerely held beliefs. Among other things, I believe in a family-centered lifestyle, in child-led learning, and in the necessity of my children's education being an integral part of their lives. I believe that if I live according to my convictions, I will be better protected by them than by attempting to comply with regulations that I feel violate my rights. —*Laura,* Texas

. . .

The Bottom Line

To sum up, your legal situation as a homeschooler depends on what state you live in and how state and local officials enforce the laws concerning compulsory attendance, private education, and homeschooling. Which form the statutes take in your state—whether they require registration, a notice of intent, regular evaluation, or advance approval—can be less important than how they are enforced.

To keep your homeschooling legal worries to the minimal level they deserve:

- Know what your state's law says. Read the statutes that apply to you, talk to other homeschoolers, and join a state homeschooling organization that monitors the regulations affecting homeschoolers.

- Learn what potential problems for homeschoolers exist in your state. Learn how other homeschoolers have dealt with them successfully, and plan how you'd respond if faced with them yourself. Don't wait until after the fact to learn what your options could have been.

- Don't automatically assume that any explanation of homeschooling legal issues you hear or read is correct. Whether the opinion is that of a school official, a lawyer for a homeschool legal defense organization, a legislator, or another homeschooler, you need to check it out for yourself. Laws concerning homeschooling are usually complex; clear and definitive statements on legal issues usually leave out something important.

- Don't let worry about legal issues distract you from the everyday business of homeschooling. When homeschoolers object to rules that require them to document their children's learning or to have their kids tested on a regular basis, it's because such requirements often interfere with that learning. If you're changing your whole approach to homeschooling because of your state's legal requirements, you're probably worrying way too much about the law.

> If you're changing your whole approach to homeschooling because of your state's legal requirements, you're probably worrying way too much about the law.

- Don't be shy about your homeschooling. You don't have to announce it to everyone you meet, but visible homeschoolers help make homeschooling familiar and acceptable to the general public. With enough of us around, the public may eventually understand that homeschooling can be fun and exciting, as well as effective, and we'll find we have active support even from families who would never themselves choose to homeschool.

CHAPTER THREE

Structure, or Can We Wear Our Pajamas to School?

S O YOU'VE DECIDED homeschooling may be what you want for your family. You're convinced that your children can grow to be competent and well-adjusted adults through homeschooling, and you're satisfied that it's legal. Now comes the big question: What do you do all day?

The popular image of homeschooling, of course, shows children sitting at the kitchen table, working diligently on their workbooks, with Mom carefully supervising while she bustles around cooking dinner. Although undoubtedly a few families do fit that image, a great many homeschoolers would not recognize themselves or home-schooling in that picture and would be dismayed at such a limited idea of homeschooling. There are a wide range of approaches to learning at home, and it may take you some time to find the style that best suits you and your family.

Theories of Learning

What you do all day will depend largely on your beliefs about children and about learning. If you believe, to use some common (even overused) metaphors, that children are blank slates to be written on, or empty buckets to be filled with facts and figures and ideas, you will take a much different approach to homeschooling than you would if you view children as growing plants to be nurtured.

One fundamental determinant is what you believe of the child's nature: Are children naturally innocent and good, or inherently savage and corrupt? Another factor to consider is how children learn best: Must they be formally drilled on material to learn it, or can they acquire skills and knowledge less formally?

Dozens of educational theorists, from philosophers such as Socrates and Rousseau to researchers such as Howard Gardner, have addressed these issues, and many of their ideas influence homeschoolers as well as traditional educators. A little familiarity with some of the ideas most popular among homeschoolers will help you make sense of the wealth of available materials when you begin to make choices for your family.

Jean Piaget and Cognitive Development

The work of Swiss educator Jean Piaget has been tremendously influential among educators during the past several decades. As a result of his direct observation of children learning and working, he proposed that children go through several distinct stages of cognitive growth. First comes the sensorimotor stage (birth to two years), during which the child learns primarily through sensation and movement. At the preoperational stage (ages two to seven), children begin to master symbols such as language and start to be able to form hypotheses based on past experiences. At the concrete operational stage (ages seven to eleven), children learn to generalize from one situation to similar ones, although such reasoning is usually limited to their own concrete experiences. Finally, at the formal operational stage (eleven years and older), children can deal with abstractions, form hypotheses, and engage freely in mental speculation. Although the rate at which children progress through the stages varies considerably, the sequence of stages is consistent for all children. Therefore, to be appropriate and effective, learning activities should be tailored to the cognitive level of the child.

More recent researchers have begun to question the specifics of Piaget's research, and some view his analysis of cognitive development as limited, focusing too much on the growth of logical skills to the neglect of other aspects of mental development.

Rudolf Steiner and the Waldorf Schools

Waldorf education is named after the cigarette factory whose director asked the Austrian philosopher Rudolf Steiner to develop a school for the children of his workers. Steiner divided children's development into three stages: to age seven, children learn primarily by imitation; from seven to fourteen, feelings and emotions predominate; and after age fourteen, the development of independent reasoning skills becomes important. Waldorf education tends to emphasize arts and crafts, music, and movement, especially at younger ages, and textbooks are eschewed in favor of books the students make themselves. Waldorf theories also maintain that the emphasis should be on developing the individual's self-awareness and judgment, sheltered from political and economic aspects of society until well into adolescence.

Montessori and the Prepared Environment

Italian physician Maria Montessori's work emphasized the idea of the prepared environment: Provide the proper surroundings and tools so that children can develop their full potential. Montessori materials are carefully selected, designed to help children learn to function in their cultures and to become independent and competent. Emphasis is on beauty and quality, and that which confuses or clutters is avoided. Manipulatives are made of wood rather than plastic, tools are simple and functional, and television and computers are discouraged. As important as the materials themselves is their arrangement, ready for use when needed; children will not learn from even the best materials if they cannot find them to use them.

Charlotte Mason: Guiding Natural Curiosity

Charlotte Mason was a nineteenth-century educator who advocated informal learning during the child's early years, in contrast with the Prussian system of regimented learning then in vogue. She recommended nature study to develop both observational skill and an appreciation for the beauty of God's creation and extended that approach to teaching history and geography through travel and study of the environment, rather than as collections of data to master. She felt children learn best when instruction takes into account their individual abilities and temperaments, but she emphasized the importance of developing good habits to govern one's temperament and laying a solid foundation of good moral values.

Holt and Unschooling

Educator John Holt wrote extensively about school reform in the 1960s, but by the late 1970s he had concluded that no reform would make schools effective places for children to learn. Although he originally proposed the word *unschooling* simply as a more satisfactory alternative to *homeschooling, unschooling* now generally refers to a specific style of homeschooling, in which learning is not separated from living, and children learn mainly by following their own interests. Children learn best, he argued, not by being taught but by being a part of the world, free to explore what most interests them, by having their questions answered as they ask them, and by being treated with respect rather than condescension.

Gardner and Multiple Intelligences

Psychologist Howard Gardner argues that intelligence is not a single unitary property, proposing the existence of "multiple intelligences." He identifies eight types of intelligence: linguistic, musical, logical-mathematical, spatial, naturalist, bodily kinesthetic, interpersonal, and intrapersonal. Because each person has a different mix of these intelligences, learning is best tailored to each individual's strengths, rather than emphasizing the linguistic and logical-mathematical approaches traditionally used in schools. A bodily kinesthetic learner, for instance, might grasp geometric concepts presented with hands-on manipulatives far more easily than she would if they were presented in a more traditionally logical, narrative fashion. A teaching approach that recognizes a variety of learning styles might encourage many individuals now lost by conventional methods.

The Practice of Learning

Theories are all well and good, but how do you put them into practice? Although some homeschoolers may find a particular theory exactly fits their needs and beliefs, most will pick and choose from a variety of ideas and develop a routine specifically to suit their own family. Often the process takes some time, and the routine is adjusted as children grow and new interests and abilities develop. Homeschoolers often take several years to realize that finding a routine that works is really an ongoing process and that what works when a child is six can be cumbersome and counterproductive at ten or thirteen.

Often families who start out with a fairly rigid structure find themselves becoming more relaxed and flexible as they grow more comfortable with homeschooling, whereas those who began with an informal and casual style may discover the need for more structure. Sometimes structure for a specific topic or two, such as math, is enough, and everything else is learned more casually.

Let's consider some typical structures for homeschooling. I'll briefly describe each, along with some of the advantages and drawbacks, and then, in the next few chapters, we'll look at some examples of how they work for some real homeschooling families.

"School-at-Home"

This is the approach most people assume when they hear talk of homeschooling and it is the one most like traditional school. Children usually have a set schedule and assignments each day, and their work is evaluated and graded. The family may purchase and use a packaged curriculum, which comes complete with textbooks and assignments, along with grading and record-keeping services. Or the parents may put together the curriculum themselves, selecting textbooks, preparing lesson plans, and testing and grading all on their own. Although school-at-home can require several hours of work daily by the student, the time is still likely to be considerably less than would be required in school, because little or no classroom management is required to deal with the children of a single family.

> Although school-at-home can require several hours of work daily by the student, the time is still likely to be considerably less than would be required in school . . .

Advantages

- With its close resemblance to traditional schools, this approach is familiar and easy for most people to understand.

- Tasks and responsibilities are clear-cut and straightforward.

- Evaluation, usually in the traditional form of letter grades, is easy and in terms easily grasped by school officials if and when a child opts to attend school.

- A complete packaged curriculum relieves the parents of much research and planning and of worry that some important topics might be missed.

- Some families like using a grading service because it keeps family relationships out of the grading process.

Drawbacks

- A packaged curriculum is often rigid and inflexible and may make no allowances for differing interests and abilities.

- Assignments can be dull and repetitious, and students can develop "motivation" problems and resist completing schoolwork.

- With a set amount of work to be covered during the school year, the student may have insufficient free time to explore any topics in depth.

- If parents are doing their own curriculum development and lesson plans, they may have to work several hours each day preparing the next day's lessons. If the family has several children, the work load is multiplied accordingly. With varying ages of children, there may be little in the educational program that could be shared among them.

- School-at-home can be the most expensive homeschooling option, especially if you purchase a complete package and discover it does not work for you and your family.

- Some families who differentiate the roles of parent and teacher have trouble keeping the two functions separate.

Unit Studies

Unit studies, like so much else to do with homeschooling, vary enormously according to who is using them. Unit studies can be more or less formal, more or less lengthy, more or less comprehensive. Basically, the idea is to use some topic of interest as a jumping-off point for a complete "unit of study." For example, if your daughter sees a TV program on dinosaurs and wants to learn more about them, you could create a unit study on dinosaurs. You might find some appropriate books at the library, visit a natural history museum, and find other dinosaur-related activities. A good dinosaur unit study might include vocabulary and spelling words, math activities (figuring out sizes of dinosaurs relative to your house, perhaps), geology, biology, art (drawing or sculpting dinosaurs), and many other traditional school subjects all woven around the central topic of dinosaurs.

Commercial unit study packages are widely available. Unit studies on Laura Ingalls Wilder's *Little House* books and on the American Girl history books are popular. Several companies also produce entire curricula based on unit studies. Konos, for example, centers its units around various character traits, such as patience, trust, and obedience. Such programs can contain huge selections of activities and resources from which to pick and choose, making them far more flexible than traditional packaged curriculums.

Advantages

- Unit studies are a way to tailor your curriculum to your child's specific interests, reducing potential boredom and restlessness, especially if you allow your child to help plan activities.

- Because of the variety of possible activities, unit studies can be adapted to use simultaneously with children of different ages and with larger groups of children when families try co-operative learning.

- Unit studies are inherently flexible and can last as little as a few minutes or as long as several months or more, depending on the depth of the student's interest.

Drawbacks

- Unit studies can be just as dreary as the dullest packaged curriculum. It's possible to take a child's merest offhand remark on a topic and, with a blizzard of worksheets and readings and field trips, completely crush whatever interest existed.

- Sometimes it's difficult or expensive to find materials for some activities you'd like to try.

- If your child's interests change before the unit is completed, and if you're not willing to drop it for a new topic, you may have to deal with a bored or resentful student.

"Eclectic" Homeschooling

Eclectic homeschoolers are the middle-of-the-roaders, the folks who mix and match their methods to suit their needs. They may tackle some subjects in a highly structured manner and leave others for their kids to pick up as they happen to become interested in them. The structured subjects, typically math and writing, are usually those that parents are unwilling to risk having their children learn more informally, either because important concepts could be missed or because the parents feel the topic requires an ordered, sequential approach.

Eclectics pick materials from a variety of sources. They may purchase a curriculum and use only parts of it, forgoing any grading or record-keeping services. They might devise their own materials or adapt existing materials.

· · ·

We don't adhere to any particular educational philosophy, at least not consistently. The past two years we have actually purchased a few textbooks, which the girls selected based on their interests or preparation for an upcoming trip. For instance, we are casually studying American history in preparation for a trip to the east coast, and our older girl decided to tackle algebra, so we bought a text that serves her needs well. But the girls' main curriculum at the moment seems to be pen-pal letters, both e-mail and the old-fashioned way. —*Barbara*, California

. . .

Advantages

- Learning can be tailored to the interests and needs of the child.

- Parents can assure themselves that material they believe to be essential is covered thoroughly.

Drawbacks

- Kids sometimes resent the mandatory portions of their curriculum.

- Other advantages and disadvantages depend on the specific choices eclectics make.

Unschooling

Unschooling, also known as "natural," "interest-initiated," "child-led," or "learner-led" learning, is a deceptively simple concept that defies easy definition. Those of us who consider ourselves unschoolers are often baffled when people have a hard time understanding what we do because it's a process that makes perfect sense once you've been at it for a while.

Unschooling is learning through everyday life. Instead of a schedule with textbooks and formal lessons, unschooled children simply do the things that interest them. For homeschoolers who come to the idea while their children are still quite young, the idea is a natural: Any child who can learn to walk without formal instruction in stepping and standing and learn to talk without comprehensive formal lessons in grammar and syntax can certainly handle simpler skills like reading and arithmetic.

This laissez-faire approach is often misinterpreted as benign (or not so benign) neglect. But even the most extreme unschooler would agree that learning does not happen in a vacuum. Children learn to walk and talk because people around them walk and talk, and children want to be able to do the things they see their parents doing.

Just as a child would not learn to speak a language he never heard spoken, he would not learn to read if he never saw the printed word or grown-ups reading.

> Any child who can learn to walk without formal instruction in stepping and standing and learn to talk without comprehensive formal lessons in grammar and syntax can certainly handle simpler skills like reading and arithmetic.

But by observing adults and older children around him, a child gradually picks up skills that interest him. Often the process is nearly invisible: Suddenly, seemingly out of the blue, your child simply does something he couldn't do the day before. With skills like reading, the process is pretty visible: The child notices symbols, signs, logos, and letters and asks questions about sounds and meanings. He asks how to spell his own name and the names of his family and friends. He listens to stories read to him (often the same ones endlessly) and begins to pick out words he recognizes in the text. Eventually, he begins to read on his own, and his reading becomes rapid and fluent faster than seems possible. The whole process can take as little as a few months or happen more gradually over several years.

The process translates to other subjects as well. Unschooled kids learn arithmetic by using it: counting, cooking, shopping, budgeting, measuring, building. Writing comes, not from assigned essays or find-the-error exercises but from purposeful writing: thank-you notes, letters to relatives and pen pals, journals and diaries, stories, poems, essays—all kinds of writing. Many unschooling parents, looking back on their own school experiences with writing, find themselves astounded at the volume and quality of writing their children willingly produce on their own.

Interest sparked by such activities often leads a child to seek more information. Unschooling parents become experts at helping their children find resources for learning what they want to know. They find the best libraries with the most helpful librarians, museums with curators who love to share their knowledge, and business people willing to let kids learn what their businesses are like. Unschooling parents sometimes even find textbooks for their kids who've decided that's the best way for them to learn what they want or need to know.

. . .

We live our lives. We go to the library often. We read to each other. I search out all manner of things I think my children might be interested in and leave them where they are accessible. When my children are curious about things, I help them find out what they want to know. The children decide what they will learn, though I expect their own decisions are shaped some by what they see to be important in our lives. Where I do have hopes or expectations for what they will learn, I try to make sure they see me putting that kind of knowledge to use. We've never had a formal lesson and don't plan to, unless one of the children wants to.
—*Laura,* Texas

. . .

I think it is really important for the parents or at least the homeschooling parent to set an example of interested learning. I can't imagine expecting my kids to become interested and active in a wide variety of activities if I didn't have a life. It also gives them the freedom to seek their own paths because I am not on top of them all the time—I am pursuing my own interests. Homeschooling can be very liberating to everyone in the family and can become a way of life that will not necessarily change when the kids move out. —*Jill,* California

. . .

Unschooling demands a great deal of faith and trust by the parent, which can be difficult for those of us who are used to the American habit of judging and comparing our children's grades and test scores. Learning happens according to the child's schedule, not ours, and an unschooling child can appear to the casual observer to be doing "not much" or "nothing at all." Most unschooling parents, though, who try logging every single activity their kids tackle over the course of a day, or a week, find themselves overwhelmed and impressed by the amount of actual learning that occurs even in the most casual approach to education. And because it is undertaken at the child's instigation, it is neither rote nor boring, and it is understood more deeply and retained far longer than material learned because it was assigned by someone else according to an established formal curriculum. Unschooled kids can quickly exceed their parents' knowledge of or energy for a particular topic and may need outside assistance.

Advantages

- Learning becomes a natural part of life for unschooled kids, not something someone else does for them or something confined to a particular place or time.

- Unschooled kids tend to be curious and tenacious at finding ways to satisfy their curiosity.

- The informal nature of unschooling allows flexible schedules and the maximum adaptability to each child's skills and interests.

- Because they are actively involved in determining how they learn, unschooled kids tend to become quite self-reliant and self-confident.

- Even more than most homeschoolers, unschoolers have the time and energy to explore topics in depth, to think and ponder and dream, and even just to be bored for a while.

- Watching your kids so eagerly learning can move you to dig into a few topics to explore for yourself; learning for its own sake can be hard to resist.

Drawbacks

- Unschooling can make parents and other relatives very nervous. Having faith that your child will learn to read is an entirely different matter from sitting back and letting her do it at her own pace.

- Self-directed learning does not lend itself to traditional assessment methods or grade levels. Demonstrating and documenting learning can be tricky and takes planning if the child will eventually enter school or attend college.

- Unschooling can be sneakily expensive: You don't purchase formal curriculum packages, but you buy interesting books and tapes, and "stuff" for hobbies and projects, and perhaps pay for specialized lessons. If you're not careful, the costs can add up all too quickly.

A Note on School Calendars

You may start out homeschooling assuming that you'll stick to the traditional September-to-June school year. Most homeschooling regulations assume your school year starts in the fall; notices of intent, private school affidavits, and other such forms are usually due for submission sometime during the period from mid-August through early October. Homeschool suppliers hit the conference circuit and advertise their wares heavily in the homeschooling periodicals during the summer on the assumption that most homeschoolers are then reviewing and choosing their materials for the coming new school year. Sticking with the conventional school calendar is convenient, if nothing else.

Most often, more structured homeschool families are the ones who conform to the traditional academic year. After nine or ten months of tightly scheduled work assignments, the entire family is often more than ready for a break. Some families won't do any teaching or learning over the summer, whereas others may opt for something like an unschooling style for the warmer months.

But many homeschoolers find that they prefer to develop their own academic calendars. Some structured homeschoolers like to continue homeschooling continuously throughout the year because they feel their children learn better and retain more knowledge without a long summer break. These homeschoolers find they need to do less review and can cover more material more quickly and thoroughly than on a conventional schedule. With a year-round schedule, they also have more flexibility to drop the work for a few days because of illness or even for a few weeks at once for an off-season vacation.

Unschoolers may also prefer a year-round calendar, just because they always have a hard time telling the difference between school days and vacation days anyway. If everyday life is full of opportunities for learning, labeling some days as school days and others as vacation days seems arbitrary and pointless.

> If everyday life is full of opportunities for learning, labeling some days as school days and others as vacation days seems arbitrary and pointless.

Other homeschoolers take a more prosaic view of their school year and tie it to the legal requirements of their state. Where homeschooling regulations require 180 days of instruction, or 875 hours, or whatever the relevant statute demands, they make their school year the length of time necessary to meet that legal minimum. During that portion of the year, the family is careful about recording all learning activities properly, with everything neatly categorized by subject and grade level as required. Once the statutory minimum is reached, the family simply quits keeping the "official" records and goes on homeschooling according to their own interests and plans rather than the state's.

Finding your preferences for your school calendar is pretty much a trial-and-error process. You can assume you'll use the traditional schedule and then realize in June that you're all having too much fun to quit learning, or you can do just the opposite—plan to go year-round and then suddenly opt for the summer vacation, without any earthshaking consequences. Or you can try different calendars each year—perhaps by the time your children are eighteen, you'll figure out which suits your family best.

Finding Your Own Structure

Figuring out which parts of which ideas will work for you is not easy. Often the ideas you find most attractive and expect will best fit your family don't work for you at all. Or they work for a year or two and then suddenly seem ridiculous. Just remember that your kids are growing and changing and the relationships among you all are changing as well. It's unrealistic to expect homeschooling to remain the same in the midst of those changes.

> Just remember that your kids are growing and changing and the relationships among you all are changing as well. It's unrealistic to expect homeschooling to remain the same in the midst of those changes.

One of the hardest notions for most of us parents to let go of is the idea that there is one correct solution, one right answer that will solve all the problems and answer all the questions. Inevitably, we sometimes question our choices for our kids and worry that we could and should be doing a better job for them. It's a fine line between always searching for the best solution for the way our kids are today and constantly second-guessing ourselves and our kids. Homeschooling is a process, not a product. It's a process that never ends as long as our kids are still learning, and if we do it right, they never stop learning, even after they leave home.

CHAPTER FOUR

Assisted Homeschooling, or Do We Really Need Any Help?

GATHERING INFORMATION ABOUT your legal options and about various philosophical approaches to learning is an obvious step in deciding how homeschooling will work for your family. But closely tied in with the legal and philosophical issues involved with homeschooling is the matter of logistics: Will you carry on independently, or will you use one of the ever more numerous options now available to assist you?

It used to be that options for homeschooling assistance were few and fairly uncomplicated. There were a few nationally known correspondence schools to choose from, fewer still private school programs specifically designed to cater to homeschooling families, and perhaps a few similar programs available within your state or locally. In some areas you might have found a school district that had an alternative home study program, perhaps evolved from the district's continuation school.

In the past few years, though, with the rapid growth of homeschooling, the number of options has exploded. Families looking for assistance and support for their homeschooling are faced with a dizzying array of choices, both public and private: correspondence schools, independent study programs, umbrella schools, charter schools, cyberschools, co-op schools, and more. Scores of companies offer everything from traditional textbook-based "complete curriculum packages" and "literature-based unit studies" to specific courses taught online and CD-ROMs alleged to contain "everything your child needs to know."

Suddenly homeschooling is big business, and lots of curriculum companies and private schools are more than willing to tell you that their way to homeschool is exactly what you need and will happily supply you with their perfect package—for a price. And the public school system is getting into the act with charter schools and their various relatives, offering what advocates call the best of both worlds: the resources of the school system combined with the independence of homeschooling—with expenses paid by your state's taxpayers.

Finding your way past all the ads and hype to the content, structure, and style of homeschooling that works best for your family is no easy task, and the job won't get any easier. Like every other homeschooling decision you make, this one depends on what your family is like and how you view learning and your kids. Your financial resources and the time and energy you're willing to devote to homeschooling will also influence your decision.

Private Options

Private options run the full gamut of philosophical and pedagogical approaches, from the most traditional to completely child led, from complete curriculum packages and mix-and-match programs to "cover schools," which merely maintain records for you. If you're interested, a program is probably available to fit your needs.

Correspondence programs tend to be fairly traditional in their course offerings and instructional approach. Typically, assignments are returned for evaluation and grading as they are completed. Some programs require an outsider, such as a teacher or librarian, to administer any required tests, although increasing numbers offer the option of submitting assignments, examinations, and evaluations through e-mail or a Web site. Some allow enrollment on a course-by-course basis, while others require enrollment for an entire semester- or year-long course of study. It's not uncommon, though, for private programs to allow either part- or full-time enrollment, whichever best suits the needs of their customers.

> Private independent study programs tend to be fairly adaptable to individual needs and usually allow the parent to have a substantial role in developing and carrying out a learning plan, including the choice of materials.

Private independent study programs tend to be fairly adaptable to individual needs and usually allow the parent to have a substantial role in developing and carrying out a learning plan, including the choice of materials. The more traditional programs tend to be affiliated with conventional classroom-based private schools, although several, such as Clonlara, are quite flexible and supportive of less structured approaches to homeschooling. Schools created specifically to serve the homeschooling market (also commonly referred to as "umbrella schools") fall everywhere along the continuum of learning approaches and styles, so it shouldn't be hard to find one to suit your needs if you're leery of going it alone. You can also usually choose the level of support you want, from "teacher-proof" daily lesson plans to simple record maintenance. In many cases, the program assigns a "resource teacher" or "educational facilitator" to each of its enrolled families to oversee their participation and act as a liaison with the program. The exact parameters of this relationship depend on the program and its arrangement with each enrolled family.

Advantages

- Enrollment in a private program may relieve families' concerns about compliance with their state's legal rules for homeschooling.

- Some private programs are accredited by recognized accreditation agencies, which can sometimes ease the college admissions and job application processes.

- Private homeschooling programs can reduce or even eliminate the burden of creating a curriculum and collecting learning materials.

- Evaluation and record keeping are overseen by the private program resource teacher and administrator.

- You have a built-in support group in other enrolled families.

Drawbacks

- Tuition, other fees, and materials for private homeschooling programs can be expensive.

- The private program you choose may turn out not to suit your needs as well as you expect; you may be reluctant to abandon your investment even when the program obviously no longer meets your needs.

- Relying on a private program may keep you from developing confidence in your and your children's ability to tackle homeschooling on your own; conversely, as you develop more confidence in your homeschooling, you may chafe at assistance or supervision you feel you no longer need.

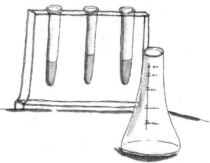

You should find out as much as you can about any program that interests you. Talk to other families who've been with the program for a year or more and, if possible, even to families who've left the program: Are the staff friendly and supportive of your educational goals? What kinds of evaluation or testing do they use? Can you work with their requirements? Do they provide transcripts or diplomas if you need them? Do they fully comply with your state's regulations?

Public Programs

The number and variety of homeschooling options available through public school systems have mushroomed over the past five years. Such independent study programs offered by public schools vary a great deal, from those originally intended to accommodate students expelled or suspended from regular classrooms, or students diagnosed to be in some way "at risk" of failure, to new ones designed especially for homeschoolers. Some seek merely to prepare high school students to take and pass the GED, and others work hard to spark genuine interest in learning in their students. Usually, there will be some sort of contract between the teacher/school and the family about what work and support is expected from each and how the student's work will be evaluated.

One relatively new option for homeschoolers is the charter school. The charter school movement began as a way for public schools to experiment with different approaches to school reform. Sometimes charter schools are brand new, independent schools; sometimes they take the form of a smaller school within an existing school. In all cases, the participants—usually teachers, often also an administrator or two, parents, some-

> You should find out as much as you can about any program that interests you. Talk to other families who've been with the program for a year or more and, if possible, even to families who've left the program.

times local businesspeople or community leaders—draft a "charter" to govern the school. While the exact rules vary from state to state— and not all states yet allow them—charter schools are generally free of most of the legal rules and regulations that apply to conventional schools and can thus be quite innovative. Many, like magnet schools, are based on themes such as science and technology, the arts, or vocational fields such as business or food service, or adopt specialized educational approaches (e.g., Waldorf or Montessori). A number of charter schools around the country have begun experimenting with programs for homeschoolers.

California's homeschooling charter schools, for example, have proved to be extremely popular with homeschooling families. Some enroll several thousand students and offer a wide variety of field trips, short-term cooperative classes, parent education workshops, and learning materials. Other charter schools are smaller and focus on particular learning philosophies or instructional themes, or they combine homeschooling with one or two days of optional on-campus activities.

> While the exact rules vary from state to state—and not all states yet allow them—charter schools are generally free of most of the legal rules and regulations that apply to conventional schools and can thus be quite innovative.

Like private homeschooling programs, most charters and other public programs assign each family to a supervising teacher or facilitator who advises on curriculum and materials, offers ideas and suggestions, and maintains student records based on reports submitted by the parents. The frequency of meetings with facilitators and the complexity of the records maintained depend on the rules of each charter. The experiences of different families even within the same program may vary substantially depending on the facilitator assigned and may vary from year to year as both personnel and regulations change.

For home independent study programs, charter schools, and other public school options, it's especially important to find out how flexible the program and its administrators are and how supportive its district personnel are. Lack of such support or increased regulation from the district or state level can often bring startling changes midyear and leave you stuck in a program you dislike intensely. If you have any doubts, think about alternatives just in case you need them.

Advantages

- Charter schools, home study programs, and other public homeschooling options are indisputably legal means of complying with your state's compulsory school attendance laws.

- Public homeschooling programs charge no tuition; program expenses are funded by the school district or other public education agency.

- Public programs can provide your family with learning materials—even long-term loans of computers, musical instruments, and other big-ticket items—you might otherwise be unable or unwilling to pay for.

- You have a built-in support group in other enrolled families.

Drawbacks

- As with private programs, the public program you choose may not be as well suited to your needs as you expect.

- More or different record keeping than you are comfortable with may be required.

- Many public homeschooling programs require standardized tests or other means of student assessment, which many families find irrelevant or even disruptive to their approach to learning.

The Do-It-Yourself Approach

Remember that comment at the beginning of the introduction to this book: "I know someone who homeschools, but I could never do it myself—it'd be so much work." With the plethora of public and private options, and plenty of marketers eager to tell you what you "need" to do a good job homeschooling, it's all too easy to think you can't handle the job. But many families eschew both public and private programs and choose to homeschool independently of charter schools, independent study programs, or curriculum vendors. Such homeschoolers run the gamut from school-at-homers to unschoolers, but they are united in their belief in their ability to provide their children with an appropriate and effective education. Some come to independent homeschooling after trying one or more forms of assisted homeschooling; others start out on their own and never see any reason to change.

Independent homeschoolers take responsibility for their children's education. They choose their materials, they decide how and when to use them, and they decide how to evaluate the success or limits of their homeschooling program. They decide whether to join a local support group, whether to become involved with cooperative learning projects, conventional youth groups, or community organizations.

> Many parents homeschooling independently find the whole process daunting at first but gradually realize that learning to rely on their own judgment is as much an education for them as it is for their children.

Many parents homeschooling independently find the whole process daunting at first but gradually realize that learning to rely on their own judgment is as much an education for them as it is for their children. Once they realize that there are no right and wrong answers to the question of how to homeschool, that the process of figuring out what works continues for as long as the homeschooling, they begin to enjoy the process of trial and error.

Advantages

- Independent homeschooling is completely flexible; learning can be completely tailored to the needs of the individuals involved.

- The family is totally responsible for creating and implementing their homeschooling program.

- Working independently helps the entire family develop enormous confidence in their abilities.

- Learning can be completely integrated into the whole family routine; outside schedules impinge only as much as the family chooses to let them.

Drawbacks

- Bearing complete responsibility for creating and implementing a homeschooling program can be more than some families are comfortable with.

- Expenses for books and materials can be unpredictable.

- Depending on the state of residence, independent homeschooling may leave some families concerned about their legal status.

Some Real-Life Examples

How do homeschoolers decide how much homeschooling help they want? How do we figure out whether we need assistance getting started? How do we know what will work for our own families? For most homeschooling families, the choices are never easy and are continually reevaluated. The easiest way to begin to see how the process works is to look at a few families to see how they handle things.

• • •

My children are now nineteen and fifteen. We've been home-schooling for sixteen years, if you count the preschool years, and have lived in three different states over those years. For twelve of those years we homeschooled on our own, without using any formal curricula or umbrella school; we are unschoolers. Four years ago we moved to Florida, a state which requires annual evaluations. This move also coincided with our daughter's reaching high school age.

We chose to enroll with Clonlara then for several reasons. Overall, I guess, was my insecurity. I didn't want our decision to homeschool to have a negative impact on our children's futures. If paying out tuition for a few years would give them a transcript and high school diploma from an accredited school, it seemed like a small price to pay. I wanted the doors to be open should our daughter decide to go to college. Then there were those annual evaluations required by the state. Our son is a "special needs" child and does not do at all well on standardized assessments. I also wanted to keep an extra layer between my family and the school district so that the district would have no way of identifying him as "different," and Clonlara's philosophy avoids labeling students. We enrolled with them for four years, until my daughter graduated. We are now using West River Academy in Colorado for my son's remaining high school years because he has outgrown the state-required evaluations that Clonlara had handled, the costs are far less, and the philosophy more nearly fits my own.

For us, the advantages were: (1) It appeased my mother, since she then thought we were doing things in a more traditional way; (2) We didn't have to change what we were doing, just how we recorded it; (3) Clonlara provided the annual evaluations (although I did most of the work for that in the form of a narrative report and providing a portfolio of work); (4) My daughter had no difficulty with college applications and in fact was accepted by all the schools to which she applied. I didn't have to write her

recommendations as guidance counselor, nor did we have to jus-
tify what we did in our homeschooling; (5) I could avoid dealings
with our local school district; (6) She has a transcript and normal-
looking high school diploma ("dorky" is her description, but what
diploma isn't?), and she will always have the choice of not explaining her homeschooling in the future if she so chooses.

As for disadvantages, cost was a big one. The tuition went up
dramatically over the time we were enrolled, and we saw no corresponding increase in service. Each family was assigned to what
was first called a "support teacher" and later a "contact teacher."
Our first one responded rapidly—within two weeks—and generally had good suggestions. However, we had three different teachers assigned over the four years, and it felt as though I was
constantly retelling our story. I disliked the lack of continuity.
Our later teachers were much slower to respond to my inquiries
(months, at times), and I found their suggestions trivial—things
I'd thought of long before and already tried. My daughter especially resented having to keep track of the time she spent on various activities in order to document her "credit hours" and the
mandatory "community service hours." It wasn't that she didn't
want to do volunteer service; she did and still does. It was the
mandatory aspect of it. In the end, though, she earned substantially more credits than the required minimum (she had more
than 40; 22 were required).

In the end, I felt like a traitor to the unschooling community
for having used Clonlara as a crutch, despite their contention
that they are strong supporters of unschooling. It also feels as
though what we did was "buy" a diploma. It's a little hard to explain, but I suppose Clonlara became just another institution that
was there to shore up my confidence that what I was doing was

right. I should not have needed it. How
do I help those who are coming up
behind me to stand on their own legs if
I resorted to that crutch?

I was also uncomfortable philosophically with Clonlara's advice to my daughter that she present herself to prospective col-

leges as a private school student. It may have made the admissions process easier, but it always felt a bit dishonest to me.

So why are we continuing to use West River Academy? Mostly because it allows us to document the fact that our son is a full-time student should our health insurer ever ask. He will be a full-time student for many years to come, but we need that piece of paper to document it, especially after he turns eighteen. With West River, all we are required to do is fill out the application and write a brief annual report. —*Carol,* Florida

. . .

My son chose to sign up for a Spanish class and science workshops. There is an Alpine Wilderness Experience offered as well, which will take one day a week and will fulfill all the time requirements for on-site participation. We will most likely do this, as we'll be going up to the pass for snowboarding, snowshoeing, skiing, rock climbing, nature studies, etc. Friends who took this class last year loved it.

I'm taking this whole thing a day at a time and will not hesitate to turn tail and run if I find anything I don't like. Our program "expects" us to participate in testing. However, the law allows us to opt out by giving written notification.

So far, the program is progressing swimmingly. Much to my unschooling heart's surprise, my son loves his Spanish and science classes and wants to sign up for music appreciation and shop class, too. I'm enjoying the camaraderie of hanging out on the site with other homeschooling families, and my three-year-old daughter certainly likes playing with the other kids.

I may start teaching a half-hour "kindergarten" class twice a week, because there are parents who want some sort of fun group experience for their younger kids. There would be just about enough time to have a short circle time, with songs and finger-plays, and a story or two. The cool part about this is that my three-year-old is welcome to participate and my ten-year-old wants to help out, too! —*Barb,* Washington

. . .

Being part of our charter school has worked so well for us that my husband has become an educational specialist there. This has been great! Many of our homeschooling friends' children have become his students, and we've been able to set up some wonderful small group classes—horsemanship, art, and science—using creative people in our community.

I also like all the educational supplies. I only check out what we can use. The extra books, musical equipment, and science kits have really benefited my children.

Some close friends and family members who would never before have considered homeschooling have signed their children up with our charter school. For these families and many others, being part of a charter school is the only way they would homeschool. They like the assistance and support of a credentialed teacher and would feel uncomfortable homeschooling alone.

We are homeschoolers, even though we are part of a charter school. If at any time I feel I am giving in or conforming to a system that will not benefit my children, I will immediately withdraw them from the program. —*Elizabeth*, California

• • •

One mid-May weekend, I just happened to buy a newspaper, and just happened to come across an ad that read "Homeschoolers! We can help!" I called the number given and got an answering machine which told me, "Welcome to IDEA—Alaska's newest statewide homeschooling support program," which turned out to be part of the Galena City School District.

I spent the next three days speaking with the principal about IDEA, his educational philosophy, how he saw the program helping homeschoolers . . . [and eventually] I chose to enroll my children. We were the seventh family to enroll.

We're rapidly approaching the 2,000-student mark now.

The fact that our program is fairly new (now entering its second year) and the fact that it is a public school program present challenges and some drawbacks, but on the whole, for most of us it is a great opportunity. In areas where state laws or district regulations are more restrictive, I'm not sure I'd want to participate in a program of this nature and probably would not. While there is the twice-yearly written report that must be done, I haven't witnessed any interference in what, how, and with what materials my children learn. Many of our certified teachers are also either current or past homeschoolers, too.

The bottom line is that they let the parents know going in what's required, offer quite a few benefits, and let the parents choose to accept or decline what they offer. If you accept the benefits, you also accept the requirements. No getting around them—but for those who can live with the requirements, the benefits are very good. —*Monica,* Alaska

• • •

I'm listed with both our local and state homeschooling organizations as someone to call with questions about homeschooling. One question I get often is "Where do you buy curriculum?" I take a deep breath and say, "I don't." There is usually silence on the other end of the line.

When I began my homeschooling journey—when my son was two—I went to the library and checked out every book on homeschooling I could find. I went to homeschool conferences. I talked to people. When my informal play group decided we needed to disband because our toddlers needed to go to preschool for "socialization" and "kindergarten preparedness," I knew I needed to make some homeschooling friends.

Fellow homeschoolers have been a wonderful resource. We all can hang out together and share our favorite books for both adults and children. We can talk about our latest interests and hobbies. I can call someone during the day and invite them over.

I like the idea of doing what we want, when we want, the way we want. I like the idea of being a pioneer, of going where no one has gone before. Yet I find that many of my homeschooling friends are joining the increasingly popular charter schools. Most of them say it is for the money and the security of complying with government standards.

I don't understand how homeschooling costs so much money. The charter schools state that the money must be used for consumable goods, so many of my friends sit together talking with this glow about what neat "guaranteed success" product they are going to buy with their free money.

So instead of sitting your child down in your lap and explaining to them how to tie his shoe, you can go buy a book to help you teach this. Later you can buy products to teach your child to read. There seems to be a whole industry built on the phrase "don't try this at home."

Well, we do—and without fancy how-to books or videos. We do what I have always done: go to the library, make friends, and ask questions. —*Jennifer*, California

• • •

Making the Choice

One unexpected element in deciding whether to use a public or private program or homeschool independently is the political impact of that decision. Many new homeschoolers, especially, are startled by the vehemence with which their decision, one way or the other, is greeted by other homeschoolers. Some very structured homeschoolers, happy with their videotape or CD-ROM (or even satellite-delivered) curriculum, view independent homeschoolers as irresponsible laggards who give the homeschooling movement a bad name. Libertarian homeschoolers who believe that American society would be better off if there were no publicly funded education at all declare that homeschoolers who use publicly 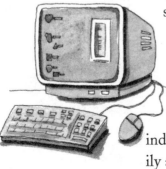 supported programs are falling into a trap by which the government will restrict options for all homeschoolers. Independent homeschoolers see some charter program homeschoolers as greedy for educational goodies they only want because they are "free." Those in public programs in turn wonder why anyone would choose independent homeschooling, when so much support is readily available.

At times, the controversy over the various forms of assisted homeschooling takes on an almost religious fervor. Families involved with public programs especially can find themselves ostracized by local support groups unable or unwilling to grant that there are legitimate reasons—financial, pedagogical, philosophical—to choose such programs. But independent homeschoolers have good reason to be concerned about the effects of large numbers of homeschoolers choosing some form of assisted homeschooling. Support groups that have existed for years have found their memberships dwindling as homeschoolers flock to charter schools and other similar programs. Independent homeschoolers worry about the possibility of tightened homeschooling regulations restricting homeschooling to some sort of "official" homeschooling program and losing the right to homeschool independently.

Much of this debate is simply the result of rapid growth and change within the homeschooling movement. Many more families are coming to homeschooling from the public schools than before, and many have only just begun to explore their options. There are more companies seeking to sell products to homeschoolers, and more homeschoolers looking for materials. With the public school pendulum swinging ever more quickly and widely between standardized curriculum guidelines and experimental programs such as charter schools, homeschoolers will undoubtedly have more changes to contend with, and probably more cross-over between conventional and alternative approaches to education will occur.

The stresses on existing homeschooling organizations will increase as the homeschooling population changes and adapts. With

> With the public school pendulum swinging ever more quickly and widely between standardized curriculum guidelines and experimental programs such as charter schools, homeschoolers will undoubtedly have more changes to contend with, and probably more cross-over between conventional and alternative approaches to education will occur.

so many programs—both public and private—seeking to enroll homeschoolers, often by limiting information about competing programs, state and local support groups will have to work hard to maintain open communications among all factions of homeschoolers, to make sure that information about all available choices reaches all homeschoolers.

Some suggestions for navigating the growing maze of options:

- Talk to lots of other homeschoolers about any program you consider. Ask them why they chose whatever option they use, whether they've tried others, and, if so, why they changed.

- Don't assume that anyone who tells you that their program is "the best available" or "your only legal option for homeschooling" necessarily has your best interests at heart. Remember to ask what's in it for them if you go along with their advice.

- Even if you choose to use a public program, join a state homeschool organization if one exists where you live. Such groups are vigilant observers of changes in statutes and regulations to do with homeschooling, and they will do their best to keep you informed of anything that might affect your rights and options. (See Chapter 11 for more about such groups and the services they provide.)

- Above all, don't believe for an instant any group or individual that insists that their way of homeschooling is the only way or the best way. Only you and your family can decide what works best for you.

CHAPTER FIVE

Money and Other Practical Matters

W E'VE TALKED ABOUT some of the legal implications of homeschooling, about theories of learning, and about how homeschoolers try to put some of those theories into practice, but there are also lots of practical considerations when you're getting started homeschooling. How much does it all cost? Can families really afford homeschooling in today's economy? Do you need a special room for your "school"? How do you organize all your learning materials? In this chapter we'll take a look at such practical considerations.

How Much Does Homeschooling Cost?

No one can predict what your exact financial outlay for homeschooling will be because so much depends on the choices you and your family make about your style of homeschooling. You'll definitely find that homeschooling entails more expense than conventional public schooling but also that it will cost considerably less than the annual $2,000 to $10,000 per child that private school tuition typically runs.

The least expensive option is a public school program tailored to homeschoolers. The most conventional of these require no expenses that would not also be expected in regular classroom programs because the materials and program are so similar except for most work occurring at home under parental supervision. Those programs that allow more flexibility in choosing materials are often a bit more expensive because they may only provide or reimburse for certain "approved" texts and materials, or they may establish a yearly budget limit for each student. If you choose to use other texts than the program recommends, you may end up having to cover the costs yourself. Some programs offer equipment, such as microscopes or computers, for loan during school terms (and sometimes over vacations, too). Also often provided are "consumables"—items such as paper, pens and pencils, workbooks, and so on—although, as with the other materials, supplies may be limited to specific amounts each school term.

> Those programs that allow more flexibility in choosing materials are often a bit more expensive because they may only provide or reimburse for certain "approved" texts and materials, or they may establish a yearly budget limit for each student.

Private homeschooling programs vary mainly according to the services they provide. Some programs, such as Calvert, mainly sell complete curriculum packages. In 1998, the average tuition for a complete Calvert curriculum for a single grade ranged from $285 for kindergarten to $530 for the upper elementary grades, with its advisory teaching service (grading, testing, record maintenance) costing an additional $220. Calvert also offers "enrichment" courses such as music and foreign languages at $70 to $200, with reduced rates for several individuals enrolling together.

Other programs, such as Alpha Omega Publications (a popular Christian-based program), sell individual courses and books as well as complete packages. In 1998 Bridgestone Academy, Alpha Omega's correspondence affiliate, charged a $100 placement and registration fee and $750 tuition for four core subjects (English, math, history, and science), with electives an additional $200 each. Bridgestone also offers reduced rates for multiple enrollments.

Homeschoolers at the high school level often use conventional correspondence courses available through public and private universities. Such courses are relatively expensive, typically $100 to $300 per course; textbooks and other required materials may or may not be included in the course fee. For homeschoolers who desire formal credit in specialized topics, particularly in mathematics, sciences, and foreign languages, such courses can be well worth the extra expense.

Less structured private programs may offer per family pricing rather than per child or per course. In 1998, the Waldorf-based Oak Meadow School offered enrollment for an entire family at about $425 per year; curriculum packages (mainly storybooks, novels, and activity guides rather than formal textbooks) range from $165 to $330 according to grade level. Families can simply purchase curricular materials from Oak Meadow, or they can opt for one of several levels of academic support: enrollment with standard curriculum, enrollment with individualized educational plan ($150 IEP fee plus teacher and materials), and enrollment with portfolio evaluation ($35 to $45 per twelve to eighteen lessons completed). Teacher assistance for grading, record keeping, and general advice fees ranged from $290 to $400 per year.

Clonlara School is extremely flexible with its services and specializes in helping unschooling families with its Home Based Education Program (HBEP). Its 1998 fees for record keeping and curriculum advice were $550 for one student, $575 for two or three students, and $600 for four or more students per family. Books and other supplies are additional and vary depending on the type of program you and your family choose. Clonlara's Compuhigh courses are available online to students enrolled in its HBEP at $50 per one-unit course.

Public school distance learning programs are rapidly becoming more available. Eugene, Oregon–based CyberSchool offers high school credit courses worldwide over the Internet in a variety of subject areas. Typical English courses, for example, include Advanced Placement English, creative writing, and "All the World's a Stage" (Shakespeare I) at $300 per class per semester.

Costs for unschooling families are almost impossible to predict, but most families estimate they spend somewhere between $300 and $1,000 for the entire family. Many families buy lots of books, crafts, games, toys, and other items without keeping official track of whether what they're buying is "educational" and can count items such as computers as general family purchases rather than as specifically educational. (Some of us deliberately avoid trying to calculate educational expenses, fearing to see the grand total.) Especially with younger children, though, it's difficult to say that such expenditures differ much from those for conventionally schooled children. Because so much of what unschoolers do falls into the category of everyday activities, for which most of us already have the materials we need, unschooling can be done on a shoestring, if necessary.

> Because so much of what unschoolers do falls into the category of everyday activities, for which most of us already have the materials we need, unschooling can be done on a shoestring, if necessary.

Fiscal restraint is, however, a good characteristic for most homeschoolers to develop. Especially when you're first starting out, it can be tempting to buy every nifty and interesting item you come across, just because you think one of your kids might really enjoy it. Too much of that sort of impulse buying can wreak havoc on your household budget, and such items often end up unused in the backs of closets or in the boxes for the next garage sale.

The Single-Income Family

The vast majority of homeschooling families find that their educational choice has one major and almost unavoidable financial consequence: the necessity of living on one income. For many parents considering homeschooling, the idea seems impossible: How can a family survive on one income and still lead any reasonable kind of life? Many parents never seriously consider the homeschooling option because they assume the financial problems it presents are insoluble.

It's mainly a matter of setting your priorities and deciding what you truly need instead of just assuming everything you need. Just as new moms consider the finances of returning to work after the birth of a child, you'll need to figure out your expenses. Your costs will be less in several obvious areas with a parent at home full-time:

- Day care expenses will be eliminated.

- Transportation expenses will probably be reduced substantially. Eliminating a regular commute means you'll no longer need the monthly bus pass, or you'll be reducing wear and tear on the car and paying less for gas and insurance. You may find that you can get rid of one car entirely.

- Work clothes become unnecessary. Even in many retail jobs, work clothes can be a significant expense (and most of us adapt quite easily to T-shirts and jeans instead of suits and ties).

- Food costs are reduced. Not only will the at-home parent be eating fewer lunches out, but the entire family may eat at home more just because they spend more time at home. Cooking at home is substantially less expensive than eating out.

You may find that having one parent at home will be less of a financial hardship than you expect, and the advantages it offers in being available and able to do more with your family will make it well worth the difference. And there are plenty of ways to keep your expenses down without feeling like you're missing out. Most homeschooling families find that they end up doing more things together as a family and spending less time at such traditional American pastimes as mall crawling. Relatively low-cost activities such as reading books, making music, going on picnics, getting together with friends, and gardening become interesting and satisfying pursuits. Homeschooling parents sometimes also find that their children's (and even their own) wants become less peer driven and follow their own interests more than the latest popular trends in toys and fashion.

> Homeschooling parents sometimes find that their children's (and even their own) wants become less peer driven and follow their own interests more than the latest popular trends in toys and fashion.

Many homeschooling families become devotees of thrift shops and yard sales, finding everything from clothes and toys to books and hobby equipment at outrageously low prices. This can be a terrific way to try out new interests without risking much money on whether the attraction will last. A few families enjoy the challenge of doing as much as possible on as little money as possible: buying secondhand goods, bartering, growing their own vegetables. Most don't take things to this extreme, of course, but a few savings here and there add up to quite a bit over the course of a year.

Books and newsletters such as the *Tightwad Gazette,* the *Cheapskate Monthly,* and the *Frugal Corner* offer plenty of advice and suggestions for cutting expenses, and several maintain Internet sites as well.

Alternatives to Stay-at-Home Mom

At least 90 percent of the time, the stay-at-home homeschooling parent is the mother. Most often, hers was the job that provided the lesser income and hers was the easier career to forfeit or postpone. Many homeschooling parents, though, find it ironic that their unconventional educational choice results in such a conventional, traditional lifestyle, at least superficially, and work hard to avoid indoctrinating their kids with gender stereotypes. They may opt to rotate all household tasks among all family members, so that no one person always cooks or cleans or mows or fixes the car, or cares for the kids.

Of course, alternatives to Stay-at-Home Mom exist. Some families opt for Stay-at-Home Dad, if the wife's income is better or the couple simply prefers a less traditional allocation of duties. Rare these days is the local homeschool support group without at least one homeschooling father in regular attendance at park days and field trips.

Frequently, the at-home parent will develop some sort of work at or from home to generate extra income. More than a few parents who take to selling books and other materials for homeschoolers, at first just for the wholesale discounts, find themselves with a full-fledged at-home business on their hands. Others, with occupations such as computer programming, accounting, word processing, or writing, find working at home a satisfying solution.

• • •

After I closed my retail business when my oldest daughter was born, money was very tight. My husband was in a teacher credential program and working only part-time. We did some brainstorming and together created a business where he is able to teach something he loves, and I can do what I love—grow a business with my daughter at my side. We marketed our kung fu school to after-school day care programs, day care facilities, and private schools so our daughter could be with us while we worked. In eight years, we have seen our business grow and change as well as our family. We've had two more daughters, and the girls help now with all aspects of the business: mailing, bookkeeping, inventory control, setting up class equipment, and designing newsletters. Not only have they learned the basics of math, reading, and writing while working along with us, they've learned one of the most important skills—how to pursue your passions in life. —*Elizabeth,* California

• • •

Sometimes both parents are employed outside the home, working different shifts so that one or the other parent is always home with the kids. Or they may work out arrangements for their children to spend part of the day or a few days a week with a grandparent, another relative, or other homeschooling families.

Organizing Your "Schoolroom"

State regulations may cover what children must learn or how many days of instruction are required, but they don't dictate the physical conditions for learning within your home. Unless you operate a licensed family day-care facility or teach other families' children in your home, there are no specific requirements for furniture, lighting, ventilation, or other items typically covered in school building codes. Physical arrangements for homeschooling are as varied as all the other aspects of homeschoolers' lives.

> Physical arrangements for homeschooling are as varied as all the other aspects of homeschoolers' lives.

Some families convert their dining room, a basement room, or an extra bedroom into a formal classroom, complete with desks, shelves, globe, and flag. Surplus school desks are often available through school districts, or families may prefer either several small tables or one large one instead. A computer or a VCR and television can be useful additions.

Other families opt to provide their kids with desks in their own rooms, leaving them the option of working there or somewhere in the common areas of the house. Or each child might have a plastic milk crate or file box to stash schoolbooks and supplies, so that all school materials can be easily found and moved wherever needed.

Unschooling families and those using some type of unit studies, in which materials are often shared among everyone in the family, generally prefer to have everything where the whole family has easy access. A good-size, sturdy table in the family room, along with an old dresser for storing craft supplies, are common sights in these homeschoolers' houses, along with lots of boxes and bins and tubs for Lego blocks and other toys. And no homeschooling family ever seems to have anywhere near enough shelf space for books.

Housekeeping and Other Complications of Daily Life

New homeschoolers are often startled when they first arrive at a support group meeting held at the home of an experienced home-schooler. They walk in to see a spotless house, with books and maga-zines carefully organized and shelved, toys sorted by types and carefully stored in bins. They marvel to see no signs of dirty dishes waiting to be washed or laundry waiting to be folded. They immedi-ately wonder what they are doing wrong and despair of ever learning to cope with all the tasks that need doing every single day. How do experienced homeschoolers manage it all?

Basically, we don't.

We are the people whose kids ask, when they see the vacuum cleaner out, "Who's coming for company?" Like everybody else, we run the dishwasher when we are out of clean dishes, we wash the win-dows (maybe) when we can no longer see through them, and we're happy when there's a path clear of small, pointy plastic toy parts through the living room. Nine times out of ten, the experienced homeschooler's home will have been cleaned up especially for that support group meeting, which was the perfect excuse for getting it back into manageable shape.

Whatever your homeschooling style, there is one incontrovertible fact about homeschooling: Your kids are home for most of the day every day. Even with outside lessons, Scouts, field trips, sports, and outdoor play, your kids will be at home far more hours than schooled kids, and your house will show the effects of their presence. As we homeschoolers often tell each other with our tongues firmly in our cheeks, our houses look lived in.

Here are a few things you can do to keep your surroundings bearable:

- Make it clear among the entire family that keeping the house livable is everyone's job. Everybody lives in the house, the family is a cooperative enterprise, and everybody needs to work together to make it function. With everybody pitching in at the same time, the worst chores are less like drudgery and get done quickly. Even the smallest children can help in some way, and letting them get into the habit while they are still young enough to want to help is worth the extra time and energy it takes.

- Try frequent short bursts of straightening and cleaning. Small children, especially, enjoy making a game of seeing how much they can get cleaned up in a quick five- or ten-minute drill. A couple of short drills each day can help keep the creeping clutter at bay.

- Become a devotee of container housekeeping. Baskets, clear plastic bins with lids, and file boxes on casters are endlessly useful for keeping things sorted and stored. Having Lego bins, a Barbie basket, a crayon tin or art box, and so on, makes clearing up clutter a matter of scooping items into the proper containers and getting the containers back to their shelves or under the appropriate beds. An old dresser in the dining room can be viewed as a permanently established set of bins, although the contents may change from action figures and crayons to model kits and watercolors as your kids grow and their tastes change.

- Try scheduling specific tasks for specific days. Instead of doing all the housework on a single day, spread out some of the tasks a bit: laundry on Monday, mowing the lawn on Tuesday, vacuuming on Wednesday, and bathrooms on Thursday. Or, just do everything often enough so that the whole house job only takes an hour or two once a week.

- Most important of all: Lower your standards! If you're feeling guilty because your house is only clean when you have friends (or your in-laws) coming over, stop and think about who your ideal spotless house is for. If the house is for you and your family to live in, you'll eventually find your own balance between cleanliness and clutter. If you want a showplace, you might want to find an apartment you can all live in so you don't get the house messed up.

CHAPTER SIX

The Primary Years: Reading, 'Riting, and 'Rithmetic

I T'S ONE OF the questions homeschoolers dread. People curious about homeschooling always ask it and always seem to suspect we're trying to hide something when we can't answer it very well: What's a typical homeschooling day like?

The problem is that every day is different, and no day seems really typical to us. It's the accumulation of days and activities and projects that make up the pattern of our learning. "Education" for us comes not in individual segments but in the aggregate of activities new and old, in combinations and imitation and recombinations and inventions. It's too hard to single out any one day as representative of the entire process.

That said, I asked the question anyway, of a few dozen homeschooling friends and acquaintances, except that I broke it down into more manageable pieces: How do you homeschool? Do you use a purchased formal curriculum, are you a rabid unschooler, or are you somewhere in the vast territory between? Do you have set hours, are you flexible, or do you eschew formal lessons entirely? Who decides what's to be learned? What resources do you use, where do you find them, and how do you use them? If you're homeschooling more than one child, do you work with them together or separately? How does your learning/teaching style or your routine differ for each child, or does it? How much and in what ways has your homeschooling changed as your children have grown and matured?

Fortunately, most homeschoolers love to talk about what they do, and I had no lack of answers. This chapter, focusing on younger children, and the two following, on older children and on teens, will begin to give you a glimmer of what homeschooling life can be like. Take these firsthand accounts as examples of possibilities, not as models. No family will have quite the same needs and interests, but many will give you ideas you can adapt and use for yourselves. Also, keep in mind that few homeschooling families will conform exactly to the structures outlined in the last chapter; although one approach may predominate, bits and pieces of others will also be used.

> For younger children—those to about nine or ten years old—the emphasis is usually on gaining the skills fundamental to further learning: reading and writing, computation, finding information, whether it be in books, on the Internet, or from individuals on a personal basis.

For younger children—those to about nine or ten years old—the emphasis is usually on gaining the skills fundamental to further learning: reading and writing, computation, finding information, whether it be in books, on the Internet, or from individuals on a personal basis. Far more important than any specific subject matter is simply learning how to learn.

At these young ages, one of the biggest divisions among homeschoolers is that between those who believe in starting formal learning as early as possible and those who believe that formal learning is best delayed until the child is eight or ten or even older. Educators such as Glen Doman (*How to Teach Your Baby to Read*) suggest starting formal lessons with babies and toddlers, on the premise that very young children can learn far more quickly and capably than is usually expected of them and that to delay such instruction is to deprive them of opportunities to perform at their best.

Raymond and Dorothy Moore are probably the best-known advocates of the later-is-better approach. The Moores' 1975 book, *Better Late Than Early*, summarizes research supporting their contention that children are not physiologically ready for formal learning until age eight to ten. They suggest that waiting allows children to gain the maturity and logical skills necessary for formal work and prevents them from becoming frustrated and discouraged by attempts to handle material they are simply not yet ready to understand.

It is quite common for homeschooled children, especially in the more flexible approaches, to learn to read as young as age two or three or to delay to age eight or nine, or even as late as age twelve. Because of the individualized nature of homeschooling, whatever style the family uses, late reading is far less of a handicap to further learning than it would be in a conventional school setting. Because schools rely so heavily on text-based instruction, we tend to forget that there are plenty of other ways to acquire knowledge. A not-yet-reading homeschooled child can watch TV and videos, be read to by family members, ask questions of friends and family, and acutely observe everything surrounding her. The late reader frequently blossoms suddenly into a capable and independent reader, moving quickly into fluent reading beyond the level normally expected at her age. Because the lack of independent reading skill does not hamper other learning to the severe degree that it might in a conventional classroom or damage the child's self-

> Because schools rely so heavily on text-based instruction, we tend to forget that there are plenty of other ways to acquire knowledge. A not-yet-reading home-schooled child can watch TV and videos, be read to by family members, ask questions of friends and family, and acutely observe everything surrounding her.

confidence, the late-reading homeschooler remains an eager and interested learner.

The Formal Approach: School-at-Home

Alisanne and Todd live in New Jersey with their daughter, Kassy. Todd, formerly employed in the corporate headquarters of a large research company, is now on permanent medical disability. Alisanne ran a business at home before Kassy's birth and plans eventually to do so again. Kassy spent a year in nursery school three times a week before beginning homeschooling.

• • •

We have a room that we've set up as our "schoolroom." We do daily lessons that take about two to three hours. Our daughter, an only child, is six. We homeschool year-round and generally six days a week.

I try to have fairly set hours, or Kassy would take all day to do her lessons. I have recently been aiming for starting by nine o'clock and finishing by noon. If we finish by lunch time, much more of the day is left to do other things.

I have a freeware lesson planning program that I keep on the computer and use to plan our week. I wrote a curriculum that I use to keep track of our overall objectives. I do an assessment approximately every six weeks to determine whether our learning objectives are on track. Currently Kassy is mostly doing second-grade work, but she has first-grade handwriting skills that slow her down. But she is only just six.

We use Saxon math. Kassy will be finishing *Saxon Math 2* in late May, and we'll start *Saxon Math 3* in June. We used *Sing, Spell, Read & Write* for an overall phonics approach to reading but have finished it. We are now using various beginning readers because Kassy did not like the readers that came with the phonics program. This year we purchased a copy of *Comprehensive Curriculum of Basic Skills—Second Grade,* and Kassy has been working through that to cover English, spelling, and such. We haven't decided yet whether to use one for third grade.

. . .

Beverly, her husband Michael, and their five children (fourteen, eleven, ten, six, and four) live in a Nebraska suburb. Michael is in the military and is the only member of the family employed outside the home. They've been homeschooling the four younger children since the fall of 1993; before then, the three oldest children attended a private Christian school.

. . .

Our homeschooling day begins in the morning. After taking my oldest daughter to school, I get the next two oldest children up out of bed. They spend the next hour eating, dressing, and diddling about. I write a weekly schedule for each child on the computer. They are allowed to work at it at their own pace but must get through Monday's work by the end of Monday. In the past I tried listing a week's worth of assignments and letting them choose when to work on them. They would leave the least liked subject for last. Fridays became torture days. So we switched back to daily schedules. They are allowed to work ahead and take the next day off if they want to. We usually stop our school work for lunch at 12:30. We usually spend an hour on lunch. The kids fix their own lunch and clean it up. After lunch, they do schoolwork until they are done. Usually that is no later than 2:30. The rest of the day is theirs to pursue their own interests. We have lots of computer games, books, and other games. They also like to go outside and play with the neighbor kids. Once a month we go to homeschool group followed by roller skating. We also attend a play once a month.

We use a certain amount of curriculum, and the rest is good books or other resources. The only curriculum I don't tinker with is their spelling program and their vocabulary program. These are both workbooks they enjoy doing; if they didn't enjoy them, we wouldn't be doing them. For math we use Saxon with lots of other stuff thrown in. Fridays we do either mental math or math games. Science and social studies are done as units.

During the summer I choose books, kits, or projects on the subjects I plan to teach. We read the books out loud and discuss them. The kids work on the projects or experiments as independently as possible. They keep science notebooks to write definitions of terms and to write about their experiments.

This year we are studying world geography. We spend six or seven days exploring a region of the world. The children select a country to study in depth. I write questions that they can answer when writing about their country. They use the CD encyclopedia, books from the library, and the Internet to find information about their country. They are learning to take notes on note cards and use them in writing a report. We also use the Internet to find music files and recipes. Each day we read about a different cultural group in the region we are studying. When we do history, we do it as a combination of biography and other books. We've used the Greenleaf Press Famous Men series for studying Egypt, Greece, Rome, and the Middle Ages.

I started out teaching separate science and social studies to each of the kids. After one year of doing this, I came to my senses. We have since done all science together. My second daughter is extremely bright and had no difficulty working on the same level as her older sister. My son as a second grader was just along for the ride. I required no written work of him. This year he has his own science notebook and is required to write reports for geography. I expect a good deal less from him in terms of a report. He is learning to read a paragraph and then write a sentence that restates the main idea of the paragraph. He writes these sentences on index cards that we sort and then copy to write his report. By the end of the year I expect him to have a good facility with this.

Next year I will have a kindergartner who will probably be getting his first dose of American history from biographies. I have a number of famous American biographies written on a second-grade reading level with extra activities to make the story come to life. With his older brother also studying American history, we may decide to act out some scenes from American history.

We also do a variety of extra activities. For example, now we are reading stories by Shakespeare from Charles and Mary Lamb's *Tales from Shakespeare*. We use this reading to practice the kids' narration skills. We are also learning Spanish using the Learnables tapes. We select a composer of the month to study. For art appreciation we are studying architecture this year. I have a number of children's books on architecture that we are reading, and later this year we will read some of David Macaulay's books.

. . .

The Eclectics: Finding What Works

Karin and Frank live with their three children (nine, seven, and six) in a North Carolina suburb. Both adults are college graduates; Frank works outside the home, and Karin handles the bulk of the home-schooling. They started homeschooling their oldest child, Duncan, this year; the two younger children will join him at home next year.

. . .

I do a combination of school-at-home and structured un-schooling, if that makes any sense.

I am using the Hirsch book—*What Your 3rd Grader Needs to Know*—right now. I use it as it is, but I skip around in the book depending on interest level and connections between subjects. For instance, we read the poem about Paul Revere's ride, and then we worked on American history dealing with the Battle of Concord, the Boston Tea Party, Bunker Hill, and so on.

I like it a lot. It covers a lot of things that I know my children were not covering in school. Also, I am learning (or re-learning) things that I don't remember now either. I am a little panicked, though, because the Hirsch books only go through the sixth grade!

Our schedule is flexible, but usually we do structured stuff (book reading, worksheets, and so on) from 10 A.M. to 2 P.M., and then he has two hours or so in the afternoon to do artwork, watch educational videos, play computer games or educational stuff.

We both decide what he learns. I want to cover everything in the book, and we try to build on something that we have learned before, but if he prefers to do science one day or not do math another, I tend to let him have his say. It all gets done eventually. I do a lot of suggesting, though.

We have three children, but two are in public school until June. Then I will be homeschooling all of them. Our plan is to have one hour of one-on-one time with each child, and one hour each of computer time and unstructured time for each child. (They will rotate "stations" every hour.) Then we'll have one hour of time all together when we'll either work on something that everyone is interested in or read aloud or something. Of course, this sounds good in theory—I'm not sure yet, but I think it will work out for us all right.

My child has become a much happier young man since he's been homeschooled, and that's why we have decided to home-school everyone.

* * *

Shari and her husband Tim have three children: TJ, ten; Bekah, seven; and Phoebe, three. They currently live in Alabama, although because of Tim's work they have moved fairly frequently and have lived in several states. Aside from some preschool for TJ, none of the kids have attended school.

* * *

Our homeschooling has become a bit more formal as our kids have grown; that is, we become more formal with each child as they seem ready.

We don't do much of what the world would call school before the age of nine or ten. Bekah, for example, gets read to a lot, we cook together, play some math games. She plays on the computer a ton, and we do have a phonics program and Miquon math workbooks, which get some use. She loves science and is forever looking through science books. We purchased a number of *Peterson's Field Guides* coloring books for her as well.

Phoebe demands school, so we give her the Cuisenaire Alphabet Book when we're doing math. We don't think of her as formally homeschooled, either.

Tim and I talk openly and freely with the kids about our ideas about education and what we believe makes a well-educated person. Their lives, for the most part, are filled with educated people, not all of whom have fancy degrees. Anyway, we decide together, based on discussions, which materials we'll use. TJ gets input; we get the final say. That is, until he throws a fit over a stupid choice I've made. Then we back up and start again.

We're believers in classical education, I suppose. Not classical methods, just the content: solid historical foundation, awareness of important figures in Western culture, lots of good music and art, and why we think it's good. We introduce a wide variety of world studies as well, but our focus is very much the importance of Western civilization on our modern-day lives.

As far as resources go, I keep my eyes and ears open, sift through what I believe to be the best stuff, and order every July or August. We also buy lots of good books and computer games all year. We spend our days informally scheduled. A schedule can be easily and guiltlessly interrupted by a phone call (though we do try to avoid this), bread baking, a field trip, whatever.

Here's a typical day:

Get up; do chores; eat breakfast sometime before 10 A.M.

Then Bible reading (TJ reads stories to the girls and me), math, any phonics work, writing, literature (we're working through a book where one day TJ may narrate a story back to me and another day write a paragraph or memorize a poem), history (reading and time line work). Science is done with Dad on weekends.

By noon or so, we're usually done and tackle more chores (the girls have effectively destroyed the house by now), eat lunch, run any errands, go to the park, or hang out and veg. With any luck, TJ may pick up a book or magazine at some point. I don't watch and don't always want to know.

I usually fix dinner while making lunch, so that's put away so Tim can throw it in the oven after he picks the girls up from the pool, where I usually stay with TJ while he works out (sometimes I swim, too). That's from 5:30 to 7:30 P.M. Then home, dinner, reading aloud, and so on. Network TV for me and Tim from 9 to 10 P.M. Bed if I'm fortunate enough to have Phoebe and Bekah both asleep. (Otherwise, that's my job, because Tim has to get up at 5 A.M. and I can sleep until . . . well, 8 A.M. or so, if I need to.)

. . .

Doug and Patricia live in a California suburb. They mix and match their homeschooling styles for their eight-year-old daughter, Emily. Patricia works outside the home, and Doug is a stay-at-home dad. Emily has never attended school.

. . .

Our homeschooling is relaxed. Emily does a lot of reading in many areas—nature, animals, science, and some biographies. She watches a local PBS station that has shows on science and literature.

We are in the vast territory between either extreme in terms of structure. We are soon to be using a math curriculum to see how she responds to it. We've heard of a good English curriculum that we will be checking into also. However, having said that, we don't have Emily sit down on a regular basis and do a certain number of pages each day. Our daily schedule is very flexible. Sometimes we focus on math or writing or art or spelling or geography. It depends on how she's feeling and how I'm feeling. We also go to the library, take trips to museums, park days, and art and gymnastics classes.

We have enrolled her in a local charter school. This is so we can have access to the funds they offer for educational materials. The school is designed with homeschoolers in mind, and we are not forced to follow any set time line or curriculum.

As the at-home parent, I'm the one who initiates most of the "homeschooling." However, my wife is a big influence in that she offers many ideas for projects and for keeping Emily's interest engaged in various areas of learning. It is clear to me that we are a homeschooling family. We all—including Emily—give input into Emily's homeschooling.

. . .

Tina and Fred have been homeschooling for almost two years. They have a six-year-old son and a three-year-old daughter.

. . .

We're a bit of both unschoolers and structured schoolers— we definitely use a piecemeal approach. We have *Alpha-Phonics* for reading, plus we pieced together reading material for him to practice on, like first readers, a couple of used A Beka books, and so on. For math, I got a workbook from Bob Jones and borrowed the teacher's guide from a neighbor who had it already. We're almost done with it, and I'm going to look into Saxon math next. For science, we subscribe to a monthly newsletter, we have all kinds of science experiment books, and we have several science CD-ROMs, plus some in history and geography. We pretty much use what we have as is, unless, as in math, we skip drill pages if he already knows the material.

We used to have set hours, but now we have approximate hours. If we miss, I don't sweat it, because I plan on schooling through the summer. I think it's not good to take so much time off, so I'm planning on one week on and one week off. We'll see how that works. (Just about everything is first time because we've only been homeschooling for two years, and as our son gets older, the way we do lessons changes.)

We both decide what's to be learned. I'm not flexible as far as the reading and math—I decide we do it, but he has input on how we do it. Everything else he has a say in. If he's not interested, we look for other ways to learn whatever it is. There are really so many interesting ways to learn about the world around us, that it's not hard. We go on field trips, regular trips to the library, and on the Internet, of course.

. . .

Freeform Learning: Unschooling

Jennifer and David live in California. David works for the state, and Jennifer writes frequently for local and state homeschooling support group publications. Their two children (eight and six) have never attended school.

· · ·

Honestly, our day begins earlier than I would like—around 6 A.M. After David makes a hot breakfast and leaves for the office, we settle into our un-routine. While I tidy up the breakfast things and catch up on my e-mail, the children play. Play is still our work and usually involves Legos, drawing, painting, hand sewing, or reading to themselves or each other.

After I have had "my time," I read aloud to the children, which is something we have been doing forever. We especially like series books about real families. We have thoroughly enjoyed the *Little House* series and the *Little Britches* series. Right now, we're reading the *Redwall* series. After I have read for a while, we snack and are ready for something else.

That "something else" varies according to the weather, mood, play date, and local support group calendar. Our local group often has at least one activity a week, whether it be a skate day, park day, or library day to focus on. I am a homebody and at this time feel it is important to be at home, so I try not to schedule more than one other play date a week. I feel very strongly that it is important to learn how to get along with each other first. When we do have what I call "quiet days at home," we do many things together and separately. For example, I may show my son how to macramé and then go on to a sewing project of my own.

Often interests at home have turned into group activities. Both my children showed an interest in playing chess, which led to our family forming a chess club within our homeschooling group. One Saturday each month a different family will host a chess club get-together. This helps all the children, regardless of age or gender, learn about chess and sportsmanship.

The children are allowed to watch one PBS program in the afternoon and then it is the dinner thing. Food is also very important to us, and we usually have done some cooking together during the day. It is important that everyone have a role and feel needed, so there is a lot of bustling around in the kitchen. Everyone having jobs also avoids the martyred-mom complex.

After dinner, David often works in the garage on projects. We just finished remodeling our kitchen, and he made the cabinet doors out of stained glass. While he worked, the children watched and later made some stained glass window hangings that they entered in the state fair.

The day ends at 8 P.M. with family story time.

. . .

Melissa and Kevin homeschool their four children (thirteen, eleven, nine, and seven) in a small Northern California city. Kevin works outside the home; Melissa volunteers extensively in the community.

. . .

We are unschoolers given to frequent panic attacks.

Until the kids are ten, we don't do anything that is not child led, but at that point we start enforced writing and arithmetic. We spend our days as we please around our out-of-the-house schedule: gymnastics, karate, science club, art class, Meals on Wheels, soccer. We have no set hours, although it seems easier to get things done in the mornings.

My husband and I work together on what are important things to emphasize—the kids still do as they please. I try to have them all do quiet work at the same time. We try to involve as many as possible in games and chores and activities, but everyone needs individual time, too.

. . .

Linda and Brad live in Hawaii with their three children (twelve, nine, and five). Linda is an at-home parent, who is also active in a state and island homeschool support group; Brad is a physician. They decided to homeschool when their first child was six months old.

• • •

We are definitely way over on the unschooling end of the spectrum. We don't use a package and are not connected with any sort of school. We don't have set hours or formal lessons except for Suzuki violin lessons that Katy requested earlier in the year. She was offered music lessons before but didn't have any interest until then. She and I started lessons, and because we were playing, first Robert and recently Emily requested violins so they could play.

This year a sort of routine has arisen around the outside lessons. Tuesday: family violin lessons followed by grocery shopping and errands. Wednesday: art class and library day. Thursday: homeschool park day twice a month. In previous years we didn't have any regular schedule, so this is new for us, but I decided the routine was helpful so the other days could be "free" days.

Occasionally there are other classes or field trips arranged by us or offered in the community—for example, a six-week American Sign Language class I arranged for some homeschool friends at the request of my oldest, or a two-week intensive course in "Animation for Young People" at the local university during the summer.

Otherwise, the rest of our learning is quite informal. The children spend large blocks of time working on things independently—reading, drawing, making all sorts of things, writing stories, writing to pen pals, sewing, using the computer, playing piano, and engaging in all sorts of imaginative play with dolls, little figures, pretend restaurant, and so on. These are initiated by the children and frequently carried out with only minimal help from me. Katy and Em learned to read without any formal instruction.

There are also times when I work with them directly. They ask for math all the time, so I try to come up with appropriate math games that they love. We like math (and Grandpa is a retired math teacher), so we have lots of books on math. In the last year or so, we got some math workbooks (Key Curriculum), which we use very flexibly. The children also ask for help or feedback on their writing or help with a particular project. I suggest activities, resources, and projects I think they might be interested in, but it's up to the children to decide what actually looks good.

Finding resources is the fun part. I usually consult them before buying materials, but I bring home lots of library books that look interesting to me even if they wouldn't pick them out themselves. Some of these they find are more interesting than they thought, and others are returned unread or read only by me. That's fine with us.

> No matter how inventive and persistent we are in trying to apply our favored techniques, our children can always equal that invention and persistence in resisting what does not work for them.

One thing that's changed is that I'm no longer averse to using curriculum materials like the occasional workbook or textbook. In the past I wouldn't even have considered them. Don't get me wrong: I still think there are far too many bad ones and problems with too heavy a dose of even the good ones, but now I will use them if they meet a specific need, and then we still use them very flexibly. I believe you have to see what's called for in each individual situation rather than think there is one best way to do things, whether it is using workbooks or rejecting them. Of course, this sounds obvious, but there are all too many people stuck in their thinking about this.

• • •

Linda highlights a common stumbling block for many homeschoolers who start with a particular philosophy or methodology in mind. Whatever your approach, it's important to keep your focus on your children and what works best for them, whether it fits into that favored methodology or not. No matter how inventive and persistent we are in trying to apply our favored techniques, our children can always equal that invention and persistence in resisting what does not work for them. It's far easier and far more effective to tailor your tools and techniques to your child than to try to force your child to adapt to unsuitable tools.

CHAPTER SEVEN

The Middle Years: Exploring the World

DURING THE "MIDDLE" years—from nine or ten through twelve—children begin to explore subject areas in more depth. Most kids have got reading figured out, and they're eagerly investigating a wide variety of subjects. Many homeschooling parents alternate between pride and dismay as their kids quickly outrun prepared lessons or their parents' own knowledge. Their amazement at their kids' enthusiasm and abilities is often equaled by exhaustion and a sense of helplessness as they ponder trying to keep up with the voracious learners their kids have become.

This is also the age at which kids may begin to focus on one or two intense interests, often to the exclusion of other activities if allowed. Even with the most formal, structured approach to homeschooling, most kids will have time to develop and explore interests and hobbies in great depth. Many who do so might never have found the time to even discover such intense interests under the normal load of work and activities demanded by conventional schooling.

Kids at this stage also begin to think about career possibilities and about specific things they will need to know to become competent adults. Many opt to develop specific skills to reach longer-term goals: The child interested in engineering focuses on math skills she will need. The budding entrepreneur tackles marketing basics. The would-be artist concentrates on building his technical art skills or digs into the computer tools becoming necessary today. Even some of the most informal unschoolers begin to take more formal approaches to learning.

But we're still talking about kids here. Even the most serious kid will not be constantly focused on long-term goals, and those goals can change from year to year or even month to month. This can be disconcerting to the parent whose ambitious dancer suddenly discovers a passion for architecture, but the process of learning about and exploring a few subjects in depth is worthwhile in itself; figuring out what you are definitely not interested in is just as valuable as finding your real interests. Looking back as adults, it's easy for most of us to see the value of digging into a few topics in depth—for many of us, that kind of exploration could have saved us several semesters of college-level work or even years in less-than-satisfying jobs.

> Many homeschooling parents alternate between pride and dismay as their kids quickly outrun prepared lessons or their parents own knowledge.

School-at-Home

Trudy and Tony homeschool their three children: Anthony (eleven), Rachel (ten), and Sariah (five).

· · ·

There is so much we want to learn, we do not know when to quit! We start at 8:30 in the morning and if no one gets carried away, we usually quit around 2:30. (But somebody always gets carried away.)

We use several different curriculums. Language arts for the fourth and sixth graders is Alpha Omega, but if they can test out of a book, they do not have to do it. For our kindergartner, we're using McGuffey and a very expensive Macmillan curriculum I purchased years ago when I taught preschool. It's great, but it's really too expensive to buy for just one person.

For math, we use Saxon and Alpha Omega, and for science and social studies, we use Konos. We do the Konos all together, and I really like that. On a lot of the Konos topics, the Internet has been very helpful. The kids are writing reports on birds right now. The local library has just one book on each of these birds (the California condor and the purple marten), but the Internet has tons of information.

For Spanish, we use whatever our local library has or trade lessons with someone who speaks Spanish. We won't purchase any more handwriting books because Alpha Omega covers so much handwriting in their workbooks that we've been doing overkill.

Our hours are set, but they're not in stone. We don't try to do all of these things every day.

Our children are much more stable, polite, and confident since we brought them home. The house is not as straight, and Mom weighs ten pounds more.

. . .

Ava and Steve, and their ten-year-old daughter, Sher' Rie, live in a suburban community in South Carolina. They found that Sher' Rie had been confused by too many differing reading programs when she attended school and that she had little confidence in her own abilities.

. . .

We homeschool all year-round and are coming up on our third year this way. This has worked well for us. It allows us to take time off when we want or need to, and it's easy to adjust a year-long schedule when you become sick and lose a week of school. For the first two years, we stuck with the school schedule, and I always felt it was too binding.

We have a family room over our garage that we use as our schoolroom. Many days our lessons carry us elsewhere within our home and yard. I use a wide variety of curriculums, but lately we have been using more Rod and Staff than the others. We've used A Beka in the past and still occasionally pull the history and science books out to use as resources.

I've liked most of the curriculum I bought after the first two years. It took time for me to find the right stuff at the right speed for Sher' Rie.

Sher' Rie has had many difficulties with reading; however, she is doing much better. For about three months this year we did nothing but field trips and reading, and she made a lot of progress with her reading skills. It's great to see her finally enjoying what she reads.

We've never stuck to a rigid schedule. We're now trying to get ourselves into an 8 A.M. to 12 P.M. schedule for our structured schoolwork, and set up all field trips for afternoon times.

I decide what is needed to help Sher' Rie in areas where she's having problems. I choose her curriculum and make the decisions about what is to be taught and when. However, I do allow room in many areas for the things Sher' Rie wants to do.

We have a computer that I'm starting to use for information from other homeschoolers. Eventually Sher' Rie will learn a lot about the use of the computer, and she, too, will be able to use it as a resource.

I use the public library for many, many books and programs they offer: music CDs, tapes and books for children, many educational videos, computers with programs for children, books on tape, artwork, phonics reading program, magazines, and newspapers.

Sher' Rie is a kinesthetic learner. When we first started, I was just using textbooks, trying to teach her visually and aurally. My teaching style has slowly changed since then, allowing more hands-on activities and lots of field trips.

• • •

Eclectics: Balancing Exploration with "Basics"

Tammy and Jack are Texas suburbanites; their two boys (thirteen and ten) attended only preschool and kindergarten. Tammy is the at-home parent.

. . .

I have tried just about every approach to learning there is. Currently, we are in "unit study mode," and it seems to be the most productive of all.

Essentially, we study when we want to. My youngest may only do math two days a week, but when he gets going, he tends to do a week's worth of work in a day. We don't do the same things every day, though I sometimes feel that we should. We prefer to continue with whatever we happen to be enjoying at the moment rather than cut ourselves off in what feels like midstream to go on to the next subject. At first this bothered me, but as I began to look at the way I study when I have something to learn, I saw that this is actually the more natural approach, at least for me and mine.

I do specific work (math, for example) with my two sons separately, and we do the general things together. For instance, we are using Greenleaf's history together. This month's unit study is early Texas history.

We're quick to run for the encyclopedia if we see something on TV (or crawling around outside) that interests us. I've come to realize in recent years that learning really is something that happens all of the time and it is wrong to limit it to the "classroom." The parent who won't bother to help her child find the answer to a question simply because the answer isn't "needed" right then is making a terrible mistake. When this is the approach used,

> Essentially, we study when we want to. My youngest may only do math two days a week, but when he gets going, he tends to do a week's worth of work in a day.

learning becomes equated with school, and it seems inevitable that school becomes a bad word. In other words, we seem to be "doing school" at all hours of the day and night every day of the week.

. . .

Lisa and Greg live with their four kids in a good-size Alabama city. Sara, their oldest, twelve, attended a private kindergarten and third grade in a public school.

. . .

We go with the flow. Sara has always liked "structured" work—that is, working through a workbook or textbook. We have done some reports and some Konos units. My best friend did the whole nine yards, but we just picked over the activities and read and talked about things. I don't give tests, nor do we grade work, except for math, where we used Saxon for three years. Right now we are pulling subjects together, like ancient Greece. I picked out a few books, a video, an art project, and called it a unit.

Sara has not been reading like I wish she would, but she has been doing the twelve- to thirteen-year-old thing: turning into a teenager and sleeping a lot. Believe it or not, the older she gets, the more structured we get.

. . .

Carol and Rick live in a California suburb. Rick is employed outside the home, and Carol runs a family day-care business in their home. Shauna, thirteen, is a preschool dropout, and Rosalie, ten, has always homeschooled. Because of several physical problems (cleft lip, intermittent deafness, corneal scarring), Rosalie homeschools through a local public school independent study program.

. . .

We are interest-driven 80 percent and structured 20 percent. The 20 percent structured is piano practice six days a week and "formal" math. We have used *Spotlight on Math* up through eighth grade level, and the *Straightforward Math* series for algebra. This algebra book is so good, I am enjoying this formerly dreaded subject. My text in school was all problems and no explanations. This one is mostly clear explanations and relevant examples, with ten to twenty problems interspersed. It is a vast improvement because this is the only subject so far that I worried about my ability to facilitate. Rick is my ace in the hole: He reviews all confusing sections with both Shauna and me, so we're all on the same bus.

For reading, cooking, sewing, gardening, science, languages, history, and so on, we are interest driven, or learner led. Each girl has strong areas of long-standing interest, some of which overlap. Shauna began dance classes at not quite three. She has never taken even a summer off, by choice. She is now dancing en pointe in ballet and also does jazz and modern dance. It totals five hours of class a week now. She is also a very talented piano student and recently took a month off for the first time in five years.

Our rule is you can take whatever lessons you want from someone, but if we are paying for someone's expertise, I want us to follow her suggestions or propose alternatives, not simply ignore her advice. This means piano lessons are completely optional, but if you take them, then you are agreeing to practice as the teacher recommends and to discuss problems with her. Failing to do the latter recently led to Shauna feeling burned out. Once she realized that she had been feeling increasingly pressured by what her teacher thought were honors (invitations to play in a Bach festival and a Beethoven recital), Shauna realized she had to voice her displeasure about taking on a more intense performance schedule. She is learning to practice the fine art of negotiation: being neither passive nor aggressive, but assertive. We are finding that Shauna's at a bit of a crossroads, where the wonderful diversity of recreation and arts may need to be cut back. At the skill level she has achieved in singing, dance, and piano, more and more time is required for each, and fewer and fewer different activities can be fit in. From ages five to eleven, we were in an expansion phase, adding many new and wonderful activities. Now Shauna is in a consolidation stage—fewer things, but in more depth. It is exciting and occasionally sad. I love seeing her be truly beautiful to watch or listen to, but the attendant choices of having to drop back on other good activities causes wistfulness. There are only so many hours in a day, even for a high-energy homeschooler.

We have set hours when I am at the girls' disposal: available, but not in their faces. This time slot is 1:00 to 3:30 because it coincides with the day-care kids' nap time. It is after Shauna is fully awake and before the out-of-control "after school" schedule of dance and singing begin. Rosie prefers a more hands-on approach from me, but Shauna is only likely to appear for an assist if something in algebra really stumps her.

Our favorite resources are our World Book encyclopedia, our Macintosh computer (with CD-ROM), the library, friends, and personally selected teachers for given things. We travel extensively and just returned from two weeks in New England seeing friends and family. We frequent many museums and love local festivals of all kinds.

· · ·

Unschooling: Finding One's Passions

Deborah and Michael live in a small town near Chicago. Their oldest son, Ted (seventeen), attended school through fifth grade; Melissa (eleven) and twins Patrick and Sarah (four) have never been to school.

· · ·

The most obvious resource around here is books because they spill out of every available space. Reference books of all sorts, fiction, nonfiction, picture books. I pick up books about things that interest me, books about things my kids show interest in, books someone someday may want. I love beautifully illustrated children's books, so I'm fortunate that my twins humor me by enjoying my reading to them for hours.

We have art supplies of all kinds, from Crayola crayons to artists' pastels and charcoals. Paper of all sorts by the ton. Craft materials, fabrics, scrounged and recycled stuff for creations. Clays, inks, and paints. Wood and leather scraps. Tools of all descriptions. Some were acquired for the kids, some for the adults. The kids have access to it all, either under supervision or alone when I'm convinced they won't kill themselves or destroy the house.

We have science lab supplies, a microscope, a telescope, and hand lenses. Math manipulatives, bought and homemade. Puzzles, blocks, construction materials. Musical instruments. Tape recorders. Games. Two working computers, not counting the screamer belonging to my oldest son, the apprentice graphics wizard.

The kids all have library cards and a scheduled library trip once a week. Sometimes we'll make another trip if one of the older two convinces me it's necessary and the weather is too bad for them to bike. The little ones would be there every day if they had their way.

Deciding to deschool my oldest gave me an excuse for all this—we would have had it anyway. My choosing not to work outside the home has meant that they are all experts at finding good stuff at thrift and secondhand stores and know how to bargain at garage sales.

So far, I've only had energy problems with my oldest. He spent six years being ground down in the public schools and emerged feeling stupid and negative. Still, left alone with plenty of time and options, he eventually came to see the need for math and writing skills and asked for help. My experience so far with the others shows that kids are eager to be part of the adult world and will learn to write, read, and calculate if they see those skills used around them. So I think out loud a lot and do things like taxes, writing letters, going over the budget, whatever, when they are around instead of after everyone is asleep. I don't sit them down and give a "lesson," but I don't hide the workings of adult life, either. As for high-tech, I have to fight to get the computer, so I don't think that will be a problem. Kids don't need to know how it works (though some will want to); they just need to be able to use it.

If they don't want my help, they make that clear. If they want my assistance, advice, or ideas, I would be an awful person if I left them to their own devices anyway. If I notice what they're working on or thinking about, I often pull related books or materials out of the shelves to leave on the tables, but they are free to ignore them if they wish. I let them know about community resources they can use and provide transportation or help making contact if they want it. If they seem frustrated, I ask if I can help. If they're running along with something, I try to stay out of their way and not interfere. Sometimes I blow it, but life is like that. I've found I can shut down a child's interest if I get too involved without invitation, so I try to tread carefully. They all like me, though, so they usually invite me to share their discoveries. I just wish my oldest could occasionally get enthusiastic about sharing earlier than midnight because I have a tendency to drift off on him, having been awakened early by the bouncing babies.

> I've found I can shut down a child's interest if I get too involved without invitation, so I try to tread carefully.

. . .

Donna homeschools her three kids (eleven, nine, and five) in the state of Washington. She runs a newsletter and mail-order book company from her home. The kids are an integral part of the business, helping with sorting and mailing and daily operations, as well as testing the books, software, and other materials Donna considers for her catalog.

. . .

I believe that I am capable of imparting a love for learning, research skills, and an appreciation for life. My children are self-motivated, self-taught, and mainly experiential learners.

I read for several hours per day; they read for several hours per day. I use computers in my work; they use computers in their work. I write professionally; they write. I cook; they cook. I use mathematics in my business, and so do they.

They are ever present when I speak to sales managers, clients, and publishers on the phone. They are also present when I converse with bank managers for business advice.

Usually the adult work world is separated from family life. Mom and Dad go to work outside the home while the children attend school. I choose to work with my children in tow, and even though it is hard, it is worth it. My children humanize my business. They are constant reminders of my priorities: love, family, and work. I am there when they need me, and we are always working toward a more harmonious and loving family.

I take my children wherever I go, and that includes out-of-state speaking engagements. The more I work, the more I travel, and I am determined to keep them with me through it all. I practice all of my speeches with my children. They are with me every step of the way, from drafts to rewrites to oral practice. They know what it takes to make a professional presentation because we practice a lot (and I need their help).

My boys are learning Spanish from a native Peruvian. She conducts two one-hour classes per week for homeschoolers in her home. They are learning to converse in Spanish and, at their insistence, to read and write in the language also.

The boys study tap and jazz dancing, and Rukiya studies ballet and tap. Latif is on baseball and soccer teams, Kahil plays on a soccer team, and all three children are excellent swimmers.

$\cdot\ \cdot\ \cdot$

Looking to the Outside

The middle years are when outside lessons often become important, both for conventionally schooled students and for homeschoolers. Typical are piano and other music lessons; gymnastics, soccer, Little League, and similar sports programs; sometimes foreign language study or other relatively academic supplements. Homeschoolers often go beyond the more usual lessons and sports leagues into more or less formal mentorships and apprenticeships.

Say, for instance, that your son is fascinated by local history and wants to learn more about it. You may discover that, in your small town, few books are available to provide information. How does your son follow his interest? There may be a small local museum or historical society, with a curator or researcher willing to "mentor" your child in exchange for help sorting papers or cleaning shelves, or simply for the pleasure of working with an interested student. Or a child interested in computers, to take a common example, may be allowed to hang out in a small computer store to pick up what she can in exchange for general help around the place.

> Homeschoolers often go beyond the more usual lessons and sports leagues into more or less formal mentorships and apprenticeships.

Such arrangements can take some digging to set up, and not every situation will work out to everyone's satisfaction. Although some adults will be pleased to work with anyone with a genuine interest in their field, others will be unwilling to even consider working with a child, no matter how levelheaded and focused. Sometimes the problem is incompatible personalities, in which case the best thing to do is to start again with another individual. Other times, the problem is simply that expectations and responsibilities were not clearly understood by all parties, and the situation may be salvageable.

Some suggestions for making informal mentorships and apprenticeships work:

- Make sure your child is genuinely interested in pursuing a mentoring arrangement and that he has a clear idea of what he would like to do. Don't push him into something because "it would be good for him"; neither he nor the mentor will be happy with the arrangement.

- A younger child may need you to make the initial contact for her and will probably have no idea where to start looking for an appropriate mentor. Use all your friends, neighbors, and relatives to help: You may find the individual you are looking for among them, or one of them may know "just the right person." It's always easier to start with a referral; even the individual unfamiliar with the idea of working with a child, or even unwilling at first, will at least listen to a proposal from someone he knows. If the friends-and-neighbors route comes up empty, you can try your local librarian, an appropriate professional society, or perhaps a local college or university professor.

- Be very clear about the terms of any arrangement, and make sure they are fair to both parties. Your mentor should not and will not want to be a baby-sitter, any more than your child will want to simply fetch and carry for her forever. You will need to decide what the responsibilities of each party will be and how much time will be expected. You may decide on a limited trial period, subject to renewal by both parties, or you may opt to let the arrangement run for as long as the parties are happy with it.

- If the situation works out, you may want to ask the mentor to write a short description of the work your child has done or the skills and knowledge your child has gained. (With older children, you may want it to take the form of a letter of recommendation.) Some kind of formal record of the experience can be helpful later in finding future mentors or in completing job or college applications.

Not every homeschooled child, nor even most, will want to try a mentoring relationship. But they can be a valuable part of a homeschooled child's education and well worth considering, no matter what the field.

CHAPTER EIGHT

The Teen Years: Finding a Direction

URING THE TEEN years the differences in homeschooling approaches tend to become less pronounced, as homeschoolers begin their transition into the adult world. For most homeschoolers, that transition is more gradual than for conventional high school students, who find their days increasingly scheduled and defined by their schoolwork, jobs, and other obligations and pressured by the need to decide what comes next. Although homeschoolers must make the same decisions, they can usually take their time considering their options and dip into some of the possibilities firsthand. And they always have the option, of course, of attending high school.

Many homeschoolers start concentrating on special interests, through intensive informal study or formal coursework, volunteer work, part-time jobs, or a complex combination of them all. A teen interested in art, for instance, might sketch and paint on his own, enroll in a community college sculpture class, take an art survey course by correspondence, and do face painting at children's birthday parties and Christmas window painting for a few local businesses. Or the teen who spends much of her days on the computer may find herself writing computer shareware or designing Web pages, as she learns more and more about the systems she uses. It's not uncommon for homeschooled teens to find their interests developing into a part-time job or business, which can provide funds for technical training or college, or develop further into a full-time career.

Back to School: Joining the Mainstream

Some homeschooling families plan from the beginning for their children to enter high school after completing eighth grade. They may have reservations about their ability to give their children the kind of secondary education they believe necessary, preferring to leave laboratory sciences, trigonometry, and other college preparatory courses to more experienced professionals. Or they may believe that, after a few years of homeschooling, their children have a solid enough grounding in both academic basics and their family values to handle high school successfully. Sometimes it is the homeschooled student who prefers to try high school: to prove she can handle the work, to become more involved in teenage social life, or simply to have a change.

It's important to plan ahead if you and your child are interested in your child attending a public high school. (Private schools are often more flexible than public schools.) Oddly enough, it is often harder for a homeschooler to get into high school than into college. Many high schools have quite formulaic approaches to granting credit and are reluctant to recognize work done elsewhere according to standards too different from their own. In some jurisdictions, homeschoolers can

> Oddly enough, it is often harder for a homeschooler to get into high school than into college.

enter high school with little difficulty at the beginning of the freshman year, but they find it almost impossible to get in at the upper grade levels. A few jurisdictions allow no high school credit whatsoever for work done as a homeschooler. Others give placement tests to determine grade level and how much credit to award for previous work.

If you think your family may be interested in high school, contact the schools you are interested in as early as possible, even two or three years before your child will be ready to attend, so that you will have time to adapt your homeschooling program to any requirements. Find out whether the schools have policies concerning homeschoolers and get details. What documentation of your child's learning will they want to see? Will your child need to take placement tests? Is there specific course material your child should cover before entering high school? Are these requirements actually mandatory or just recommendations?

> If you think your family may be interested in high school, contact the schools you are interested in as early as possible, even two or three years before your child will be ready to attend, so that you will have time to adapt your homeschooling program to any requirements.

If the school you are interested in has no existing policy regarding homeschooling, ask to talk to the principal about your case. You may be lucky and find a principal with the authority and willingness to make homeschooling policy on an individual basis. If you are less fortunate, you may find yourself with no alternative but to ask the school board to create a formal policy. You may want to ask your local or state homeschooling group for help and advice on what's worked in other districts.

Once your child is enrolled, you can generally expect few problems related to having homeschooled. Your child may take a few days or weeks getting used to the atmosphere and the schedule and may have to fill in on odds and ends of a few subjects, but most homeschooled students perform well both academically and socially in high school.

High School à la Carte

Some states and school districts allow part-time enrollment for homeschoolers. If your child is interested in a specific subject or activity but unwilling to enroll full-time to get them, he may be able to sign up for just the desired courses. Courses such as chemistry, biology, or shop classes, which use specialized equipment and supplies, and activities such as concert or marching band, which require the participation of a fairly large group, are typical choices for part-time enrollees. Often, whether part-time enrollment is allowed depends on the state's rule for granting ADA (average daily attendance) funds. If the hours part-time students are enrolled do not count in the calculations to determine funding, it is unlikely part-time enrollment will be allowed.

Participation in extracurricular activities can be just as complicated. Some schools may rule on an individual basis and will have no problem allowing homeschoolers to participate in school clubs or other activities. Others will be adamant about requiring formal enrollment. Even the most friendly and cooperative schools, however, may draw the line at homeschoolers participating on athletic teams. Most high school athletic competition is regulated by state athletic organizations, which generally have strict rules governing eligibility, with detailed requirements for residency, school enrollment, grade point average, and so on. Again, it's worth contacting your local or state homeschool groups for more information; formal efforts may be under way to develop or modify policies allowing homeschooler's participation in school sports.

School-at-Home: Preparing for Independence

Jim and Carolyn live near a small town in Maryland. Jim works full-time as a computer systems administrator; Carolyn works twenty hours a week as an office assistant.

• • •

Our family has been homeschooling for the past nine and a half years using a traditional approach. We have homeschooled three children; the oldest is now in his second year at the local community technical college with his sights set on a degree in biology.

We follow a set curriculum. Our children are taught by grade level and receive a certificate at the end of the school year stating that they have satisfactorily completed the course. We feel it is important that our children have this structure.

For the elementary school grades, we use Calvert, a classical curriculum. We use the teaching advisory service as the regulations in Maryland say we should. For the high school years, we use the American School curriculum. This is a correspondence school that was originally founded to encourage adults to obtain their high school diplomas, but it is more than willing to accept homeschoolers. We don't pick and choose from the curriculum, although there are times when we might do something orally instead of in writing. Both Calvert and the American School have been very satisfactory for our needs.

We are fairly flexible on the hours but find that the morning hours tend to be best, as the children are much more alert. Our daughter, the youngest, is now in sixth grade and spends five to six hours a day on her schoolwork. She usually begins about 9:30 A.M. and is done by 2:30 P.M., with lunch and breaks thrown in. Our middle child is using American School and is a bit more flexible. He usually spends three or four hours a day (which might

include some weekends now because of his outside job). He has completed more than half of the curriculum for the high school diploma; he would be a sophomore if he were in public school, so he is well ahead of his peer group.

We do also encourage our children to learn outside the set curriculum. We use library resources, the YMCA, the Internet, and a local homeschoolers' group. Our children are all avid readers, good swimmers, have great computer skills, and interact easily with both adults and children their own age. They have taken gymnastics lessons, swimming lessons, and joined drama groups. The boys are members of the Civil Air Patrol, where each has been squadron commander. My daughter enjoys playing volleyball. We look for opportunities to broaden their experiences wherever we can in addition to their school subjects.

When the children were younger, I spent much more of my time "teaching" them. When we began, the oldest was in sixth grade and could work mostly on his own. The middle child was in second grade, and so he required my time and energy. The youngest was just three years old and learning her ABCs. As time has gone on, I have spent less and less time teaching and more time acting as a resource to my children. They prepare their own lessons every day. With Calvert, they are required to take a test every twenty lessons on the material they have covered during that period. The tests are sent to Calvert's advisory service for grading, which gives me a good idea of what they have been doing. All of the high school curriculum is written directly to the student, although I do help set up a weekly schedule for my son so he knows what he needs to accomplish for the week.

• • •

Eclectics

Margaret and Michael live with their two boys in a Northern California city. Although Margaret holds a teaching credential, the boys have always homeschooled through a public school independent study program. Michael is employed outside the home; Margaret works from home part-time.

• • •

It took several years for me to really understand differences in learning style and trust a child who prefers textbooks with questions at the end of the chapter to make sense of information. We get our textbooks for the most part through the independent study program (ISP). We follow the subject pattern of the public school with lots of latitude for following interests as they arise.

We find we have to set aside a few hours during the week to work together. I write my weekly log, and we plan for anything we need or want more of, such as time for musical instrument practice or completing a writing assignment. We let Wednesday morning ice skating account for the bulk of physical education. The elder, who has more questions in math, works on it while I'm cooking dinner and available at a reasonable regular time (as opposed to when I am working, for instance). Occasionally we take advantage of organized activities like math play days, science classes, field trips, theatrical productions, Spanish classes, and creative writing classes. Many of these are opportunities to spend time with friends as well.

There have always been periods of self-directed study on the days I had my weekly voice class and days we worked around baby-sitting other people's children. I can't remember many formal lessons—one or two in long division or cursive as they came up.

We have lots of history books, political science books, historical fiction, some natural history, anatomy, Spanish and Italian textbooks, and dictionaries, but our biggest source of materials is the library. We also borrow from friends and from the ISP.

How could I forget ITV/PBS? We use it little now, but when the boys were younger they watched so much that one weekend I announced that there would be no more TV starting Monday. On that Sunday, the third-grade Sunday School teacher told me she'd never heard such a clear explanation of photosynthesis as my child had given in class that day. I had never discussed photosynthesis with them. When he confirmed he'd picked it up from TV, I decided to start watching ITV (instructional television) with them instead of doing other things during that time. They learned about decimals and numerous other math concepts from ITV.

Generally, I work with the two boys separately, except when reading aloud, which these days is usually related to history.

Both boys became noticeably more independent in setting and accomplishing goals when they were about thirteen.

. . .

Unschooling: Jumping into the World

Lillian and Ed live in a small Northern California town. Ed's job requires frequent travel, so Lillian is usually the parent at home. Their son, now a teenager, attended a Waldorf kindergarten and another private school for first grade.

. . .

We now have a core that we try to maintain through chaotic times around here. Ethan has a basket with his math books, writing materials, pencils, and all the basic materials that he might need. He works out of that basket on his own most days for an hour here or a half hour there, but always at my suggestion so far. We do more creative and interesting things as we find the time. For instance, we play Take Off for the geography bearings, and he really enjoys related computer games like High Seas Trader. We've recently launched into an in-depth study of geography and history through books of all kinds and constant reference to a globe. These are subjects he asked to learn more about.

Ethan reads a lot of books on his own and has always been a font of information, so I haven't felt the need to get too concerned about "teaching." He also absorbs a lot from educational TV shows. Much of the time I don't even know where he's learned things. I've always provided a lot of books and interesting materials around the house, and have always read to him.

When we started, I tried to have bit of a schedule, but it never worked. It took a while to let go of the school model—a few months at the most. I knew nothing about homeschooling at the time, except what I learned from the local public independent study program. We drifted into an unschooling mode over the years, but now that he's thirteen we've become a little more concentrated. We worked with ISPs for three years, but now I don't really know why, because we always gave them a lot more information than they gave us.

Ethan's pretty easy and basically goes along with anything I suggest he should be studying, but there hasn't been too much pressure on him that way. I support what he asks to learn.

. . .

Jill, Greg, and their three children (eighteen, sixteen, and thirteen) are also Californians. Greg owns a small business, and Jill works part-time out of the home. Cristie, the oldest child, attended kindergarten, but the kids have otherwise always homeschooled.

. . .

What do we do all day? An impossible question to answer!

Today, Curtis and I did some stuff together. He is working on these polyhedrons from a kit that is kind of fun, so he did some of that and did his piano and I helped him a little. Then we took the dog out with the bike for a mile or so (always a death-defying journey for me), and he went another mile by himself. He read some of James Herriot's *All Creatures Great and Small* and a book on Pericles that he's interested in, and a chapter from *From Colonies to Country*, a volume of Joy Hakim's History of US series. We read a chapter together from Jim Lovell's book, *Lost Moon.* Curtis and I saw him on his book tour, so now we are reading his book (autographed, of course) together. We want to do a little bit on our papier-mâché project when I get off the computer.

Paul today has done some math, some drivers' ed (using a textbook), and some history. Cristie went to spend the day with a homeschooling mom who has small kids, because she wants more experience dealing with babies. She'll probably write some tonight and fit in a little Latin. Paul and Curtis just went outside to play garage hockey, a game whose rules elude me.

So, you ask, is this a typical day? No! This is one of those rare days when we are home all day, no one has anything scheduled, including me, and we have an abundance of free time. Normal days for Curtis consist of play rehearsals, orthodontist appointments, writing, playing, minutes at the piano, learning the Greek alphabet, riding in the car, reading, doing wash, going to the grocery store. Normal days for Paul are hours on his computer working on programming, or playing the latest computer game to write a review, or writing. Both Cristie and Paul take physical science and dance at the local community college three days a week, and Cristie also works on Latin by herself and is writing a science fiction novel. She works for Greg doing computer input for billing, and she lifeguards when the pool is open. We all do tai chi and shao lin but seldom together except on Saturday mornings for our lesson.

Curtis, Cristie, and I volunteer weekly at the library, shelving books or doing whatever else is needed. Paul and Cristie work one day a month getting the billing out for Greg. They all take chemistry one morning a month, and we have park day every Thursday. Twice a month we have writing club here, followed by a sign language group in which we are all learning American Sign Language. Usually we get to at least one museum a month because I am intensely interested in art and study art history. In fact, Curtis sits in on the first half hour of my art history class before his rehearsal starts, and he gets these brief views of things like Greek pottery or Roman sculpture of heads. I am always amazed at how much he remembers (probably more than most of the class, which is there for a full three hours). We also walk the dogs each day—whoever has the time—and we cook and clean, although not enough. Mostly we all live together.

> I think we have many more things that are structured learning programs now than when the kids were young, but it's mostly by their own choice that they use them.

We have never had formal lessons, although the kids have used texts at times, more so as they got older and had specific things to study, like higher math or drivers' ed. I think we have many more things that are structured learning programs now than when the kids were young, but it's mostly by their own choice that they use them.

· · ·

Finishing Early

No matter what their style of homeschooling, homeschooled teens often finish their secondary-level work and are ready to move on to something more challenging by fifteen or so. Because most states compel school attendance until at least age sixteen and often until eighteen, you'll need to check carefully into your state's regulations about graduation and diplomas. If your teen is enrolled in a private program that grants diplomas, or if state regulations allow you to grant your own diploma, you should have no problem; if not, you'll have to make sure you won't run afoul of truancy regulations.

Taking the GED (General Educational Development) exam is one option. There are five tests (writing, literature, social studies, math, and science), each about sixty to ninety minutes long. Although the tests are the same nationwide, each state establishes its own rules for who is eligible to take the tests and for minimum scores to pass. In some states, individuals are not allowed to take the GED tests until they are eighteen. A few employers and colleges, however, view a GED diploma less favorably than a conventional diploma; the armed forces, especially, limit options for GED diplomates. Some states have their own equivalency tests: California, for example, has its California High School Proficiency Examination (CHSPE), which can be taken during the sophomore year of high school. A passing score is considered legally equivalent within the state to a high school diploma. Such state-specific tests are often now honored by colleges and universities in other states as well, though it would be smart to check specifically with the institutions you're interested in.

In short, you'll need to learn what the rules are for your state. A state or local homeschool group should be able to tell you how homeschoolers where you live generally deal with these issues and can probably save you time and effort searching for the proper information. Your local library or community college will probably have information on (and possibly registration forms for) the GED and any other state equivalency programs, including test dates and fees as well as the eligibility rules.

Licenses and Permits

That major milestone for the American teen—the driver's license—can also require some advance planning for homeschoolers. Your teen may be able to take driver training through a local public or private school, or you may be able to provide the necessary training yourself. If you know a homeschooled teen with a driver's license, it's worth asking her for information before tackling your state's motor vehicle department; homeschooled teens are still few enough that accurate information can be hard to get, even from the agency that makes the rules. Where states mandate driver training requirements for schools, you may have to request a requisition form for driver education materials, sometimes by a specified date for the following school year. You should check in advance with your insurance agent to find out whether or how homeschooled students qualify for good student discounts on auto insurance.

When your teen gets a job (other than casual employment such as baby-sitting and lawn mowing), you'll also need to look into work permits. Child labor laws regulate the ages and number of hours children are allowed to work, although family businesses are often exempted from such rules. Work permits are often obtained through local public schools or directly from the state labor department. As always, your state homeschooling groups should be able to provide information to guide you.

Getting Ready for College

If your teen is considering college, it's a good idea to get familiar with the alphabet soup of college admissions tests: ACT, SAT-I, SAT-II, PSAT. The SATs and the PSAT are produced by the Educational Testing Service and are used by colleges throughout the country. The PSAT, usually taken early in the eleventh grade, is also used to qualify for National Merit Scholarships; students can also ask on the test form for information from colleges they are interested in. The SAT-I is the newest version of the SAT and contains tests of mathematical and verbal reasoning; the SAT-II (formerly Achievement) tests cover specific subject areas. The ACT, produced by the American College Testing Program, is used mainly by colleges in the Midwest and South. Any bookstore will have shelves of test preparation books for sale; many will include copies of actual past tests, which will give you the best idea of what to expect. A test preparation guide, such as those from Princeton Review or Kaplan, can also be valuable for learning to think like the test makers and developing the knack for multiple-choice exams.

> Many homeschoolers start taking community college classes during their early to midteens, usually one or two courses in subjects that particularly interest them. This can be an alternate route to establishing evidence of one's ability to perform college-level work (as opposed to relying on high school grades and transcripts).

Many homeschoolers start taking community college classes during their early to midteens, usually one or two courses in subjects that particularly interest them. This can be an alternate route to establishing evidence of one's ability to perform college-level work (as opposed to relying on high school grades and transcripts). Many colleges will accept some minimal number of college credits as equivalent to a high school diploma for admissions purposes. If, however, your teen plans to apply for scholarships for use at a four-year college, be sure to check into their eligibility rules. In some cases, too many college credits may be a disqualification for scholarships awarded to graduating high school students.

The middle teens, while there is still time to fill in any gaps, are also a good time to start the whole process of looking into college options: learning about specific requirements for programs you may be interested in and beginning to organize information for admissions applications. We'll talk more about college admissions and other possibilities for life after homeschooling in Chapter 14.

CHAPTER NINE

Evaluation and Record Keeping, or How Do We Know They're Learning?

EVALUATING AND KEEPING appropriate records of your children's learning can be one of the most daunting tasks facing new homeschoolers. What if your children don't keep up with what kids their age are doing in school? How do you prove to college officials or potential employers that they've learned enough to handle college-level coursework or the demands of a job? What about grades and transcripts and achievement tests and all the other bits and pieces that make up a student's "permanent record"?

How do you know whether they're learning what they should know?

For most new homeschooling families, this is a major concern. You worry that you won't do right by your kids, and you won't know how to tell whether there's a problem. Perhaps this dependence on an outside authority to tell us how well we are learning is an effect of our own schooling, but in no other area of our lives are we so unwilling to trust our own judgment. Consider, though, the matter of physical health: How do you tell when your kids are sick if you're not a doctor? It's easy to recognize a healthy kid, and most parents have little trouble determining when their kids are sick. At some point, parents may need professional help for a diagnosis and treatment, but noticing that there is a problem in the first place is not something most of us have trouble with.

The matter of learning is pretty much the same. It's obvious when kids are learning, and it's a rare parent indeed who cannot tell whether kids are learning as they should be. If your kids are interested in the world around them and eager to follow their interests, if they know and can do more now than they could last year, then they are probably doing just fine. If you keep at least some rudimentary records of your kids' skills and abilities, you'll probably never doubt it.

> If your kids are interested in the world around them and eager to follow their interests, if they know and can do more now than they could last year, then they are probably doing just fine.

Like every other aspect of homeschooling, the kinds of records you keep depend on your homeschooling style and your particular family's needs. In addition, the state you live in may have something to say about the form and detail of your records and may require some sort of standardized testing for your children. You may find that the information school officials want from you tells you very little of substance about how your children learn, so that information you accumulate for your own use will look completely different from your "official" records.

To determine what kinds of records you'll keep, the first thing to do is figure out who you're keeping records for:

- For yourself? You may want to have some record of milestones in your children's academic lives. Just as you might have noted when they took their first steps or lost their first tooth, you might enjoy having a record of when they first wrote their names, read their first words or first books, or figured out how much money they'd saved. On those occasional bad days, it can be nice to have something to look at to prove to yourself that they've been learning.

- For your children? Your children may appreciate having the same sort of information about their childhood when they are older, and a look back at their lives through your eyes could give them a completely different perspective on their experiences. Again, having some proof of how they've spent their time can help during those stretches when they doubt themselves and their competence.

- Education officials? Your state or school district or the administrators of your home study program may have quite specific requirements about the information you need to keep. Such requirements can be easy to comply with, or they can involve a considerable amount of work to put together.

- Admissions officials or future employers? The specific needs of these groups can be hard to predict, but you may want to collect letters of recommendation from music teachers, sports coaches, and other adults who can testify to your children's abilities and character. Any material demonstrating their suitability for a future occupation or other situation can be useful to have available if needed.

• • •

No, no, *no.* (Come on, does anybody actually give grades?) I don't keep anything specifically for records, although we have stuff around that the kids have done. I could pull something together if we needed to. —*Jill,* California

• • •

I keep a narrative journal of our daily activities and events. I also do a six-month summary for each girl, in June and December. In completing the daily narrative, the girls and I use our calendars, their personal diaries, trip records, photos, and such—anything that serves as a memory jogger to help us show the breadth and depth of what we do. The records are designed to be maximally useful for the girls—I don't write with some future school official or admissions officer in mind. I feel confident that I can write up a presentable transcript if necessary. —*Carol,* California

. . .

No records, no grades. I don't care about any evaluation—I can see how much he knows, and I can see that he compares well with his school friends. I once took him to a math center for an evaluation and suggestions and was sent away with the comment that we were "way ahead of the game" and should just continue doing whatever we're doing. —*Lillian,* California

. . .

We keep records for the charter school to show what Emily is learning each month. These records can be as simple or as detailed as we want. We don't give grades. Occasionally, Emily wants to have grades put on her papers, which we do until she loses interest in the idea. Our evaluation process is simply being aware of her strengths and weaknesses, supporting her desire and ability to learn, and giving extra attention to areas we think might need extra attention. Our goal in all this is not to intimidate or demean her, but rather to reinforce her natural desire to explore living in the world successfully. —*Doug,* California

> We keep records for the charter school to show what Emily is learning each month. These records can be as simple or as detailed as we want. We don't give grades.

. . .

Once you've got a good idea of your reasons for keeping records, you can decide which of the many options will best suit your needs. Most homeschoolers will use some version of traditional grades, portfolios, or narrative descriptions of their children's work and abilities, and many will combine all three approaches to develop a system that works for them.

Traditional Grades and Transcripts

Traditional letter grades are probably the easiest form of evaluation for most of us to understand, because most of us have had vast experience with them. They work best, of course, with a traditional, structured approach to homeschooling, with clearly defined subjects and assignments, and clearly articulated goals and objectives.

Advantages

- Letter grades are familiar and easy to calculate; they are especially suited to "objective" evaluations with answers that are clearly right or wrong.

- Traditional letter grades most readily translate homeschooling experience into terms school officials, admissions officers, and potential employers can understand.

Drawbacks

- Letter grades often convey little concrete information about how well the student actually understands and can apply the material covered.

- In conventional schools, grades are often used as a gauge for comparing students' work. Homeschool grades, however conventional they look, give little basis for comparison with other students.

· · ·

I keep a log of what we do, tracking the number of days I have recorded as "school." I grade obvious things like math papers, but I'm not overly concerned about grades at this time (third and sixth grades). Honestly, I have come to disapprove of the whole idea of grades and grade levels. As far as I am concerned, learning should happen at the child's natural rate, not according to what some textbook says, and the next step should not be approached until the current one has been mastered. (In other words, they either know their stuff or they don't.) —*Tammy*, Texas

. . .

I keep a grade book with checks to show that work has been accomplished and if a test was given, what the grade was. Grades are based on a scale and reflect the percentage of correct answers. Major projects are also graded. Those are subjective grades based on whether the child met the objectives for the project. I have also made report cards on the computer with our school name. They look very official. I have the children tested each year and put those forms in their school record folder. When we placed our daughter back in school, they were glad to have the test scores, but I felt like they thought the report cards were worthless—that parent evaluation was somehow prejudicial.

We also keep portfolios of work for the entire year. The children file their papers behind the weekly schedules in their schedule notebooks. Every nine weeks we go through them and keep the ones we think reflect improved work or excellent work.

The grade cards and grade book are really kept for extended family and officials. They provide us a means of showing educational progress in a form that they understand. The portfolios are just for us. If I were ever required to keep a portfolio for state evaluation, I would include only those papers that showed outstanding accomplishment. —*Beverly*, Nebraska

. . .

Portfolios

Portfolios are a common tool of what professional educators refer to as "authentic assessment." Instead of relying on letter grades derived from numerical scores calculated from arbitrary numbers of quizzes and tests and homework assignments to evaluate student achievement, authentic assessment provides a means of looking directly at students' work as evidence of understanding and mastery of material. Portfolios are simply collections of student work samples designed to present a reasonably accurate picture of the student's accomplishments.

Portfolio systems used in schools can be quite complex, with guidelines for choosing material to be included and complicated "rubrics"—standards against which those contents are to be judged. Unlike artists' portfolios, which are invariably samples of the artist's best work, school portfolios are often designed to illustrate the student's learning process. For example, instead of containing a highly polished essay, a portfolio might include an outline and several early drafts, as well as the finished product, to show the progress the student made in the course of completing the project.

> Unlike artists' portfolios, which are invariably samples of the artist's best work, school portfolios are often designed to illustrate the student's learning process.

Most homeschoolers take a much less formal approach to portfolios—one more closely analogous to the traditional artist's portfolio: a sampling of the best work across a wide variety of subjects and skills without attempting to evaluate it against any particular scale or rubric.

Advantages

- Portfolios can provide more meaningful information about student skills and abilities than conventional letter grades.

- Portfolios can be flexible enough to illustrate areas of strength that traditional grading systems do not measure well.

- The student can choose her best work to be included in a portfolio; her skills and achievements are usually shown to best advantage.

Drawbacks

- Because they may show only the student's best work, portfolios may not give an accurate picture of the student's real abilities. Samples may not be the student's typical product.

- Portfolios, even with clearly defined standards for judging their content, can be every bit as subjective as any other form of evaluation.

• • •

We keep many more samples than we turn in—stories, artwork, photos. Especially in the artwork category, we are being swamped by the creations of three prolific artists, so we are seriously having to re-think what we save. I make notes of good books that we want to re-member, and once a year or so, I will spend a week or two jotting down what the kids did in some detail: questions asked, topics investigated, educational shows watched, books read, and so on. Usually this takes so much time that it doesn't go on for long, and my husband points out that no administrator will want to read all that. Still, it is al-ways reassuring to see the variety and depth of things that turn up.

Grades seem pointless, so we don't give them. The kids participate in our evaluation process by telling us what they thought of the year and what they'd like to do in the coming year. This is ongoing, not done just at year-end. The children also read the reports we write and give us feedback from their perspective. On a couple of occasions, at my suggestion, they wrote a short description of some recent activities, and I included these with our progress report. —*Linda*, Hawaii

• • •

We occasionally take photographs or shoot videos for our own use and enjoyment. I keep a box for each of the children where they can save anything they choose, and I sometimes save things of theirs for myself. We don't plan to ever give grades or tests, keep logs, portfolios, or do any other formal evaluation. I enjoy keeping a journal from time to time, and I expect my children might eventually also, but these are strictly personal. —*Laura*, Texas

• • •

Narrative Evaluation

Many homeschoolers use some form of written narrative to record their evaluations of their children's work. This can take the form of journals or diaries describing daily activities at regular intervals or less frequent semester or yearly reports comparing each student's interests and abilities with those apparent in previous reports. Written narrative descriptions are particularly useful to unschoolers, whose learning may not fit easily into the categories normally used in more conventional systems.

> Written narrative descriptions are particularly useful to unschoolers, whose learning may not fit easily into the categories normally used in more conventional systems.

Advantages

- Written narrative description can provide specific and useful information about the student's strengths and weaknesses and can be used effectively for any and all subject areas.

- As your children get older and become more conscious of what they are learning, they can take a more and more active role in keeping records of their learning.

- In the absence of conventional grades, descriptive evaluations can provide useful information for school officials, even though it is in a form less familiar or convenient than letter grades or numeric scores.

Drawbacks

- Journals and diaries can be quite cumbersome and time-consuming to keep up, to the point that the record keeping interferes with the learning process. Many a homeschooler has been brought up short by a child's "Mom, can you stop writ-

ing so we can play?" and realized that the journals had completely taken over.

- Journals and diaries can be difficult to translate into conventional transcript terms because the activities they describe are
  not segmented into easily delineated subjects.

One useful adjunct to almost any form of record keeping for
homeschoolers is simply to keep a list of books
your children read. Over the years, most homeschoolers develop quite an impressive reading
list, and the accumulated titles can give you a
good start at evaluating what's been learned
over the years. With a little bit of organization,
you might even be able to build a transcript
from a reading list.

> Grades are, in my
> humble opinion,
> stupid. The only measure
> of learning is how well
> someone functions in
> society or if they feel
> themselves that they
> know something.

• • •

No grades—how do you grade life? I have
started keeping a journal of things done. It
helps with the umbrella school and it is nice to
look back at. I am lousy at it. —*Lisa,* Alabama

• • •

I keep a log of sorts. There are sections for
each subject, with books read, activities done,
and an average amount of time spent for each. Grades are, in my
humble opinion, stupid. The only measure of learning is how well
someone functions in society or if they feel themselves that they
know something. Emily does not need to prove to anyone but herself (and maybe me) that she has learned anything. —*Anne,* Illinois

• • •

I was never much of a record keeper. I find it impossible even
to record the books my children read. I do supply them with lots
of books, resources, and experiences, but I have not been able to
actually sit down and record their progress on a daily, weekly, or
even yearly basis.

What surprised me was when I read my past editorials and stories and realized that I do keep a journal. I have recorded our experiences and ideas in *The Drinking Gourd* and other publications. Phew! It's good to know that I will be able to read about our family's homeschool odyssey after my children grow up and leave home. —*Donna*, Washington

. . .

Learning to Speak Educationese

Although the learning records you keep for your own use can be written in whatever form and style suit you, a more formal approach is often useful for records kept for compliance with state or district requirements. A bit of educational jargon can go a long way to making your program sound impressive to those accustomed to more traditional approaches, and translating everyday activities into the more exaggerated versions of "educationese" can actually be a lot of fun.

> A bit of educational jargon can go a long way to making your program sound impressive to those accustomed to more traditional approaches, and translating everyday activities into the more exaggerated versions of "educationese" can actually be a lot of fun.

Imagine, for instance, how much more impressed a bureaucratically minded evaluator might be by "interactive student-oriented teacher methodology" than by plain "one-on-one tutoring." Or consider the recent classroom favorites: "sustained silent reading," which is reading done for its own sake without threat of future worksheets or quizzes, and "daily oral language," which, though actually a classroom exercise finding errors in a written sentence, sounds to most of us suspiciously like "talking."

Most families will not have to go to this extreme, of course. But if you have to keep records of your children's activities, learning and using a few of the more ordinary bits of educational jargon can make the entire record-keeping process easier. "Developmentally appropriate," "cooperative learning," "immersion," and "hands-on learning" can be applied to almost any subject matter: your twelve- and eight-year-olds can, while making cookies together, immerse themselves in a developmentally appropriate, hands-on, cooperative study of fractions and measurement.

If you're an unschooler, you'll quickly find that you can redefine your entire life as educational experiences. Going out to play can be socializational development and physical education, grocery shopping becomes consumer math and nutrition education, completing household chores develops concentration and time-on-task skills, and library trips are research instruction and resource identification.

> If you're an unschooler, you'll quickly find that you can redefine your entire life as educational experiences.

Translating everyday activities into education jargon can also be reassuring to unschooling parents who worry that their children are "doing nothing." Putting life into educational terminology makes it obvious that they are doing a great deal and that we are just not good at recognizing learning that takes place outside the classroom.

. . .

> When I get paranoid I pull out diagnostic tests and books like *Science Scope* and *What Your Child Needs to Know When.* I do that less and less the more we homeschool, however. Other than perhaps checking off the skills that the kids know, I don't keep records—although I do intend to start. —*Peggy,* Oklahoma

. . .

Many homeschoolers who must provide curriculum plans to get approval to homeschool each year find a "scope and sequence" useful. Simply an outline of what topics and skills are typically covered at each grade level, a scope and sequence can provide a structure on which to build your curriculum plan. Most are general enough that a workable plan can be developed even for those homeschoolers who, because they let their kids' interests prompt study of particular topics, are unwilling to lay out too much curricular detail in advance. Dozens of sources are available for such outlines: encyclopedia companies, state and county offices of education, teacher college libraries, teacher supply stores, Internet databases, and homeschool suppliers.

Many homeschoolers find such books as the *Comprehensive Curriculum of Basic Skills* or E. D. Hirsch's Core Knowledge Series (e.g., *What Your First Grader Needs to Know*) useful as curriculum outlines. It's important to recognize, though, the limitations and biases of such volumes. Their everything-in-one-volume approach means that facts and rote memorization are emphasized to the detriment of understanding the context and relevance of the topics covered. The Hirsch books especially are heavily weighted toward a Western European worldview, and events and culture of other parts of the world are treated only superficially.

Standardized Testing

Possibly no topic arouses such mixed feelings among homeschoolers as standardized testing. Diagnostic tests, readiness tests, screening tests, aptitude tests, achievement tests, IQ tests, placement tests, admissions tests—the list is almost endless, but the tests we usually mean when we talk about the kinds of standardized tests homeschoolers deal with fall into three main categories:

1. *Aptitude tests* (also known as IQ tests or cognitive ability tests): These tests attempt to determine the student's innate ability  or intelligence, to define what the student is capable of. Examples are the Wechsler Intelligence Scales for Children-Revised (WISC-R), the Stanford Binet Intelligence Scale, and the Differential Aptitude Test (DAT).

2. *Achievement tests:* These tests attempt to determine what a student has learned in specific subject areas, such as reading and math. Examples include the California Achievement Test (CAT) and the Iowa Test of Basic Skills (ITBS).

. . .

The last standardized test Shauna took was in first grade while we were with an ISP. Her adviser pushed us into doing it. I have said, "No, thanks," every time that standardized testing has been offered to either girl since. Shauna scored from fifth- to eighth-grade level in all areas, and the ISP adviser wanted her to be the poster girl for "how good the program was." I feel that, then as now, school people are eager to take credit for any learning that a child has demonstrated. That was certainly the case here. They wanted to use Shauna as their star pupil for publicity purposes. —*Carol,* California

. . .

3. *College admissions tests:* These are specialized achievement tests that attempt to determine how much a student has learned and to predict how well a student will perform at the college level. The best-known examples, of course, are the SAT and ACT.

. . .

The only time I can foresee my children taking standardized tests is if they choose to go to college. If or when that time comes, I would think it wise for them to prepare for the required tests. Otherwise, I feel standardized tests are only relevant to a standardized education, and even then only marginally. Because I have rejected standardized education as inadequate and inappropriate for my children, I feel standardized tests have absolutely no value for us. —*Laura,* Texas

. . .

Unfortunately, the differences among these categories are more a matter of intent than content, and both the reliability and validity of specific tests are often questionable. A "reliable" test is one that consistently gives the same results for the same individual each time it is administered; variations in the testing conditions, the mood of the student, the humidity, the way instructions are given, or coaching have little effect on the results of a reliable test. A "valid" test actually measures what it is designed and used to measure. For instance, a test that purports to measure understanding of mathematical concepts may not be valid if it consists solely of multiple-choice arithmetic items; it probably measures only rote memorization skills.

With all their potential and actual problems, why do homeschoolers use standardized tests for evaluating their children's educational progress? Most commonly, state homeschooling regulations require regular testing of homeschooled students, sometimes annually, sometimes at specific grade levels, such as grades 3, 5, and 8. A specific test may be mandated, families may be allowed to choose from a list of approved tests, or testing may be only one of several available options for evaluation. Among states that demand tests, some require that scores be submitted to the local school district or a state education agency, some require that a minimum score be attained to continue homeschooling, and others require only that students be tested but never ask for results at all.

> Most commonly, state homeschooling regulations require regular testing of homeschooled students, sometimes annually, sometimes at specific grade levels, such as grades 3, 5, and 8.

Many homeschooling families decide that standardized tests are the least intrusive and easiest method of evaluation their state allows. Or, even when it's not required by homeschooling regulations, families may choose to have their children tested at regular intervals as a means of assuring themselves (or their relatives) that they are "keeping up" with conventionally schooled students. Others simply believe that, because standardized testing has become such a widely used tool by schools and employers, it's best to get their kids used to taking such tests as early and routinely as possible.

. . .

We have used the Stanford Achievement Test and the Iowa Test of Basic Skills. We take the test once a year in the spring. I have administered some of the tests. One year the older two girls were tested with a homeschool group. I keep the results in the children's school folders. I also announce their scores to the relatives. They usually do well on these tests, so it is a form of validating what we are doing. I don't teach to the test. I don't get the test early enough to even think about doing this. I don't really know what are considered the "normal" subjects covered in social studies or science for each grade level.

I always check the tests over after the kids take them. This gives me more information about what their score really means than the numbers you get back in the mail. I know that they missed four questions in science because we have never studied rocks and minerals. If I found they were missing questions on topics that we had studied, I'd have to think about my methods. In fact, I have changed my English curriculum because of this.

My kids don't mind taking the tests. They don't have test anxiety. I usually discuss with them how they did on each test right afterward. We talk about the things they knew because they studied "xyz" this year, and the things they missed because we hadn't studied "abc." They especially love it when they get questions right on subjects we haven't specifically studied. They do a lot of outside reading, so they really learn more than is actually on their weekly schedules. —*Beverly,* Nebraska

. . .

The idea of testing bores me senseless. What I will probably do is discuss the idea of tests with the kids. If they're interested in taking some, fine. And if one or more of my children expresses interest in attending college, I'll explain the concept of tests and let them know that it's probably a good idea to familiarize themselves with taking some before they go off to college. —*Pam,* California

. . .

Here are some suggestions for dealing with standardized tests and their consequences:

- If you are faced with standardized tests, find out what test is being used. Is the test criterion-referenced or norm-referenced? Criterion-referenced tests attempt to measure whether a student has mastered specific material. They measure the student's performance against a specific body of knowledge determined by the test makers. Norm-referenced tests compare each child's test performance with the performance of a group of students who have already taken the test. Such tests are designed to produce results along a classic bell curve, with most individuals scoring near the middle, but half above and half below the median. School districts can buy tests normed to different groups depending on what type of group (inner-city urban, suburban college-bound, etc.) they want to compare their students' scores with.

> Most test makers specifically warn against using their tests as the sole criterion for decisions that would substantially affect a student's life, such as academic tracking or placement or awarding financial aid.

- Try to find out whether the test was designed to be used for the purpose it is actually being used for. Although there is considerable debate over whether tests can truly do what they are advertised to do, many tests are commonly used for purposes they were never designed for. Most test makers specifically warn against using their tests as the sole criterion for decisions that would substantially affect a student's life, such as academic tracking or placement or awarding financial aid.

- Try to find out the margin of error for the test score. Some tests have a margin of error of 10 percent or more, which could make a major difference if that margin is ignored by those who use the test results for evaluating the success of a homeschooling program.

- Most of all, try not to give test scores more weight than they deserve. Treat tests as a screening game used by people who don't have the time, energy, or willingness to look at test takers as individuals. If your kids develop test anxiety, either on their own or from picking up on your own worries, try to keep the process in perspective. See whether there are measures available to make the testing process more comfortable for them. You may be able to have the test administered in your home or other familiar surroundings or even be able to give them the test yourself. Under some circumstances, time limits turn out to be flexible, or portions can be administered orally. It may also be possible to substitute other more appropriate tests for the one normally given, or you may be able to opt for testing through a local college psychology department or a private psychologist.

CHAPTER TEN

Finding Learning Resources

ONE MAJOR PROBLEM new homeschoolers face is finding appropriate learning materials for their children. How do you tell whether textbooks are any good? Is this grammar text widely used in schools because of its excellence or its publisher's marketing skills? Is that five-year-old biology book good, or is it out of date already? What if your child is fascinated by the late medieval history of Eastern Europe or the latest twists to superstring theory? Where do you even start looking for resources?

Experienced homeschoolers are likely to tell you that the problem is actually quite the reverse: With so many good resources of all kinds—books, tapes, museums, theaters, people, and organizations— the real problem is choosing from the wealth of available material. Where do you find the time and energy to tackle even a tenth of the interesting stuff you'd like to dig into? How do you choose?

Fortunately, you're not alone. First and foremost, your children will help you with selection, whether you want their help or not.

Your kids will be fairly adamant about what works and doesn't work and will be more than ready to let you know what they think. Their complaints may be fairly direct, as in "This book is really lame, Mom. I wanted something by someone who actually knows something about quantum electrodynamics." Or their criticism can take a less overt form of reluctance or resistance, as in the daily or hourly whine of "Mom, can't I wait and do this tomorrow?" In the long run, it's easier on everyone if you encourage the direct complaints. Usually, kids have good reasons for disliking particular materials and, with a little prompting, will happily share them with you, along with lots of suggestions for what would work better.

If you're a member of a local homeschooling group, you've also got a whole range of opinions and experience to draw from. In all but the smallest groups, you'll usually find someone who's tried whatever you're interested in and can tell you about his experience with it. Whether the experience was positive or not, the information will probably help you decide whether or not to use the material for your family. You may be able to borrow books or manipulatives for a firsthand look, or you might even find used copies to buy. Support groups are also excellent sources of information about useful stores and catalogs as well as local resources such as museums, galleries, nature centers, and more.

> Your kids will be fairly adamant about what works and doesn't work and will be more than ready to let you know what they think.

Textbooks and Other "Educational" Materials

Conventional learning materials such as textbooks are usually easy to find. If you're interested in the type of texts used in the schools, you can check with your local school district or county office of education to learn whether it has a curriculum library. Sometimes access to such libraries is limited to public school teachers, but often the public is also allowed to peruse school materials there. County offices of education often also maintain media and technology centers, from which laboratory equipment, films, video and audio equipment and tapes, or computer hardware and software can be borrowed. Availability to homeschoolers will depend on state and district regulations.

Your area may also have a used book depository, where textbooks, library books, and equipment no longer used by area schools can be purchased for thrift-store prices or are free for the taking. Textbooks are sometimes too worn or damaged for continued school use, but often they are just plain outdated. The best finds are usually in the library discards. Old encyclopedias, dictionaries, and other reference books are fairly common but are far outnumbered by the literature: historical novels, literary classics, just plain good reading. As with any thrift shop, you'll have to make regular visits to keep up with the changing stock, and you won't necessarily find something worthwhile on every visit.

You may decide you want to order textbooks directly from the publisher. Some educational publishers will ask for a school purchase order or for an order on your school letterhead. (Many homeschoolers, especially in "private school" homeschooling states, find a ream of school letterhead a worthwhile investment for such cases and for other occasional correspondence.) Others are happy to sell textbooks to homeschoolers but draw the line at teachers' guides and answer keys. Some refuse to deal with homeschoolers at all, while others have set up divisions specifically to serve the homeschool market.

Also worth checking out are local teacher supply stores. Most homeschoolers won't be interested in the endless racks of seasonal bulletin board decorations and "Great Job!" stickers, but many such stores also carry lots of supplementary materials for science, math, and literature. Usually, you'll also find an assortment of paper and other consumables: colored construction paper, newsprint both blank and ruled for various grade levels, poster and finger paints, pens, and pencils. You'll also find lesson planners, grade books, and teacher calendars, which you might be able to adapt for your own record keeping.

Dozens of catalog businesses are aimed at the homeschooling market—with more popping up every day. Some mainly carry books about homeschooling; others carry mainly curricular materials. Some aim at particular market segments, such as unschoolers or Christian homeschoolers, and others concentrate on a specialized subject area, such as math or science. Appendix C includes a list of some popular homeschool suppliers, both general and specialized.

Over the past two decades, homeschool suppliers have tended to be small operations, often home-based businesses started by homeschooling families. Recently, as homeschooling has become more popular and well known, larger companies have entered the market. Some carry materials previously unavailable directly to homeschoolers and others carry the more popular products of smaller companies but undercut their prices. If you tend to enjoy the more obscure resources, you might want to make a point of patronizing the smaller companies, even for those items available elsewhere, just to help keep those interesting but obscure items available.

A relatively new element in the homeschooling market in recent years are the independent dealers. These are individuals who sell a particular company's line, rather like Avon or Discovery Toys representatives. Dorling Kindersley and Usborne Books are especially active in the homeschooling market, fueled largely by homeschooling parents who sell the books so they can afford to buy all the volumes they want for themselves.

Libraries

Libraries are the homeschooler's favorite resource, and most homeschoolers probably could not survive without them. It is a rare homeschooling family within reach of a library branch whose members are not regular patrons. Libraries are tremendous resources for books, magazines, videos, pamphlets, community information, and more—and libraries make few rules about who is allowed access to it all. Libraries function to make their information accessible, and you don't have to be in a certain grade or pass a certain test to be allowed in. If you've got a library card, you've got what you need.

. . .

We use the library a lot. Several librarians there know us now and are very helpful. We check out lots of books and videos. —*Beverly,* Nebraska

. . .

We use the public library so often that we know all the staff by name. We are there twice a week, for thirty to sixty minutes per trip. —*Carol,* California

. . .

Most librarians are familiar with homeschooling and enjoy working with homeschoolers. Many homeschoolers schedule their library trips during the slower hours before the arrival of the after-school crowds with term papers due, so they are often recognized as homeschoolers. Librarians tend to be responsive to the needs of their patrons, so many have made it a point to find out what homeschoolers need and want in their libraries, with the result that most libraries carry at least a few homeschooling books and a pamphlet file. Librarians also help homeschoolers find resources through interlibrary loan and from other sources.

Libraries are the homeschooler's favorite resource, and most homeschoolers probably could not survive without them.

Homeschoolers often end up as volunteers at the library. After all, if we're spending so much time there and getting to know the stacks so well, we're bound to pick up the classification system pretty quickly and become fairly proficient shelvers of books. Homeschoolers also get involved helping with story hours and other children's activities and often prepare library displays on homeschooling and other topics. With tight, even shrinking, library budgets in many areas, some homeschoolers have become fierce advocates and supporters of their library systems. Others, with regret, have found themselves looking elsewhere for what they can no longer find at their library.

. . .

We have not used the library system as often as we used to, mainly because we prefer to buy books that are more current than anything the library has to offer these days. We do still go to the Friends of the Library annual sale, though. —*Barbara,* California

. . .

Local public libraries are not the only libraries homeschoolers find useful, however. Don't forget college and university libraries in your area. Although they may not have the multiple copies of the latest fiction or self-help bestsellers your local library branch has, their collections will be larger and more comprehensive, especially in academic areas the colleges specialize in. College and university collections of periodicals are usually extensive, with many more specialized journals available on microfilm and microfiche. They may also have special collections on local or regional history or other topics. Check to see whether your local college libraries have programs for local residents to obtain library cards; access to their resources can be worth any fee involved.

Don't forget college and university libraries in your area. Although they may not have the multiple copies of the latest fiction or self-help bestsellers your local library branch has, their collections will be larger and more comprehensive, especially in academic areas the colleges specialize in.

Community Resources

Far from being the sheltered, even antisocial, misfits of the old popular image, homeschoolers, with their flexible schedules and unquenchable thirst for learning, are active participants in community life.

. . .

My kids and I love to take classes in the community. In the past few years, they have studied piano, drums, voice, theater, karate, dance, swimming, art, skiing, flying, and skating. We are involved in Girl Scouts, youth band, and a children's theater company. We often attend concerts and the ballet and visit museums everywhere we travel. —*Barbara,* California

. . .

Homeschoolers involve themselves with various community resources on several different levels. First, and most common, is simply making use of services offered—for instance, taking a class at a museum or buying a product from a local business. Next, homeschooling families or support groups might arrange to visit a local factory to see how furniture is made or take a tour of the local blood bank to learn how it works. Individual homeschoolers may work as volunteers or apprentices within the community, often finding such opportunities after exploring many options. Finally, some facilities may in turn provide services for homeschoolers after they've had experience with homeschoolers working as volunteers for them.

> Far from being the sheltered, even antisocial, misfits of the old popular image, homeschoolers, with their flexible schedules and unquenchable thirst for learning, are active participants in community life.

Don't expect every business or museum to be eager to work with homeschoolers. Some relatively bureaucratic bodies simply haven't any official policy for dealing with homeschoolers and so won't even try. Some will be completely unfamiliar with homeschoolers, and a few will have had a bad previous experience with a rowdy bunch and decided not to have anything to do with homeschoolers ever again. Most who are hesitant are simply used to working with school groups, typically one grade or age at a time, and are a bit puzzled when faced with handling a mixed-age group of homeschoolers.

One homeschooling mother talks about a common difficulty her local support group deals with:

. . .

In general, resources like museums, local theater and symphony, and so on, have welcomed homeschoolers and have treated us at least as well as school groups, sometimes being even more flexible to accommodate just a few families, or our request to bring entire families rather than just one grade or age level.

But a serious problem here is the lack of available space for informal groups (with no money) to meet. We use the city parks, which usually work out nicely for outdoor space unless it rains. Indoor space for projects or meetings is not inexpensive or easy to come by. When space is available, it is usually more than we can afford or requires liability insurance or lots of paperwork.

The parks and recreation department has been particularly unhelpful in making facilities such as gyms or multipurpose classrooms available to us. We've asked, but they make lots of excuses and always seem to have a reason (meeting, staffing problem, and so on) that we can't have a particular room on a particular day. I say "excuses" because when we turn around and ask, "Well, what days are available?" they continue to be vague and say things like "Well, we might have a staff meeting, or we might not be here." Also, they favor organized sports. They can't fathom why parents would bring their children to our park gatherings if we don't offer instruction in sports or league play. And they once allowed a league to use the gym the same day we had a permit for its use. Though mistakes do happen, there's been a clear pattern of not working with us. Our name was clearly marked on the scheduling calendar and we had confirmed the dates in advance, so I know they just decided that a basketball league was more important than a small group of homeschoolers. And yes, we have tried calling elected city council members and talking to administrators. We were then grudgingly offered some dates and lots of hoops to jump through, and in the end we decided not to do that again.

. . .

All homeschoolers use community resources to some extent, but unschoolers are especially interested in finding ways to connect learning with the everyday details of life. Try looking at your community not just as the place you live and work and shop but as a collection of opportunities for learning. Consider a few of the possibilities you may be able to find within a short radius of your home.

> Try looking at your community not just as the place you live and work and shop but as a collection of opportunities for learning.

Bookstores and Other Retailers

Bookstores run a close second to libraries as homeschoolers' favorite resources. New books, used books, any books on any topic can become a part of a homeschooling curriculum. Trade books are often better information sources than many books specifically intended to be educational. Other retailers similarly useful as "curriculum" suppliers are toy stores, computer software and hardware dealers, hardware stores, nurseries and garden supply stores, and so on.

Any retail operation can be an interesting place to visit, just to see how businesses work: How do employees spend their time? Where does the stock come from? How is inventory tracked? How do the owners decide what their customers will buy? Even the most routine shopping trip can supply bits and pieces of the answers to such questions.

Museums and Other Cultural Institutions

Museums, although overtly educational, are like libraries in that there are no prerequisites for learning from them. You can pick and choose from their offerings, spending all your time in one gallery and ignoring the rest if you like. (And while you're taking your time with whatever parts interest you, the odds are good you'll also see a classroom group rushing through in small groups to complete the worksheets they've been assigned to make sure they see everything they're supposed to see.) Many museums offer classes and work-shops, and some will be happy to customize their offerings for an in-terested homeschool group.

One option often available from historical museums now is what are called environmental living programs (ELPs), known more fa-miliarly as living history programs. Some museums and historic sites have year-round programs, with docents acting the parts of residents of the exhibited site and period. Other programs are designed specifically for student groups. Typically, students study the period enough to create a character or adopt a real historic character to play the part of. During the ELP event itself, the students wear appropri-ate costumes, perform tasks typical of the period with the equipment of the museum, and answer visitor questions as their characters. ELPs can be a terrific way either to spark interest in a historic period or to consolidate previous study.

Check with local museums and historic sites for information on ELPs in your area. You'll probably have to put a group together for a program; most student ELPs are designed with classroom groups in mind. Most ELPs are happy to work with homeschoolers, though; homeschool groups often have a much higher adult-child ratio and put considerably more energy than many school groups into making the event authentic.

Performance groups such as theaters, symphonies, and ballet companies may also have something to offer in addition to their reg-ular performance schedules. Their regular school outreach program may also be available to homeschool groups, and you may be able to arrange to:

- Take a tour of the group's rehearsal or performance sites
- Attend a regular or dress rehearsal
- Talk with some of the performers about their work
- Volunteer to be ushers, stuff envelopes, or do other necessary work for the group

Manufacturers and Other Businesses

Many manufacturing concerns offer tours of their plants. As with retailers, visits can be both to view the material, techniques, and equipment used to manufacture the product and to see the kinds of workers and jobs necessary to operate such a company. Depending on the type and size of the business, you may also be able to arrange to "shadow" workers for a couple of hours or an entire day.

Medical Facilities

Most hospitals have formal volunteer programs and many have tours, but don't stop there. There are nursing homes, assisted care homes, blood banks, medical laboratories, physical rehabilitation centers, hospices, limb prosthetics makers, and more. And don't forget your own doctor or dentist, or even your veterinarian, who might be willing to give your family the full tour or an opportunity to help out for a few days to see what his or her work is like.

Educational Facilities

Homeschoolers in educational facilities? Of course. A surprising number of homeschoolers volunteer in their local schools, although the extent to which they can do so is often affected by the attitudes of local school officials or teachers, or by the degree to which they perceive a need for extra help. Private schools are often more flexible in allowing volunteers, especially young ones, on campus.

• • •

Some friends (a mother and ten-year-old daughter and the daughter's friend) volunteer one morning a week at a public school. They work with some of the first graders who aren't reading yet. I gather it's been a positive experience for both the volunteers and the students.

From what I've heard, our own local school hasn't been too receptive even to parents of classroom children volunteering, so I don't get the impression they have a welcome mat out.

It seems more likely that we'll volunteer someplace other than a school when our youngest is a little older. —*Linda,* Hawaii

. . .

Shauna has volunteered in the classrooms of two of my day-care kids because she walks them to the private Lutheran school that they attend. The kindergarten teacher that both kids had is especially friendly and loves to have Shauna's help with projects. We have found the other teachers to be less flexible as Elise moved into first and then second grade. Shauna thinks her freedom "bothers the other teachers a bit," and they aren't as comfortable with it, especially because they are young and in-experienced. The kindergarten teacher is in her late forties and very relaxed. The first- and second-grade teachers are in their early to mid-twenties. Shauna wrote a thirteen-page journal chronicling her adventures in bringing Elise to first grade. The teacher there insisted that Shauna "drop Elise off and leave, like all the other parents do." Elise preferred to have Shauna spend a minute helping her hang up her backpack and arrange her things. Shauna negotiated with the teacher on many occasions during the year and finally outlasted her, more or less. She also brought the teacher fresh strawberries from our garden, which may have helped win her over a bit. Shauna is not obsequious or fearful of adults, and some teachers dislike this, to be perfectly frank. —*Carol,* California

. . .

We don't have anything to do with the local schools, although I have many friends at the Christian school my children used to attend. That school has a band open to homeschoolers that my oldest daughter will probably join next year. It is a small school, so adding in homeschoolers for extra activities really makes sense for the school. —*Beverly,* Nebraska

. . .

As Beverly notes, private schools are sometimes willing to work out arrangements for homeschooler participation in some activities, sometimes with volunteer work as a quid pro quo. Specialized schools, such as those for vision- or hearing-impaired students or for the developmentally disabled, may also be willing to have home-schoolers as volunteer teacher aides.

Government

Civics class has nothing on actually watching the government at work. With so many levels to choose from, it could take years to begin to grasp how it all works. And though watching government work can be fascinating, it's not nearly as interesting as participating, especially if you have an issue you care about promoting. Here are some ideas for you and your kids:

- Visit your congressional representative's district office.

- Attend a general session or committee hearing of your state legislature. Pick a bill to follow through the legislative process and watch what happens to it through the entire session.

- Attend a meeting of your city council, county supervisors, school board, or planning commission.

- Attend a trial for a day or from jury selection to verdict.

- Attend an appellate court hearing.

- Visit a police or fire station.

- Write to a government official on a topic important to you and your family. Try to decide whether the response is a form letter or a more personal response. Write back. Make it a regular correspondence.

- Look into the possibility of your child working as a page for a legislator or other elected official.

- Write to a candidate for elective office, explaining your views on her political stand on an issue important to you.

- Volunteer in a political campaign.

- Take part in a peaceful demonstration or protest of a government policy.

Sports and Outdoor Facilities

Youth sports leagues: baseball, soccer, softball, basketball—you name it, there's a sports organization that can always use coaches and equipment managers and fund-raisers. Parks and recreation departments use playground aides, lifeguards, and instructors for all kinds of classes. Nature centers need volunteers for picking up litter, maintaining trails, fund-raising, publicity, and helping with interpretive programs.

Special Interest Organizations

If one of your kids is becoming seriously interested in bees, you'll probably want to contact the nearest apiculture society, and your budding medieval historian might love the Society for Creative Anachronism. There are hundreds of hobby and special interest organizations to choose from, and their members are usually happy to share their knowledge with anyone who is seriously interested, no matter what their age or experience. If you can't find a listing in the phone book for the kind of group you want, check with your local library for their community organization files. Or try contacting the relevant department at a local college for information about local groups.

Also worth looking into are cultural and ethnic societies, if you're interested in a particular area of the world and its language or culture. Such groups usually hold regular meetings, lectures and classes, and often sponsor annual festivals featuring food, music, dance, and other aspects of the culture. Again, check with the local library or a college language department to find local groups.

Charities and Nonprofits

If an opportunity to volunteer is what you're looking for, you're guaranteed to find many to choose from in the nonprofit sector: youth groups, food banks, Meals on Wheels, the Red Cross, Special Olympics, the Salvation Army, literacy services, senior centers—the list is endless. Not only is the work educational, but it's also desperately needed.

Travel

Another minor advantage of homeschoolers' flexible schedules is the ability to travel at any time of the year. If you want to take a trip, you don't have to hit the road with most of the rest of the country sometime between Memorial Day and Labor Day. Traveling during the off-season not only gets you out of the crowds but can also save you money with off-season rates as well. Just imagine: late fall and early spring trips, leaves turning or blossoms in full color, and perfect weather.

With travel, you can take the "we are there" approach to history and geography. You can design a themed tour for yourselves—follow the Oregon Trail, visit Revolutionary War sites, or try finding routes of the Underground Railroad. Or, you might just visit a particular area and explore what it has to offer.

. . .

We have crossed the United State five times, three by train. We take the Charles Kuralt approach, seeing the back roads and interesting locals. We go on all the tours—maple sugar making, candle factory, cheese making, lumber mills, and so on—that we can find. Our favorite reference is the AAA TourBook for each region. It has helped us find countless great places, events, waterfalls, fairs, festivals, museums, and colorful characters. —*Carol,* California

. . .

The Internet

No discussion of learning resources today would be complete without mentioning the Internet. The Internet is vast and varied, ranging from the unbelievably impressive to the abysmally useless. Fortunately, dozens of search engines are now available to help sort through the ever-expanding glut of FTP and Web sites. Just to tantalize you, here's just a tiny sampling of what's available, from large institutional sites to those created and maintained by individuals. (Uniform Resource Locators [URLs] are given in Appendix C; Internet resources about homeschooling are covered in the next chapter.)

- VolcanoWorld Home Page—a great earth science resource; even includes a "Volcano of the Week" feature.

- The Smithsonian Institution Home Page—visit all the Smithsonian Museums online, including the museums of American Art, American History, Natural History, the American Indian, Air and Space, and the National Portrait Gallery.

- The Exploratorium—San Francisco's great hands-on science museum online.

- The Library of Congress—the vast resources of the Library of Congress at your keyboard: the "American Memory" photo database; Thomas, the congressional bill database; current exhibitions; library services and research tools; and the Library of Congress catalogs.

- Natural Math—an intriguing collection of activities and ideas for learning math with an unschooling approach instead of traditional rote methods.

- World Wide Arts Resources—from the Metropolitan Museum of Art in New York City, a huge, worldwide database of Internet resources on the visual and performing arts, architecture, film, literature, and more.

> The Internet is vast and varied, ranging from the unbelievably impressive to the abysmally useless. Fortunately, dozens of search engines are now available to help sort through the ever-expanding glut of FTP and Web sites.

- Bad Astronomy—one determined astronomer's valiant attempt to document and counter the ever-growing body of misinformation about astronomy brought to us by Hollywood and the news media; with links to other astronomy and general science sites.

- The United States Civil War Center—an impressive (and ongoing) attempt to collect all Civil War–related links found on the Web.

- Virtual Renaissance—travel back in time to a Renaissance town at this virtual living history site, complete with historical characters to guide you (and plenty of links for learning more).

- The Human Languages Page—links to over 1,800 language-related sites on the Web—online lessons, translating dictionaries, native literature, software, and more.

- The Quotations Page—a catalog of Internet quotation resources as well as a large-scale quotation site itself.

- Great Writers and Poets—links to writer's personal pages and pages about writers, lists of literary awards, and more.

- Digital Librarian—"a librarian's choice of the best of the Web."

- My Virtual Reference Desk—a mind-boggling collection of links to newspapers, magazines, dictionaries, shopping, sports, almanacs, and other reference sources.

- Cornell Theory Center K-12 Gateways—links to resources in math and science, arts and social sciences, and others for educators.

- The Halls of Academia—from the TENET Resource Center, links to sites for careers, history, art, government, home economics, geography, multiculturalism, science, and more.

- Bizarre Stuff You Can Make in Your Kitchen—a fascinating collection of recipes, mostly from books of the 1930s through the 1960s, for the traditional (volcano, slime, prop blood) as well as the less common (cloud chamber, Leyden jar, Tesla coil, glowing pickle).

CHAPTER ELEVEN

The Homeschooling Community

L ET US IMAGINE you are lucky enough to have an ideal situation for homeschooling: kids who are enthusiastic and eager, a supportive family, friends who think you and your children are amazing, a state law that is no trouble to comply with, a community full of libraries, museums, and other interesting places, and a school district that is happy to offer access to resources and activities as you want them. How could you possibly need anything more?

How could you not? No matter how supportive your family and community are, there will be days things don't go right, days when you think you were crazy to have even attempted homeschooling. Or sometimes you'll worry that things are actually going too well, too smoothly, so that you start to think you must have missed something, something important that you're not dealing with. Now and then you'll have days when only another homeschooler can tell you what you need to know or give you the perspective you need.

None of us, of course, lives in that ideal world where no one ever questions our judgment in choosing to homeschool. Occasionally, all you'll really want is a few hours to be around people you don't have to keep explaining things to. You'll be tired of telling your mother that yes, her grandchild is learning to read just fine, and explaining yet again to the neighbor down the street that no, your kids don't need to be at school today or any other day because you're homeschoolers. And your kids will enjoy getting away from that one kid down the block who insists that they must be stupid because they don't go to school.

Fortunately, you can get advice and support and just plain companionship from your fellow homeschoolers in many ways. You can join a local support group, a state association, or even a national organization. You can read any of a dozen homeschooling magazines or join half a dozen Internet newsgroups and mailing lists. And you can take your family off to one of the many homeschool conferences held each year, where you can wallow in being surrounded by homeschoolers who, for that weekend at least, constitute a local majority.

Local Support Groups

Local homeschooling support groups come in many flavors and styles. Finding a group that suits you depends on what type of activities you're looking for, what kind of atmosphere you prefer, and, to a large extent, what size community you live in. Many homeschooling resource books and magazines include contact information for local support groups, although such information is sometimes out of date because of membership turnover and the tendency for groups to split and reorganize. To find current information on existing groups, try asking your state's homeschooling organizations for regional or county contact people. You can also check your local library's community organization file or, if your area has them, take a look through the free parenting monthlies, usually found at bookstores, grocery stores, and restaurants, for listings of local homeschool groups.

All but the smallest towns or rural areas will typically have at least two groups. Usually, one will be specifically Christian, probably fairly conservative, although not any particular denomination. The other group will not especially care about your religious beliefs, except that if your beliefs are somewhat exotic you may find yourself tapped as an interesting new educational resource.

Groups can consist of a few families or have several hundred members. They may be informal almost to the point of anarchy or highly structured. Some offer more activities each month than any one family could dream of participating in, whereas others schedule only one or two events each week. Most groups fall somewhere within the following range:

- Highly informal: As many as two or three dozen families get together at regular intervals for park days. Individuals may schedule field trips, workshops, or other activities and open them to the rest of the group. Usually there are no formal officers or business meetings, although one person puts together a short newsletter with information on the events scheduled for each month.

- Moderately structured: The group chooses officers to perform various functions, typically a chairperson, a secretary, a newsletter editor, an activities coordinator, and a new member contact person. Sometimes the officers will be elected, but often anyone who volunteers for a job will be eagerly accepted in the position. To the park days, skating days, and miscellaneous field trips of the smaller group, this group may add one or more evening meetings with a guest speaker or discussion topic, a "mom's night out," a teen meeting, Scouting or 4-H groups, group discounts to performances or amusement parks, or ongoing cooperative classes in art, science, math, or other topics.

- Highly structured: Depending on the location, this type of group can have several hundred to a few thousand members. The large size often means that the group is divided geographically into smaller "chat groups," which function more like the smaller support groups. Officers may be elected by the membership, or the organization may be formally incorporated as a nonprofit organization whose governing board appoints officers. There may be several publications, perhaps separate newsletters for adults, teens, and younger children, or for each region. Additional activities can include choirs and bands, sports teams, and an annual curriculum fair or small conference.

. . .

Until this year I had never been involved with a support group. I really like the way [it] is run. It offers things that are difficult to do on your own. The group meets once a month. The older children belong to a 4-H club, which the teens staff. My children are working on a baking project and a model rocket project. They have activities for the younger children, too. The parents meet together to go over monthly news and then listen to a guest speaker. Guest speakers usually speak on practical topics, like how to fill out the state forms or make a transcript for your high school student. After the meeting we usually go with friends to get our Book-It [a national pizza chain's reading incentive program] pizzas and then go roller skating in the afternoon. It makes for a fun break in our normal routine. —*Beverly,* Nebraska

. . .

It may take a while to discover whether you are comfortable with a support group. Each group has its own personality. Some are friendly and welcoming to newcomers; members will be eager to get to know you and get you involved in their activities. Others, not wanting to push you into things you might not be interested in, will let you make all the overtures. Park days and other mainly social events can be daunting to the newcomer who arrives full of questions about homeschooling. Everyone knows everybody else and is talking a mile a minute about everything but homeschooling, and the newcomer starts out feeling isolated and unwelcome. Often, all you'll need to say is, "Hi, I'm new here," and you'll be taken firmly in tow and introduced around. Eventually the conversation will get back around to homeschooling.

That conversation can turn out to be one of the most valuable aspects of joining a local support group. You'll meet other new homeschoolers and families who are more than willing to share their experience with you: books and materials they've tried and liked—or found completely useless—learning problems they've faced and dealt with, or just the odd bits of local lore such as which library branches have the friendliest librarians. Many families have books and toys they've outgrown and are willing to sell, swap, or lend. And of course, a few people always have ideas to share with you, whether you're interested or not.

Many support groups, especially the smaller ones, have habits and traditions they are not even themselves aware of. The parents at park day may automatically move their blankets and chairs to follow the shade on a hot day, leaving the inattentive newcomer wondering whether she has cooties when she doesn't figure it out immediately. Or they may assume that newcomers are just getting a handle on things and don't bother to ask whether you're interested in helping plan activities. If you have questions or concerns, it never hurts to ask questions to clear things up.

Some groups restrict their membership or their leadership positions. You might be required to be currently homeschooling rather than just considering the idea. To serve as an officer, you might have to have been a member for some minimum period or agree to some kind of statement of philosophy. Most commonly, a religiously oriented group might require a signed statement of faith, although there have also been a few groups that require acceptance of a statement of educational philosophy. Such requirements can definitely help you decide whether that particular group is for you.

You may find that the first group you contact doesn't suit you. Maybe the members feel a bit too free to tell you all that's wrong with the way your family homeschools, or there's an unstated philosophy you don't agree with. Maybe you feel pressured to participate more than you'd really like, or perhaps you just don't like the people much. Don't hesitate to try other groups; you may find that some are targeted more to specific ages of children or to particular approaches to homeschooling.

If you are unhappy with the existing groups in your area or can find none, you can always start your own group. Post notices in likely places around town: libraries, food co-ops, churches, teacher supply stores, and so on. Send a notice of your group to your local paper's community calendar editor. (Again, don't forget those free parenting monthlies.) It might turn out that there are several homeschoolers in the area who've just been waiting for someone else to take the initiative in starting a new support group, or you might attract just one or two responses. Don't get too discouraged if you don't get a huge response; one or two new friends may be all you need.

> Don't hesitate to try other groups; you may find that some are targeted more to specific ages of children or to particular approaches to homeschooling.

• • •

The support group that I started when we first began homeschooling is still going strong more than a decade later, but we moved after the first year. There were two existing support groups in our new city, neither of which suited my family's needs. We helped to start another one that has been wonderful for us. The group is organized as a cooperative, and since it grew rapidly, we have had lots of energy and talent contributed by the members. We have co-op classes, field trips, family gatherings, skating and park days, but most of all, friends for me and the girls. —*Barbara, California*

• • •

I gave a luncheon talk about homeschooling to a local [community] group and met a like-minded homeschooler. She and I started Wildflower Homeschoolers; she did the newsletter and I helped host the meetings. Over time, our support group has developed two sides—the homeschooling side and the food co-op side. Most of the people are in both groups. We've done many field trips that were fun . . . but park day has disappeared as an officially organized event. The group is at a bit of a crossroads: too much geographic mobility and overextended schedules. Constant turnover as jobs take families away has been the hardest obstacle. The group is evolving. —*Carol,* California

· · ·

If local groups turn out to be completely unavailable or unsuited to your needs, check into some of the publications and Internet resources described later in this chapter.

State Homeschooling Organizations

Far too few homeschoolers take advantage of the services offered by state homeschooling organizations. Basically, state groups are watchdog organizations, formed to monitor the legal status of homeschooling within a state and to keep members informed of potential changes that might affect them. Most also provide information about homeschooling to government officials, educators, the press, and the general public, and many sponsor large homeschooling conferences.

> Far too few homeschoolers take advantage of the services offered by state homeschooling organizations.

Just as there are often several local groups in an area, most states also have two or three organizations. As with the local groups, typically one state group will be uninterested in its members' religious affiliations (or lack thereof) and one will be explicitly Christian. Often more important than an organization's religious orientation, though, is its basic approach to providing information. Some groups view their purpose as providing you as much information as they can collect, so that you can make informed decisions about how you choose to comply with your state's regulations. Others take a more prescriptive approach, informing you of the proper steps you should take to be a responsible homeschooler.

A useful state homeschooling association will provide most of the following:

- A newsletter, typically published bimonthly or quarterly, to keep members informed about legal and legislative news that might affect homeschoolers and provide current information on local groups and newly available resources. Many state newsletters also include book and magazine reviews, curriculum ideas and recommendations, and plenty of members' personal experiences and opinions.

- A network of regional or county contact people, who provide information about the services the association offers, refer people to local support groups, and answer general homeschooling inquiries. They also work to pass local information, especially any problems homeschoolers have with local school officials, back to the state group.

. . .

[When] I became a county contact, I began to receive phone calls from prospective and current homeschoolers. I now also get calls from researchers, newspapers, professors, and others who are curious about homeschooling. I do get the occasional phone call expressing terror at swimming against the tide of society in such a basic way, but usually gentle reassurance is all that is needed.
—*Carol*, California

. . .

- A legal or legislative committee or coordinator to collect and collate information on the legal status of homeschooling in the state.

(See Chapter 2 for information on the kinds of problems most likely to develop.) This is the job most groups consider their fundamental purpose: keeping up with any potential changes and making sure that members and other homeschoolers throughout the state know about them early enough to deal with the troublesome ones. If you're at all politically oriented, this can be a fascinating committee to volunteer for.

- A published guide to homeschooling in the state. This should include, at minimum, an overview of the rules governing homeschooling, possibly including the text of applicable statutes and regulations, advice on dealing with officials, a listing of local and regional contacts or local support groups, and a good general homeschooling resource list. Advice on choosing curriculum and other materials, information on learning styles, potential field trips within the state, and other more general information can also be included. Depending on the size and prosperity of the group, the energy and perseverance of its board and members, and the complexity of the state's rules, this publication might be a few photocopied pages stapled together, a good-sized pamphlet, a massive loose-leaf binder, or a full-fledged book.

- Other services or activities. These might include regular (usually annual) conferences or curriculum fairs, campouts or other social gatherings, ID cards for homeschooled kids, yearbooks, and "graduation" ceremonies.

Most homeschooling organizations are run by unpaid volunteers and will eagerly welcome volunteers to share the load. (If you've had trouble finding other homeschoolers, volunteering with a state association may be just what you need.) Many homeschoolers serve as board members or local contacts for years and long ago ceased trying to keep track of the time and energy they've put into helping other homeschoolers.

Like any other groups, homeschooling associations are occasionally wracked by internal wrangling and dissension. Such turmoil can be enormously upsetting, to both the work of the organization and the digestive tracts of the affected volunteers, but the essentially healthy groups eventually survive and thrive. In extreme cases, dissenters may split off to form a new organization, which only gives the state's homeschoolers more options to choose from.

Here are a few suggestions to help you get the most from your state homeschooling association:

- Remember that most are grassroots organizations operated by volunteers and barely make ends meet. Although most are happy to try to help you with questions and problems, don't expect the people you contact to be able to drop everything to do so. They will likely view their role as helping you to help yourself.

- If your state group has any projects that even remotely interest you, volunteer to help. Its effectiveness is completely dependent on its members, and the more who help, the more the group will have to offer.

- Make a point of actually joining the organizations you find useful. Too often, homeschoolers will say they appreciate the legal and legislative work a group does and are glad it's there, but they aren't really that interested in the politics of homeschooling. If you want the support a state group provides, give it the support it needs from you.

National Organizations

National homeschooling organizations, so far, have not been terribly successful. Although several attempts have been made to found useful groups at the national level, organizers have often found that most homeschoolers do not see much need for support at that level.

Part of the problem is figuring out what a national homeschooling organization would be for; education is regulated at the state level, so national groups have usually been little more than referral services to state and local organizations.

The National Homeschool Association (NHA) describes itself as existing "to advocate individual choice and freedom in education, to support those who choose to homeschool, and to inform the general public about home education." Mainly, the NHA publishes a small quarterly newsletter and a homeschooling information packet, refers inquiries to state groups, and holds yearly national conferences, usually in Ohio, Kentucky, or other midwestern states. It also sponsors regional conferences, although not in every part of the country every year. NHA conferences are usually campout-style and are meant as opportunities for homeschoolers to talk to each other instead of listening to speakers or viewing vendor displays. If this type of gathering appeals to you, you'll have plenty of opportunity for discussing homeschooling and other topics in depth: The typical NHA conference is attended by fewer than 100 people.

> NHA conferences are usually campout-style and are meant as opportunities for homeschoolers to talk to each other instead of listening to speakers or viewing vendor displays.

In 1995, Mark and Helen Hegener tried a new approach, with the founding of the American Homeschool Association (AHA). It was intended mainly as a trade association for businesses serving the homeschool market, although there were also membership categories for individuals and for homeschooling support groups at all levels. After its first year, the AHA changed its structure from a membership organization to a service organization focusing on information gathering and networking. Today it maintains a Web site, publishes an electronic newsletter, runs e-mail discussion lists, and offers a collection of resource files on a variety of homeschooling topics.

Of more interest to most individual homeschoolers are a variety of national special interest groups. Most at least publish a newsletter and provide resources for their specific topic; some also hold conferences, maintain lending libraries, or conduct online discussion groups. General state and national homeschooling groups usually maintain lists of such groups and can point you in the right direction if you have a specific interest.

These topical groups fall into several categories:

- Religious groups, such as the Jewish Home Educators' Network, the National Association for Mormon Home Educators, the Muslim Home School Network and Resource, the Jewish Home Educator's Network, the National Association of Catholic Home Educators, and many others.

- Political groups, which may focus on education reform from a homeschooling perspective (e.g., Alliance for Parental Involvement in Education) or concern themselves with broader political concerns (e.g., Homeschoolers for Peace and Justice).

- Support groups for homeschoolers with physical or learning disabilities (e.g., the National Challenged Homeschoolers Association).

Conferences, Workshops, and Curriculum Fairs

. . .

Conferences? *Yes!* They are fabulous, absolutely essential!
—*Barbara*, California

. . .

I haven't seen a need [to attend any]. I don't want a curriculum and I don't have to worry about meeting requirements yet, and that seems to be what most of these events are geared toward. —*Pam*, California

SETHSA (Southeast Texas Homeschool Association) has the Gulf Coast Home Educators Conference every year. It's huge, with nine or so workshops going on all day for two days as well as an enormous exhibit hall.

· · ·

I have attended a number of conferences and curriculum fairs. I really enjoy these. I have learned a lot in the workshops I have attended. I love browsing the fairs and seeing what is available. My favorites are the book stalls by companies like Greenleaf and Lifetime Books & Gifts. I have an extensive library and love discovering new books. —*Beverly,* Nebraska

· · ·

I *love* curriculum fairs and have driven as far as 250 miles to go and work at one. I usually get paid in materials or wind up using my pay to buy curriculum. —*Peggy,* Oklahoma

· · ·

I try to attend two every year. SETHSA (Southeast Texas Homeschool Association) has the Gulf Coast Home Educators Conference every year. It's huge, with nine or so workshops going on all day for two days as well as an enormous exhibit hall. I love it! I also attend the Christian Life Workshops every year. The exhibit hall is smaller, but Gregg Harris brings in a great many products himself and the actual sessions are always helpful. Between these two conferences, I am usually able to get the vast majority of what I will need for the year. —*Tammy,* Texas

· · ·

I've been to a ton of them. Most have been really fun, overwhelming, exhausting. —*Shari,* Alabama

· · ·

My wife and I have attended two conferences; they have both been enjoyable experiences for us. The greatest benefit has been the support and assurance that we were doing the right thing with Emily. These conferences were attended by almost a thousand people each, and the sense of healthy community was strong enough to feel. We walk away more certain and committed to the idea of homeschooling than when we entered. —*Doug,* California

· · ·

It's hard to overstate the value of the feeling Doug mentions. Even the most experienced and confident homeschoolers are often surprised at the boost in morale that seeing a thousand (or five thousand) homeschoolers together in one place can give. Knowing intellectually that thousands of homeschoolers are out there somewhere does not have quite the same impact as actually seeing a good number of them in person.

Just to have a couple of days during which most of the people you see and talk to are people who believe that homeschooling is an obvious and natural educational choice is surprising. The effect is astonishing—just find a nice, comfortable seat somewhere and listen to bits of the conversations passing by. You'll hear stories and debates and jokes and ideas and more stories, and underlying every one of them is the basic assumption that homeschooling is an effective and reasonable educational choice. The lift you get from that kind of affirmation is exhilarating.

And if you're one of those of us who occasionally begin to feel like something of a community oddball—either the only homeschooler or the only "different" homeschooler in town—the right conference can be extremely comforting. No matter how offbeat you feel, there will always be someone whose approach to education and learning you'll think is even more outlandish than your own.

There are several categories of gatherings I refer to loosely as conferences. Let's start with the more modest affairs and work our way up to the really huge events:

> No matter how off-beat you feel, there will always be someone whose approach to education and learning you'll think is even more outlandish than your own.

- Curriculum fairs: These can be swap meets hosted by local groups or full vendor exhibit halls sponsored by local, regional, or state groups. Any speeches or other formal presentations are usually made by vendors explaining their products. In addition to formal curriculum materials, the products exhibited can include books, games, toys, and software.

- Homeschooling seminars: A number of speakers give workshops on different aspects of homeschooling at various locations throughout the country. Such workshops are usually hosted by a local group; any exhibit hall is usually limited to materials chosen or approved by the workshop presenter. Among the most popular of these presentations are Raymond and Dorothy Moore's Family and School Seminars and Gregg Harris's Christian Life Workshops.

- State or regional homeschool association conference (small-scale): The smaller full-fledged homeschooling conferences concentrate on workshops presented by experienced homeschoolers and may or may not include an exhibit hall. Typical topics include getting started with homeschooling, learning styles, and college admissions for homeschoolers. Such conferences are often held at small colleges, with dormitory-style accommodations sometimes available.

> Conference styles vary as much as any other aspect of homeschooling organizations. To determine whether you're likely to enjoy any particular conference, consider the organizer or sponsor.

- State or regional homeschool association conference (large-scale): The bigger state conferences schedule two or more nationally known homeschooling speakers to supplement a wide variety of workshops. In addition to a large exhibit hall, you may find a technology room demonstrating the latest in computers and software. Banquets, dances and entertainment, homeschool "graduation" ceremonies, and possibly programs for teens and younger children may round out the program. These larger conferences are usually held at colleges, convention centers, or large hotels with conference facilities, and can attract audiences as large as five thousand.

Conference styles vary as much as any other aspect of homeschooling organizations. To determine whether you're likely to enjoy any particular conference, consider the organizer or sponsor. Take a look not only at the conference materials but also at the organization's other literature, especially its newsletter. Odds are, if its publications appeal to you, so will its conference.

The most enjoyable and useful conferences take a smorgasbord approach to designing their program: They offer a wide variety of speakers and workshops with the idea that most people are bound to find something interesting. Here are some suggestions for making the most of a conference:

- Don't expect to agree with everything you hear or all the speakers to agree with each other. If you attend with the idea of finding some new, provocative ideas for your family, you'll get more out of the experience.

- Don't concentrate so much on the formal program that you miss the opportunity to meet and talk with other homeschoolers. There will often be informal gatherings of special interest groups, and serendipitous encounters can turn out to be the highlight of the weekend.

- Do plan your budget. Depending on the companies that choose to exhibit, you could easily spend several hundred dollars cruising the exhibit hall. Try to have a good idea of what you want to find and how much you're willing to spend. (On the other hand, be flexible. You may find something that is simply unavailable elsewhere, and you'd regret passing it up for months after the conference.)

Homeschooling Support in Print and Electronic Form

If you're the type who prefers to get your homeschooling support in print rather than in person, you have dozens of magazines and newsletters to choose from. Or you can frequent homeschooling forums online with the major commercial services such as America Online, on independent BBSs, and on Internet newsgroups and mailing lists.

Magazines and Newsletters

In 1980, there were only two or three homeschooling periodicals to choose from. Now at least a dozen good-sized magazines are available, with new ones trying to break into the field every year, along with dozens of newsletters targeting specialized slices of the homeschooling community. Among the best known or most interesting:

- *Growing Without Schooling* (GWS) is the granddaddy of homeschooling periodicals. Founded in 1977 by John Holt, it focuses on unschooling or child-led learning. Although it includes reviews and occasionally interviews of interest to homeschoolers, the bulk of it consists of letters from homeschoolers sharing their experiences and ideas. GWS can be enormously helpful to the nervous unschooler just getting started.

- *Home Education Magazine* (HEM) is the magazine to read if you want to know what homeschoolers across the country are talking about. HEM addresses a broader range of homeschooling styles than any other homeschooling magazine, giving its readers a bit of the flavor of the debates within a movement full of opinionated people. Mark and Helen Hegener, editors and publishers, include articles on education philosophy, the politics of education reform, curriculum ideas, along with regular columns reviewing books, movies, and software and some lively opinion columns. If you'd like an overview of the American homeschooling movement, HEM is worth a look.

- *Practical Homeschooling* (PHS) is the flashiest of the magazines serving the Christian homeschooling market. Glossy, cluttered, and chatty, it emphasizes curricular approaches to home education. Many of its regular columnists are themselves curriculum developers or popular workshop presenters, and fully half of each issue is devoted to product reviews. Editor-publisher Mary Pride writes colorful and opinionated articles, and she sprinkles jokes and hints in the margins throughout the magazine.

- *Homeschooling Today, Homeschooling Digest,* and *The Teaching Home* also serve the Christian homeschooling market. *Homeschooling Today* is probably the friendliest of the lot, providing lots of helpful, hands-on curriculum ideas. *Homeschooling Digest* is an attractively laid out quarterly (e.g., all advertising is grouped at the back) "for serious homeschoolers," with more abstract articles on developing Christian character and moral values along with curricular and legal advice. *The Teaching Home* is also fairly serious, with articles on record keeping and curriculum, reviews, and a topical focus section in each issue. In many states, a supplement published by one of the state's Christian homeschooling associations is bound into the magazine.

- *F.U.N. News* is a quarterly newsletter for unschoolers. Editor–publishers Billy and Nancy Greer focus on a specific topic—geography, foreign languages, math, sports and fitness, and so on—in each issue, with print and Internet resources, and ideas for activities.

- *At Our Own Pace: A Newsletter for Homeschooling Families with Special Needs* includes reviews of books, articles, materials, and methods, as well as interviews with subscribers who have children with disabilities ranging from autism and learning disorders to cerebral palsy and post polio syndrome, and letters from parents. Jean Kulczyk publishes this eight- to twenty-page newsletter irregularly; subscriptions are free, although donations are gratefully accepted.

Electronic Discussions of Homeschooling

If you've never participated in online discussions, you may find yourself taken aback at the energy they often generate. It's worth "lurking" for a bit to get the feel of things before you try participating.

Although there are thousands of friendly and helpful people on-line, many are also impatient, to put it mildly, with those who are less experienced. Unless you enjoy being the target of gratuitous insults, learn a bit of the "netiquette," lest you get yourself flamed to a crisp.

Most of the commercial on-line services have forums serving homeschoolers. You can usually find boards discussing specific topics and reference libraries from which you can download files, as well as lists of other homeschooling resources such as books, Web site links, mailing lists, and much more.

If you have access to the Internet, you can drop in on several homeschooling newsgroups: misc.education.home-ed.misc and misc.education.home-ed.christian serve the obvious constituencies, and some of the homeschooling mailing lists crosspost to the newsgroups.

There are a number of mailing lists of interest to homeschoolers, from general discussions of homeschooling to those specializing in particular areas such as religion, ethnicity, or special needs (subscription information for these mailing lists is given in Appendix A). Here's a sample:

- The Home-Ed list has lengthy discussions on philosophy, support groups, and resources, along with frequently recurring threads on kids' favorite books, whether spanking is ever justified, and whether television is a useful educational tool or a promoter of idiocy and mindless violence. There is also lots of banter and joking and occasional annoying crossposts from other lists. Home-Ed is a very active list; a digest version is available for those who don't like getting several dozen separate posts daily. Home-Ed's FAQ (frequently asked questions) file contains listings for dozens of resources, both online and off, from a wide range of viewpoints.

- The Unschooling list obviously specializes in unschooling. It's a friendly, relaxing, but fairly active list, and it is also available in a digest. Also available are the Radical Unschoolers List and the Unschoolers' Circle.

- The Homeschool Train Up A Child list is for those whose (Christian) religious or spiritual values are a central motivation for their homeschooling. The Madrasah List supports Muslim homeschooling families. LDS Home Learners supports Mormon homeschoolers, and the Many Paths List was started by a Christian mom and a Pagan mom who wanted a homeschool discussion group that welcomed all religious viewpoints.

- The Home-Ed Politics list is devoted to discussions of the politics of education, broadly defined. The level of activity varies enormously: Home-Ed Politics can be almost inactive for weeks until a new issue prompts a flurry of vehement discussion. During its active stretches, a little bit of Home-Ed Politics can go a very long way.

- The Aut-2b-home List is a private, moderated list for parents homeschooling kids with disorders on the autism spectrum. The ADD/ADHD List is for parents homeschooling kids with attention deficit/hyperactivity disorder.

Similar to mailing lists but less interactive are electronic newsletters, which also cover a variety of topics from general to specific:

- The *AHA Online Newsletter* is sent the first week of every month with news and information, articles and essays, networking, and other resources.

- *Chart & Compass* is a monthly newsletter for anyone interested in letting their children learn at home.

- *Edusource Web Reviews* offers Internet learning resources.

Dozens of specialized homeschooling mailing lists and newsletters are now available. It may take a bit of lurking to find the group that suits you, but more lists are started all the time. Many of the major homeschooling Web sites maintain lists of mailing lists, or check Liszt and other lists of lists. One of the best sources for homeschooling mailing list and newsletter information is Karen Gibson's "Homeschooling Email Lists, Newsletters, etc." Web site.

The number of excellent Web pages on homeschooling has exploded in the last few years, and more pop up all the time. Joining Jon's Homeschooling Page, one of the oldest and best homeschooling Web sites, are Ann Zeise's Mining Company homeschooling pages; Kaleidoscapes, hosted by Kathleen Iuzzolino, Cafi Cohen, and Karl Bunday; and dozens of other new and interesting sites.

CHAPTER TWELVE

Coping with the Rough Spots

MANY NEW HOMESCHOOLERS find themselves dazzled and discouraged by conversations with longtime homeschoolers. The veterans can intimidate by being so helpful: They seem to have everything perfectly organized, their houses are always clean, their kids are bright and eager and always geniuses, and they have plenty of time to answer your questions and solve your problems. Worst of all, they never, ever have bad days homeschooling.

We all have bad days, of course. We worry if we're doing our best for our children; we become immune to dust and cobwebs; we start to think our kids will never stop bickering; we can't figure out how to fit everything we have to do into our days; we just plain run out of energy. We all have our bad days.

Homeschooling veterans, though, do have the advantage of experience. We're past that stage when the novelty of homeschooling lets us believe that any problems are simply because we're new at it. We know and expect we'll hit those stretches when nothing seems to go right. We expect we'll get through them, and we begin to recognize them as normal. The symptoms become familiar, and we develop strategies for dealing with them.

Parental Panic Attacks

Parental panic attacks are a staple of the homeschooling life, especially if you lean toward the unschooling approach. They occur when you've been talking to other homeschoolers or reading about them in a magazine or newspaper, and you realize that your children just don't measure up. They won't graduate from medical school by the age of twelve, they don't speak five languages fluently, they show no signs of starting their own businesses that will make them independently wealthy by sixteen, and they've not yet published Nobel-quality work on recombinant DNA. In fact, you're not even sure they could make their beds regularly if you didn't remind them. And it's all your fault. It's because you chose the wrong math book, or didn't read aloud to them enough, or maybe just don't have the right stuff to make a success of homeschooling.

> We know and expect we'll hit those stretches when nothing seems to go right. We expect we'll get through them, and we begin to recognize them as normal.

. . .

I go through the idea that I should be giving Sara more information—making her "study" some of those important things like the Punic Wars. Lots of times she already knows what I try to tell her. I do wish she wanted to study more on her own, but I'm not going to force it down her throat. —*Lisa,* Alabama

. . .

As a product of the public schools, I find I still get anxious at the beginning of the school year. We should get busy and do something. I think of all the public school kids sitting for hours with paper and pen. It always passes if I wait long enough. Then I can see what Emily is truly learning and I calm down. —*Doug,* California

. . .

It's only happened a few times in eleven years, but like everyone else I've had a few moments of insecurity about my children's progress. It's only happened when I've thought about comparing them to what might be expected for "grade level." —*Linda,* Hawaii

. . .

I've worried extensively about TJ's reading. It didn't seem natural that he'd be such a late reader. God's funny that way. I never thought of sending him to school, but I did worry a lot! I've worried about Bekah's and my relationship. It's tough. I've wondered if she might be better off in school. Then I watch her wiggle at the computer or do something else because of her highly kinesthetic personality, and I remind myself that surely she's better off at home. —*Shari,* Alabama

. . .

The effects of extreme parental panic attacks are pretty predictable. You resolve to reform your whole approach to homeschooling. If you unschool, you'll start daily drills in arithmetic and grammar and spelling. If you use a packaged curriculum, you'll dump it for another better curriculum package or maybe jump whole-hog into unschooling. Usually, whatever changes you make will last no longer than a week, and your kids may let you know within hours or even minutes that you've totally lost your mind.

Once you've survived a few of these attacks, you realize that you're not usually worried about anything substantive about your homeschooling. They're just the sort of general worry that hits most parents every so often, except that the worry is customized to your homeschooling situation.

Some suggestions for coping with parental panic attacks:

- Take a deep breath, and count to 10 (or 20 or 50 or 100 or 10,000). Don't make any drastic changes in your lives for a few days—wait to see if the worry just evaporates.

- Reread a favorite homeschooling book or article. Sometimes you'll find you just needed to be reminded of the ideas that got you started homeschooling in the first place.

- Talk to some homeschooling friends in your local support group or online. You'll undoubtedly find people who've been through similar situations before. They can help you put things in perspective and decide whether your worries are justified.

Skepticism from Family and Friends

It might be an offhand "And why aren't you in school today?" directed at your kids by a store clerk or a baleful glare from a neighbor when your kids play outside on a weekday morning. Or maybe it's your family: Your mother wants to know exactly how long you plan to keep at this homeschooling foolishness with her precious grandchildren, or your sister keeps giving you brochures about local magnet school programs. Or they talk to your kids: "How do you spell *prodigious?*" "Don't you get lonely not having any friends?"

• • •

For several years, I hardly spoke with my father's parents because I knew they would go through the usual spiel, and I was tired of it. We have a sort of truce now because other family difficulties have taken the focus off us, but even so. . . . —*Tammy*, Texas

• • •

Back in the beginning of our homeschooling, I was attacked by four different people in one week. It caught me completely off guard; none of these people had even asked any questions about homeschooling, so I naively assumed that they all understood. The very next week I began making phone calls to put together a countywide support group. —*Barbara*, California

• • •

I used to [hear this sort of thing], but I've gotten very comfortable handling it. The hardest is when they ask about school at home, but I liken what we do to what most people do with their preschoolers: Answer questions, provide materials, and the kids learn. —*Grace,* California

• • •

I rarely encounter hostility, and when I do, I calmly listen, state my views, and cite personal experiences to back them up. On our recent trip east, a friend's daughter asked Shauna, "Aren't you bored being at home all day? Shauna replied, "No, I love choosing what I do, and besides, I'm out at dance, book group, singing, and lots of other things. Do you ever get bored in school?" Eva answered, "Oh, yes! So often we have to listen to the teacher drone on about something I already know, and. . . ." At this point, Eva's mother shot her a look that said "Stop!" Eva's mother is a schoolteacher. Later, as we drove north to Massachusetts, we thought of Eva, languishing in sixth grade. Shauna said, "I know Eva tries to like school because she has no choice but to go, and she wants to please her mom. But I think she'd love homeschooling . . . and she probably can't even tell her mom." This was followed by a lengthy discussion about communication and how and why people say what they do. It pointed out the primary benefit of the homeschooling lifestyle: One's family is truly top priority, and we are able to be there for each other as we wrestle with problems or sort out situations. Closeness requires quantity as well as quality time. Home education facilitates this. —*Carol,* California

• • •

No hostility, but concern, from some friends and family. Luckily everyone trusts us and believes that we will be OK, but some of them still worry about things. —*Pam,* California

• • •

The older my children get, the better I handle criticism. Sometimes I find the attacks on homeschooling ludicrous. "Your children are so close to you—you'll have to let go of them sometime." "Don't turn your children into neurotics by stressing

academics too heavily." "Your children are not able to handle the
real world." (I usually hear this one from folks who haven't even
met my children.) And, of course, the infamous "Your children
don't socialize!"

Fortunately, I am too busy to respond to criticism. Our relatives are happy with the way our children are turning out, so we
no longer receive criticism from them.

It's very difficult for a school authority to challenge black
parents about homeschooling. All I have to do is roll out their
statistics on how black children are doing in school nationwide,
and they shut up. They know their results are pathetic. —*Donna,*
Washington

. . .

Skepticism? Sure, my parents are teachers, as is the better part
of my family. I trusted a pastor friend who said I'd probably be
better off just letting the tree bear its fruit, so to speak. Homeschooling caused one very painful episode and a lot of whispering
behind my back, but now TJ's so doggone terrific that people tend
to keep their reservations to themselves. Every little personality
quirk of his probably gets blamed on homeschooling, but we've
learned to live with it. In time, I'm trusting the same will ring true
with Bekah and Phoebe. Actually, the fact that Phoebe adores her
older siblings so and is so close to and dependent on them (in a
good way) bears testimony to our homeschooling lifestyle as well.
—*Shari,* Alabama

. . .

We have not had any pressure from family until this year
about our homeschooling. My husband had to field a broad array
of "opinions" from his folks this summer: my credentials to be
teaching, our children being around each other too much. My
husband was able to discuss their concerns with them without
getting upset, which I think really helped the situation. Their
minds weren't changed about homeschooling, but I think he effectively countered their arguments. They have agreed to keep
their opinions to themselves and not try to influence our children
against homeschooling. The children spent a month with their

grandparents this summer, and during that time remarks were made about the children needing to be in school. Because our oldest was returning to school, Grandma made a big deal about this, leaving our second daughter feeling like she was missing out. She later told me that she thought Grandma thought she was stupid because she homeschooled. She is extremely bright, so she knew this wasn't so. We've discussed this, and she now realizes that what Grandma has against homeschooling has very little to do with whether she or the other kids are doing well in their homeschooling. Most of the flaws they point out in our children are valid, but they would have the same problems in school. The standard that they hold up for our children is perfection. We can't possibly meet that. I don't feel that our homeschooling is a failure because our children are not perfect. —*Beverly*, Nebraska

· · ·

I've noticed a change in general acceptance and knowledge of homeschooling in the eleven years we've been at it. Seven years ago when we moved to Hawaii, we were frequently asked if it was legal; now most people we run into know a friend, relative, or neighbor who is homeschooling. Also, most people we've met have a generally favorable view of homeschooling, telling the kids how lucky they are or saying something positive about it as compared with school, whereas in the past, folks we met expressed more doubts or skepticism. This change in attitude is also found in many local educators and administrators—they've spoken very favorably of homeschooling publicly, stating that parents who choose it are very committed and are doing a good job.

My in-laws were very skeptical about homeschooling in the beginning, but over the years they've seen that the children are turning out OK, so it doesn't seem to be an issue with them anymore. They've commented on what good readers the girls are. Occasionally, they've even asked us for our advice on educational issues regarding our nieces and nephew! —*Linda*, Hawaii

· · ·

As Linda points out, skepticism from neighbors or the public is far less a problem today than it was ten or fifteen years ago. Most people have at least heard of homeschooling and realize that it is a legal option, so there are fewer problems with neighbors calling truant officers or questioning your kids' schedules. Most problems of this type are caused by simple unfamiliarity with the idea of homeschooling. Many homeschoolers find that the best way to defuse critical neighbors is to make it a point to tell them about homeschooling, about the interesting field trip they just went on, or how their kids are volunteering at the local library. Such "converts" to the concept often end up defending homeschooling to other neighbors.

> Many homeschoolers find that the best way to defuse critical neighbors is to make it a point to tell them about homeschooling, about the interesting field trip they just went on, or how their kids are volunteering at the local library.

Family skepticism or hostility can be much more difficult to deal with. All too often, grandparents will bring up the topic with the kids every time they see them, trying to prove to them that there's something wrong with homeschooling and that they would be better off in school. Even if your kids are perfectly happy homeschooling and not the least interested in attending school, this can put quite a strain on relationships, and you may have to tell your relatives to bring their concerns directly to you and leave the kids out of it.

Sometimes, skeptics will have a hard time explaining what they dislike about homeschooling. They may look at your kids and see that they are personable and friendly, competent learners, able to handle most situations they find themselves in, but they still feel they are missing something by not being in conventional schools. It may help to quit worrying about what such skeptics think about homeschooling and treat it not as your problem but as theirs. Much as we all enjoy talking about how much we like homeschooling and how well we think it works, we will never be able to persuade some people to our views. When that's the case, there's not much reason to keep trying. You may find that once you cut back on the evangelizing, your relatives will cut back on the criticism as well. And as your children grow older, the novelty of the idea wears off as the success of homeschooling becomes obvious.

Burnout

You wake up in the morning knowing that you've got to get that history chapter covered this week, your daughter only wants to sleep until noon, your son wants to watch Nickelodeon all day, your husband can't figure out why the laundry from last week isn't folded up yet, you haven't even started writing the article for the local support group newsletter that you promised by tomorrow, and you begin to agree with your daughter that sleeping in until noon has a lot to recommend it.

This is burnout.

• • •

I am getting very close to burnout now. It has more to do with the little kids, though. Five, three, and two are just too much on many days. In another year our life will be entirely different. Although I hate to wish time away, I will be glad to get out from under all the spills, nursing, and such.
—*Lisa*, Alabama

• • •

I do burn out at times, usually when I've forgotten how to say no and have overcommitted myself again. When this happens, I start looking at everything I am involved in, and all that is not essential to my or my family's well-being gets axed.

The only time I suffered from genuine "homeschool burnout" was when I tried to use a formal school-type curriculum. No one

> I do burn out at times, usually when I've forgotten how to say no and have overcommitted myself again.

had warned me that the curriculum, being designed for classroom use, was full of completely unnecessary busy work. Now I warn people to toss out half of what's in the book. —*Tammy*, Texas

· · ·

We burn out regularly—once a month or so. I back off school for a bit and wait for it to pass. I also check my eating and sleeping habits and see if there could be a physical cause or other strains on our family. I tossed out Saxon [math] because of burnout—one of the best decisions I ever made. —*Peggy*, Oklahoma

· · ·

We're lucky that we have a diverse life. Wally and I have hobbies we enjoy, and we love being parents. I think if I had to "teach" each day, I would burn out quickly. Living life? I've never had a burnout problem doing that. —*Pam*, California

· · ·

I experienced burnout working on the support group. A few years ago I felt like I was the only one keeping it going. The burnout was mainly a result of trying to do too much by myself. I tried to recruit help by listing all the things to be done, begging for help, and so on. I took it all personally that no one would help me. I had all sorts of ideas about all the activities a "good" support group should offer. But finally it dawned on me that if people don't want it enough to do it, then maybe it doesn't get done. I gave up the newsletter and put my energy into keeping a group going. I took a new approach in announcing the annual organizational meeting. Realizing what a drag it was to hear a lecture on

how everyone had to pitch in, I just focused on the neat things in the works and made it sound like they'd be the ones missing out if they didn't come. And I gave up my expectations that we ought to offer certain things.

Since then, I'm happy to say, a lot more people have stepped in to plan things, not just field trips, but we have new volunteers doing a newsletter, running a teen group, and organizing regional groups. —*Linda*, Hawaii

· · ·

Just as parental panic attacks mainly tend to afflict unschoolers, burnout tends to be an affliction that strikes highly structured homeschoolers. Keeping to a strict schedule can be stressful—particularly if the material being covered is relatively dull and difficult to adapt to individual interests or includes large amounts of busywork designed to occupy the larger number of students in a conventional classroom. It's easy to get so caught up in keeping to your schedule that you forget the schedule was designed for your convenience instead of the other way around.

If you're finding you or your children are less and less interested in keeping to your schoolwork or getting more and more crabby about it, consider making some changes:

> Just as parental panic attacks mainly tend to afflict unschoolers, burnout tends to be an affliction that strikes highly structured home- schoolers.

- Take a day or a week off to do something entirely different from your usual routine.

- Share some of the load. If your spouse doesn't help with the homeschooling, get him or her to take on some subjects. You will enjoy the break, your kids may enjoy the change in teachers, and your spouse may get a look at an otherwise unfamiliar side of the kids. Or consider working out an arrangement for a cooperative class or two with a few other homeschooling families.

- Look seriously at your routine. Is everything in your normal routine actually something you want or need to be doing, or can you drop parts of it without losing much? Do you know why you're doing most of what you normally do, or is much of it just for the sake of maintaining the routine? If the schoolwork your kids are doing is mostly material they already understand, you're probably working far too hard and might do well to consider a less structured approach to homeschooling.

Sibling Wars

All those kids stuck at home with each other all day long? Everybody knows siblings would drive each other (and their parents!) crazy if they had to spend all their time together. You can't do schoolwork with kids of vastly different ages all together, and if you try working with them separately, you're always getting interrupted to answer questions or settle disputes with the others. How can you handle a whole family of children without everybody getting totally frazzled by the end of the day?

> Everybody knows siblings would drive each other (and their parents!) crazy if they had to spend all their time together.

. . .

At first I found homeschooling a wide age range difficult. It helped once my oldest son became able to read well. I will soon have another learning to read. I think things will be different this time because I don't feel so pressured to perform. I have enough experience to relax and let the learning come in its own time. I've learned not to push. We expect our kids to help each other and to support each other. This has been such a part of their life that the younger two know they can go and ask their older brother and sisters for help and receive it. The kids get along very well together most of the time.

There is more friction between my oldest two daughters than any of the others. There is some jealousy involved in their relationship. The younger daughter thinks it's very unfair that her sister [who does not homeschool] gets things like HoHo's for her lunch, while she gets none of those prepackaged junk food treats. The older daughter is required to make her own lunch, so I have a stock of things that she can throw in a sack and run. It's purely fuss avoidance on my part. —*Beverly*, Nebraska

. . .

Well, we used to do everything as a family, with the little ones in arms sleeping or nursing while we did family projects, but that's changed as the kids have grown older. Fortunately, as the children have gotten older, they've also become more independent, so they're pretty much able to read or work on their own projects while I help the others. At four, Robert sometimes has difficulty waiting for his turn with me. I often get him started on his own projects first, or I have one of the two girls do something with him while I help the other. —*Linda,* Hawaii

• • •

Children almost always grow out of sibling problems. With toddlers and younger pre-schoolers around, older children can have trouble finding the time and space to work on complicated projects. Naptime and play dates can help, but sometimes the best solution is just to wait until the younger ones are old enough to handle things more easily.

Siblings who've just recently left school for homeschooling can be quite testy with each other. Spending more time with each other, though, usually means they get to know each other better. Sometimes, of course, this means that they get quite proficient at knowing which buttons to push to really annoy each other, but they also get better at settling their differences. Most homeschooling families report that their children get along with each other far better as homeschoolers than they ever did as schoolchildren and see that as a major benefit of homeschooling.

Most homeschooling families report that their children get along with each other far better as homeschoolers than they ever did as schoolchildren and see that as a major benefit of homeschooling.

Overscheduling vs. "Mom, I'm Bored!"

Prevalent among homeschoolers is the constant problem of a workable balance between too many activities and too few. We hate to pass up on any opportunity for an interesting field trip or speaker, but there's only so much time and energy to spread around.

. . .

I'd say being too busy is one of our biggest challenges, and this is so even though we are involved in fewer organized activities than many others. We've been consciously trying to slow down, but it seems if it's not one thing, it's another. Frankly, it seems to be a big problem for most people we know (schooled and home-schooled). I'd love to hear how other people strike a balance be-tween doing too much and opting out of activities. One thing that's helped me is to realize that it's my own thinking that does me in, rather than anything external. That is, it's my thought that I have to see a show or that it's a good experience for the kids or that I have an obligation to do something, rather than the show, class, or project for itself. —*Linda,* Hawaii

. . .

Sometimes we overschedule; sometimes we have quiet weeks. but we always make it to park day and her dance lesson. Frankly, I don't think my children saying they are bored is my problem. There are a million things they could do to occupy their time. I make a few suggestions, and Katherine has learned how to find things to do, and so has her brother. —*Grace,* California

. . .

I cannot personally deal with this one. I have not in eight years of homeschooling found the balance between too many scheduled outings and the coziness of home. Perhaps a planned community of homeschoolers? —*Melissa,* California

. . .

We are never bored. It isn't allowed. We are much better at scheduling these days, but I will admit to overdoing it in the past. —*Barbara,* California

. . .

My mom taught me never to say "I'm bored" because such foolish statements got you cleaning the garage! When bored, find something to do. That's what adults have to do, and that's real life. Overscheduling? I can tend to this, but I don't think that schooling or homeschooling makes it any different: I always have to be careful not to overschedule. —*Pam*, California

. . .

We have more of "Mom, I'm bored," in which case I point to laundry or dishes that need to be done. —*Peggy*, Oklahoma

. . .

New homeschoolers, especially those with younger children, tend to think of "exposing" kids to this and that wonderful opportunity and are unwilling to miss anything that might be in any way worthwhile. In extreme cases, parents can sound as though they're talking about rolls of film instead of about their children. That balance—between doing everything and collapsing from exhaustion—can be elusive. Some of us prefer only one or two activities a month; others are restless without one or two events each day. Most of us are comfortable with a couple of outings a week, but the comfort level changes as the weather, the seasons, and our kids change.

Don't forget that boredom can be a very useful state of mind, however. It's often the harbinger of a growth spurt and will be followed by a child's most amazing project to date. Or it may be an antidote to previous overactivity—a chance to veg out, recover, and assimilate what's gone on before. Don't be too quick to jump in with activities for the child who says she's bored. Offering suggestions usually doesn't work anyway, and by saying she's bored, she may really be saying she feels she ought to want to do something "constructive" when she really feels like doing nothing. And there's a lot to be said for learning to find one's own way out of boredom.

Don't forget that boredom can be a very useful state of mind, however. It's often the harbinger of a growth spurt and will be followed by a child's most amazing project to date.

Feeling Isolated

. . .

This is the big one right now. I have not been able to find my own friends, and Greg is working in another state. I feel trapped at home. There are a few things I can do about it, but I just haven't had the energy . . . things will probably get better. —*Lisa,* Alabama

. . .

This happens, but we're too busy to worry about it right now. My son has lots of friends on weekends and after school. Our support group keeps changing, so the problem comes and goes. —*Lillian,* California

. . .

I rather like isolation, as long as I'm choosing it. We plan/hope/dream to live on a medium-size farm with neighbors we can't see. Psychic isolation would be a problem, I think, except that I've found this wonderful community online. —*Pam,* California

. . .

Feeling isolated is why I started a support group. I know that our teenager feels isolated these days, though, because home-schooled teenagers are in short supply around here. —*Barbara,* California

. . .

Feeling isolated has actually been a concern of mine for Shauna, as the exodus of similar-age homeschooled friends continues. She denies any loneliness; I see it as my problem, not hers. She says she considers me one of her closest friends, and we do talk a great deal on our nightly three-mile walks. Rosie was jealous of this "alone time" and has opted to walk a last lap with me alone, to have her private talking time, too. She is likely to plan Christmas gifts or discuss meals she'd like to cook. Shauna is more into pondering the universe and discussing the behavior of other adolescents. She watches many of her acquaintances with thinly veiled horror, seeing the eating disorders, superficiality, and low self-esteem. She does know several girls from strong families who are "freethinking"—Shauna's word for those who haven't lost

their sense of self in the maelstrom of adolescence. These girls go to either the local Lutheran private school or to public middle school, but the difference is that their parents have continued to foster closeness in the family. All have strong, confident mothers.
—*Carol*, California

. . .

Feeling isolated, whether or not you are physically or geographically isolated, can leave you discouraged and depressed, whether it's the kids or the parents who feel it most. You may find yourselves the only homeschoolers in your area, or the only unschoolers in a community of school-at-homers, or the only school-at-homers in a community of unschoolers. In addition to the obvious palliatives, such as reading a good homeschooling book or magazine or talking with homeschoolers in your support group (if one is available), you can try these things:

- Get yourself to a good, large homeschooling conference. Seeing for yourself that there are lots of homeschoolers like you around can do wonders for your morale, and you may meet some new friends who live within a reasonable distance from you.

- Don't assume that you'll only find the moral support you need from other homeschoolers. Sometimes a long chat with any good friend will do the trick.

- Get yourself involved in some community activity you enjoy. Volunteer at the library or a food bank; join a theater or musical group; work for a political candidate. Feel a part of your community by becoming a part of your community.

"I Wanna Go to School!"

Occasionally, children will make it quite clear that homeschooling is not for them:

• • •

I began homeschooling in a temporary apartment with three children working on one small dining table. This was in my canned curriculum stage, so we spent a lot of time at that table. We were moving and had to wait on housing. When we finally moved into our home, it was such a blessing to spread out. Meanwhile, back in the little apartment I had one eleven-year-old child who did not want to homeschool. She didn't want to even be in Indiana. She wanted to go back to Omaha and be with her friends. She made life miserable for all of us. She has since told me that she did everything she could think of to make life hard for homeschooling so we would put her in school. Well, that was impossible for us to do, so she stayed home the entire time we were in Indiana. I tried everything I could think of to make homeschooling more palatable for her. I was involved in discussing unschooling online, and I thought that might be the answer for her, but she rejected it. She had been in school so long that she couldn't believe that she could unschool and not end up being stupid. She spent a good deal of time sleeping, which is a normal thing at this stage of life. She thought I was a bad teacher because I didn't force her to learn, but she also thought I was awful when I made demands on her. It was a no-win situation. Once we moved back to Omaha, we put her in school again. It was her choice. She has not changed her mind about this, even though she has found out that middle school does not give her much time for sitting and chatting with her friends. She prefers to be in a classroom. She has made modest improvements in her learning, but as far as science and social studies are concerned, she's gone back to the "memorize and dump" system of learning, which bothers me. Homeschooling without her at home is so much smoother. We actually enjoy our days. So until she's truly ready to homeschool, she'll remain in school. —*Beverly,* Nebraska

• • •

At some point, homeschooled kids who've never been to school start to wonder about what they're missing. Perhaps the neighbor kids tell them they'll be stupid if they don't go to school, or perhaps they're just curious about what school is like and whether they could handle it. Whatever the cause, it's important to deal with your children's questions before the school question becomes a major issue. Talk with them. Find out what they want to know about school, and answer as many questions as you can.

Many homeschooling parents find themselves panicked when their five- or six-year-olds announce they have no interest in homeschooling and insist they want to go to school. In most cases, kids this age have something specific they want to do. Most commonly, they want to ride on a school bus and, even when the local public school is only half a block away, insist that going to school will allow them to do so. When the attraction is something simple and concrete like a school bus ride, it's usually a pretty simple matter to deal with.

For more general curiosity about school, it may be possible to arrange to visit a classroom for a day or two. A local public school may be happy to allow such a visit, in hopes of encouraging enrollment, or a private school may turn out to be more helpful. Most homeschooled kids find the experience interesting but end up preferring to stick with homeschooling.

Some will finally decide they truly want to go to school, however, and you may find, like Beverly did, that school is the best option. At the elementary level, there is usually no problem for homeschooled children getting into school. Sometimes the child will be placed according to her age; other schools will administer diagnostic tests to determine the appropriate grade level. Typically, homeschooled children tend to score on such tests at or above grade level in all areas but math, where they tend to score high on problem-solving skills and a bit below grade level on computational skills. Most have little trouble adjusting to school academics.

The social aspects of school sometimes are a bit trickier. Some children, especially coming from an unschooling style of learning, have trouble learning *not* to take the initiative in what they do. It can take a while to develop the school habits most take for granted: asking permission to get a drink of water or go to the bathroom, or even raising one's hand for recognition before jumping into a discussion. It's a rare homeschooler, though, who does not adjust perfectly well within a few weeks (and it's also quite common for such kids to decide to return to homeschooling within a term or school year).

CHAPTER THIRTEEN

Special Circumstances

E VEN UNDER THE best of circumstances, homeschooling can be a challenge, but in some situations it can be especially difficult. In some cases, homeschooling is simply the most workable choice among several formidable options. By maximizing individual attention, homeschooling can be very effective for children with learning differences or physical disabilities. Even with the advantages it offers, though, homeschooling in such cases adds to the burdens borne by the parents and other family members. Other situations, such as single parenting or geographic isolation, present obstacles that discourage all but the most determined families from attempting homeschooling.

Learning and Physical Disabilities

It is hardly disputed that learning disabilities such as dyslexia and attention deficit disorder are greatly overdiagnosed in schools these days. Whether such conditions are even physiologically based disorders is still a matter of contentious debate among educators, psychologists, neurologists, and parents alike. Whether a particular child is learning disabled and needs special education services is just as debatable: Each child is different, and the available services may or may not suit his needs.

Many families begin homeschooling specifically because one or more of their children is diagnosed at school with a learning problem such as attention deficit disorder or dyslexia. Such diagnoses often are simply wrong. Teachers required to teach particular skills at specific ages may only note the existence of, say, frequent letter reversals and be unable to devote the time and energy to find out whether this is truly a serious problem or simply a matter of waiting a few months for the child's skills to catch up with the lessons.

• • •

We call TJ "Mr. Reversal." I think all his "g's" are facing the right way now. He just turned ten. It's been a struggle and we're keeping our eyes open to what might still be a problem. Small print gives him headaches. —*Shari*, Alabama

• • •

Other children may have problems sitting still or staying focused on the material being presented, with the result that their behavior becomes a distraction to both the teacher and other students. Some teachers may look only at such symptoms and the classroom problems they entail, without investigating underlying causes, before calling in the special education consultants. The fact that a child may behave inappropriately because of sheer boredom may never be considered.

Parents skeptical of such "diagnoses" who try homeschooling often find the problems nonexistent at home. With the individualized instruction homeschooling allows, ordinary garden-variety letter reversals can be treated as the fleeting problem they usually are, and the active child can mix in all the physical activity he needs with his reading and written work. A bored child can always be allowed to find something more interesting to do when the needs of twenty-five or thirty other children don't have to be considered.

Many children, however, have genuine difficulties learning in school, and their difficulties are not confined to the school setting. Such children obviously need special assistance, but whether a formal label of "learning disabled" will help can be largely a matter of luck, depending on the quality of the special education services in your district. A specific diagnosis can be a tremendous relief to a child frustrated by her difficulties, but all too often, "learning disabled" children gradually become discouraged and believe they are incapable of learning. Many parents begin homeschooling out of frustration with the lack of appropriate and effective services for their children's learning problems and discover that they can provide better help themselves.

If your child does exhibit learning problems, it's important to determine whether they are symptoms of a serious problem or simply the effects of a learning "difference" that may eventually disappear on its own or be worked around. Do not rely on a diagnosis made only by a teacher; although teachers can recognize symptoms and behavior and point out the need for an appraisal, they are not qualified to make diagnoses themselves. You should make sure any diagnosis comes from a qualified professional. Don't hesitate to ask for further information or get a second opinion if you have any doubts. Be aware that, even if you are homeschooling, you may still be entitled to special education services through your school district. Check with your local and state homeschool groups for advice about what programs are available to your family.

> With the individualized instruction homeschooling allows, ordinary garden-variety letter reversals can be treated as the fleeting problem they usually are, and the active child can mix in all the physical activity he needs with his reading and written work.

Although they often present challenges similar to those of learning disabilities, physical problems at least have the advantage of being relatively concrete and identifiable. You may be entitled to (and need) services from your school district, but as homeschoolers you will also have considerably more flexibility tailoring a program to your child's needs.

* * *

Rosalie was nine months old and twelve pounds when we adopted her from Korea. She has had thirteen surgeries to correct numerous birth defects including a cleft lip and palate and severe eye problems. We learned in 1994 that she has a rare syndrome called Rapp-Hodgkin form of ectodermal dysplasia. She can't sweat and is therefore very heat-intolerant. She has had more than sixty-five severe middle-ear infections, often leading to temporary deafness. Seven of her surgeries were for ear tubes. She has corneal scarring due to extremely dry eyes, no blink reflex, and no sensation in her corneas. The hearing, speech, and vision problems caused by all this have led to a merry-go-round of specialists.

> Do not rely on a diagnosis made only by a teacher; although teachers can recognize symptoms and behavior and point out the need for an appraisal, they are not qualified to make diagnoses themselves.

Our first two speech therapists were through the hospital system. Once Rosalie turned three, we were referred to the school district. Our two district speech therapists have both been great to work with. Even though we have an interdistrict transfer for Rosie's ISP [independent study program], we are still using our home district's special education services. This is because of Maureen, Rosie's speech therapist for the last three years, who is a tireless advocate for children and an all-around great human being. Maureen is funny, patient, and has been in the district for twenty-five years. She is fearless and can work the system on our behalf like no one else I've seen. Maureen helps Rosalie speak intelligibly—no small feat with a huge mouthful of constantly changing orthodontic appliances, abnormal anatomy, and teeth coming and going.

Maureen knows the whole special education system and was able to help us get referrals to the vision and hearing specialists. The reason Rosie is so challenging is that none of her physical problems stay static. Her hearing varies with the weather, allergies, and infections. Her vision with bifocals is 20/70 corrected, on a good day, and worse if it's hot, dry, or windy. Her teeth are very abnormal because of the cleft palate: two top central incisors are missing, and the remaining teeth are completely sideways and out of position. Her lower jaw is ahead of her upper by a centimeter. At age nine and a half, she is losing teeth and only replacing some of them. Eventually she will be getting dental implants for her central incisors, probably at age fifteen or so, after a surgery to bring her whole midface forward. Her story is one of hundreds of medical appointments, procedures, specialists, surgeries, and well over $200,000 so far. And she is still a smart, funny, normal kid, and one tough cookie.

The hearing specialist tested Rosie and declared her to be the "best listener and lip reader I have tested." She is on call for us if Rosalie gets into hearing problems again this winter. The last audiometry showed 80 percent hearing in her right ear and 75 percent in her left. Not bad for having needed nine sets of ear tubes and having had six ruptured eardrums. In October, the vision specialist arranged our use of a Voyager reading machine at home. Instead of having to hunt for large print books, Rosie can now place any book in the Voyager, which uses a video camera to magnify the print into any desired size. Rosie can adjust the clarity and read without fatigue. Wow! According to Maureen, we will have the use of the machine until Rosalie is eighteen. We had been having problems finding appropriate books for her: large print books are expensive to produce, and few mid-level children's books come that way. We had read everything the local library had on hand—one small shelf of classics such as *Treasure Island, Pippi Longstocking,* and *Alice in Wonderland.*

Rosalie is a very sweet, smart, and lovable person who has patiently tolerated running this maze of the health care system. She speaks with wisdom beyond her years, and only asks that the health care providers that we deal with treat her with respect. Her homeschooling experience has been vastly different from Shauna's, who has been remarkably healthy all her life. Shauna understands how scary it is for Rosalie to face surgery after surgery, even though she is usually pretty stoic about it. Shauna has a lot of respect for her little sister. She does feel twinges of jealousy at the attention Rosalie's health problems demand, but is really very understanding about it. My goal is to not create the sense that being sick is the way to get attention. I have taught both girls that "If you need attention any time, just ask for it. Please be straightforward about what you want; tell me." When Rosalie is hospitalized, I stay with her from door to door. I hold her in the operating room when they give her IV sedation and am in the recovery room as she begins to wake up from surgery. Being separated from her sister and from her mom is hard for Shauna. Her homeschooling at such times usually involves writing in detail about what she did, so she can share it with Rosie when we return home. The two sisters are very close, as I have seen to be the case in many homeschooling families. —*Carol*, California

. . .

We have two children, one with autism. Our daughter attended a generalized early intervention (EI) program for special education students for three years. EI was an inefficient use of my daughter's time. The first year, the teacher was too laid-back and had low expectations. The second year, the teacher was fresh out of college and had no idea how to educate children with autism. The third year, the teacher knew how to cater to our daughter's learning style, and we worked as a team in developing strategies, tools, and so on. That year proved to us what she could do when paired with a knowledgeable teacher. Most of the speech therapy was group work, which was wasted on our daughter because she needs one-on-one attention. She didn't qualify for occupational therapy until the end of her final year in school.

The answer became crystal-clear: My daughter was spending six hours in school, five days a week. I was working with her only ten hours a week at most due to my full-time career. Yet she learned more at home than she did at school (except for the one year with an excellent teacher). I knew this because I often had to tell the teachers what our daughter could do and show them how I "got it out of her"! Other factors played a role in our decision: She is extremely sensitive to noise, and it's hard to create a quiet learning environment in school. Even during her "good" school year, my heart broke to see her cower in a corner at a Christmas party because all the kids screamed excitedly when they saw Santa Claus. Our daughter is on a special diet, and it was very hard for school personnel to be vigilant since she was adept at sneaking food. During her school career, I had attended extensive training on educating children with autism and had even given presentations on the subject. Homeschooling promised answers to our problems: Our daughter would always have her own teacher experienced with autism, with her unique learning style in a quiet environment, with her special diet.

The results of homeschooling speak louder than words. After not seeing our daughter for two years after we started homeschooling, our relatives—some with expertise in autism as education professionals—were impressed with how social and relaxed our daughter was. She used to avoid everyone and stress out easily at family gatherings, but now she reached out to people to get them to draw for her and play with toys. Since homeschooling, her imagination, pretend play, and spontaneous language have all increased noticeably. Because she joins me on all my errands, she has learned important community skills without having to create artificial versions in the classroom. Our daughter learned to interact with a variety of people of all ages in a variety of settings through errands, library visits, field trips and homeschooling special events, and support group activities. Because she was exposed to overstimulating large-group activities in short, infrequent bursts, she learned to enjoy socializing with others in small groups and to cope in large groups.

When our daughter was in school, she was not considered an ideal prospect for mainstreaming into academic subjects: She had poor verbal skills and was extremely delayed in her preschool knowledge. Now she carries a full academic load and has advanced knowledge in music and geography. Her writing is now readable (her teachers—despite my repeated cautions—expected her to write with her right hand when she's obviously left-handed). She loves art and spends a great deal of her free time drawing, painting, and coloring—tasks she avoided at all costs before. She has extensive knowledge (for her grade level) of animals and animal classifications and enjoys science. She reads on grade level and enjoys reading in her free time.

I am at a loss to describe how much our daughter has blossomed since we started home-schooling. She has developed far beyond all predictions of school and medical personnel. Most important, she is happy with herself and is not ashamed or fearful because she perceives the world in a unique way. —*Tammy,* Pennsylvania

> I am at a loss to describe how much our daughter has blossomed since we started home-schooling. She has developed far beyond all predictions of school and medical personnel.

• • •

I have a child who would have carried a ton of labels had he gone to public school. Fortunately, we removed him from the early childhood program when he was five and avoided all those labels. I know it was the best thing we could have done for him. We were fortunate—I think—that our health insurance at the time provided some of the specialists he would have gotten from the school—occupational, physical, and speech and language therapy—for the next two years until we moved. I say "think" because it was a blessing with a cost, and I don't mean the financial cost. The more important cost to me was in the lost years when I still thought he needed professionals to ensure his development, when I did not yet trust myself and him to know and be able to do what he needed to optimize his growth and development.

What home education does is to provide a truly personalized course of study. It allows you to go with the flow, to have good days and bad days, and not fight the bad days but accept them and then do whatever you can on those days. We spent a lot of days in the park or on nature walks when he was younger, whether for his bad days or mine! I spent literally hours a day—for years—reading to him when he hadn't mastered that skill yet, reading for pleasure and for new ideas, so that his mind was fed even when reading was yet denied him. I can't tell you when he finally became a reader—he's fifteen now and it happened sometime after he was eleven, but I really can't pinpoint it more specifically. It's still slow for him, but wonder of wonders, he is reading for pleasure and always wants to be in the middle of some book or other. Right now it's Deke Slayton's autobiography, so we aren't talking children's books, either. That would probably not have happened if he'd been in school, either. Sooner or later, they would have stripped his love of reading from him in focusing on what he wasn't doing "at grade level" (many things) and ignoring those things he was good at. I still read to him, although for far less time each day. Likewise, I still "write" for him: He dictates, I help with grammar and whatever else is necessary to make it clear to the reader, and, most often, type it for him, including letters to e-mail and pen pals. Without that help, those outlets and relationships would be denied him. At the same time, his knowledge of many subjects is at or often beyond grade level because he could pursue those interests independently of the skills needed to do so on his own. No institutional school could have done the same.

Another big plus for home educating kids who don't fit into the school's niches is that they are able to maintain a positive attitude about themselves and their abilities. With luck, they never

> Another big plus for home educating kids who don't fit into the school's niches is that they are able to maintain a positive attitude about themselves and their abilities.

get the impression they have to be "fixed." I found that one of the bonuses of not having educational credentials is that if I discovered a method wasn't working, I figured the method was wrong—not the child. That approach was put aside, sometimes to be returned to later when he was ready or interested and sometimes not. I worked to find another way or simply waited for another time. We never had a shortage of other things to do, and eventually he has come to find his way with—or around—all of the basics.

We are unschoolers. I have to admit it took me a lot longer to unschool our son than to unschool our daughter whose challenges are different and more "normal," whatever that is. I remember wondering for years if he would ever show a passion for learning some particular field. It was our daughter who gave me the confidence to give up (most of) the guilt that I wasn't doing enough. I'd heard the message of the professionals all too well that he would have to be "pushed" to do those things that were hard for him. Well, they were wrong. He has worked on all those difficult things, in his own way, on his own timetable, and for his own reasons. I've also learned that what most of the professionals do is no different from what an observant, caring parent does, mostly modeling whatever skill they are trying to "teach" and trying different approaches until one works. With a lot of patience and a little research and a lot more patience, you can do it, too.

Not all situations will lead to successfully home educating a child with special needs. Every child, but especially special needs children, need their home to be a haven, a place where they know that they are loved and honored and cherished unconditionally. If the child's needs are such that the family cannot maintain this attitude and at the same time deal with the educational needs, then it's far more important that home be a haven. Some families simply need the respite that some hours away from home provide. (For us, school created more problems than the little so-called respite it gave.) If a parent's ego is too involved in the child's performance to step back and out of that performance, they may not be able to homeschool that child, whether that child has special needs or not. Some children's needs are overwhelming, and no one person could meet them twenty-four hours a day seven days a week. Sometimes you have to consider the needs of other family members and say, "This is all I can do now." For all of these and myriad other reasons, families may decide not to homeschool a special needs child while doing so with other children. Only they know what will work for them. But just as I always remind people considering home-schooling for the first time, it is not a one-time, irrevocable decision. Circumstances change; you can be alert to those changes, and the day may come when that child may come home.

> Unschooling my special needs son has been one of the best things I've done in my life. It's been good for me and the rest of the family as well as for him, and has led to amazing growth for all of us. —*Carol,* Florida

. . .

Undoubtedly, having an advocate who knows the system can be invaluable in helping to obtain the services you need. Dealing with the day-to-day challenges of serious problems can be exhausting enough without having to fight your bureaucratic battles alone as well.

Here are some suggestions for making special needs homeschool-ing work:

- Make sure your child is part of the process and understands as much as possible of what is going on. Your child can give you valuable information about how he learns and what methods and activities are most helpful, and he has the most to lose from inappropriate choices.

- Find yourself an advocate within the special education system to help you make sense of it. A private homeschooling service or school may have individuals who can help. Where no advocate can be found, you should be prepared to devote considerable energy to becoming your own expert.

- Learn as much as you can about the particular problems you're dealing with. It's especially important with problems such as attention deficit disorder (ADD), for which the causes and proper treatments are hotly debated, to get information about all the available treatments rather than automatically accepting the first recommendations you are offered. Contact any relevant support groups to find out what information and assistance they can provide.

- Learn as much as you can about the laws and regulations that apply to special education. Don't miss out on services you're entitled to, and don't feel obligated to accept those you don't want because you don't know your rights. Contact support groups who can offer you the benefit of their own experience and provide information about your options.

- Make sure you're dealing with everybody's needs in the course of dealing with a child's disabilities. Siblings who feel neglected or shut out may need more attention paid to their own problems, or they may simply need to feel their own contributions are appreciated. If the bulk of the caretaking falls to one adult, that person may need an occasional break from the routine. Occasionally, the entire family may need that break from the routine. If this means you need help from your extended family or friends, ask for what you need—folks won't always volunteer their help unless they realize there is a need.

Single-Parent Homeschooling

Take the average homeschooling family and consider everything the family members do to make their homeschooling life work: They figure out how to live on one income, they decide on learning materials, and they help their kids use them. They learn to budget their time and their money to cover the things they most want, and they usually manage to make it all work. Now think about that family again, but take one of the parents out of the picture. It may sound like an impossible challenge, but single-parent homeschooling can be done, and done quite well.

Single-parent homeschooling takes determination, organization, and, above all, help. Much depends on the kind of arrangements the parent can make for work and for child care. A lucky few may find a workplace that welcomes children; most single parents of younger children work out flexible schedules and child-care arrangements with other homeschooling families. As the children get older and more independent, child care becomes less of a problem.

> It may sound like an impossible challenge, but single-parent homeschooling can be done, and done quite well.

. . .

My children are now thirteen, eleven, and seven. Having spent their formative years at home has enabled them to care for themselves. Baby-sitting, household chores, car jumping, plumbing, cooking, laundry, and myriad other jobs are routine to them. If I have to speak or teach locally, I don't have to pay for child care. For out-of-town conventions, I either drive so the children can be with me, or I call upon a close friend or relative for assistance. —*Donna*, Washington

. . .

Like Donna, many single parents find a way to work from home. Telecommuting is one possibility, as is a home-based business of some kind. With planning and organization, the kids may be able to help out with the business, or the parent may prefer a cooperative homeschooling arrangement with another homeschooling family or two. Depending on the family history, the noncustodial parent may also be able to help out.

Consider these ideas for making single-parent homeschooling work:

- Let your kids know that your lives are a cooperative effort. For homeschooling to work while you are trying to support everybody financially means that everybody needs to pitch in, whether it's taking over some of the household chores, helping with the shopping and cooking, or simply learning when to give that busy parent a break.

- Consider your employment options carefully. If your prospects are limited, you may want to look into the possibility of further education. A few very tight years may be worth the struggle if the result is a substantially better income; financial aid or some kind of public assistance may be available.

- Look into cooperative homeschooling arrangements. You'll probably want to work with families with similar educational philosophies, so it might take some digging to find the right families. One family might have all the kids on weekday mornings, while you take them in the afternoon, or two or three full days each week might be preferable.

- If you've got the room, consider offering a college student room and board in exchange for child-care services. You'll probably have to do quite a bit of interviewing to find the right person, and you'll have to make sure everyone is clear about duties and expectations, but such an arrangement could be positive for everyone involved.

- Cultivate a network of friends and family who can help out on short notice. Get to know members of a local homeschool support group who are willing to take your kids for group events now and then. Occasionally, you'll need a break from kids and work, and your kids will need a break from you and their normal routine. Don't expect to be able to go it totally alone.

• • •

The best investment I ever made was joining my support group nine years ago. Members have carpooled my children to field trips, dance classes and performances, offered emergency care, and given me lots of support—food, money, and even a loaner car—throughout my divorce. —*Donna*, Washington

• • •

One nasty complication for some homeschooling single parents is a custody battle. Homeschooling has occasionally been brought up as an issue in such fights. Sometimes an estranged spouse uses homeschooling merely as a wedge to bargain for lower child support payments or alimony, or he may be genuinely concerned about it as an appropriate choice for his kids. Even though homeschooling is a legal educational option, courts may view it as a less desirable educational option and consider it when deciding custody arrangements. In such cases, it's definitely worth contacting homeschooling organizations for advice; they may be able to refer you to lawyers or expert witnesses experienced in such cases.

Geographic Isolation

For homeschoolers, geographic isolation spans everything from the family who lives a few miles out from the nearest town to military families stationed overseas and families sailing around the world in a fifty-foot ketch. One family finds that their kids want more contact with other kids. Another family discovers that the learning materials they want are not available where they are.

• • •

We travel nine or more months of the year for my husband's work. We spend from a few weeks to five or six months in each location, but we keep our permanent residence in Texas. It is very difficult to take along everything we'd like. We have to start over making new friends often and leave our comfortable home behind. We might eventually be subject to state regulations in locations where we spend more than a few weeks. Travel opens up a whole world of possibilities for learning, but it can make our daily lives much harder. —*Laura*, Texas

• • •

Geographic isolation keeps us on the road entirely too much! We try to keep our activities down, but end up overloaded every fall. —*Lillian,* California

• • •

I wouldn't say we're isolated in terms of finding other home-schoolers, but we end up driving a lot to see our friends. One problem is that the kids don't have any friends right in our neighborhood. So seeing their friends depends on both sets of parents coordinating schedules and driving. We used to have good friends who lived only a half mile away whom we saw often. We've missed that a lot since they moved. —*Linda,* Hawaii

• • •

Often, of course, geographic isolation is the result of lifestyle choices the family willingly makes. But whether it is completely voluntary or not, such isolation still creates problems getting along from one day to the next. Sometimes answers can be found by way of the post office and the Internet. Sometimes the only solution is in adjusting, adapting, and learning to cope with the situation.

Pen pals of all kinds can help, and pen pals these days are by no means limited to the traditional paper-and-pen version. Online services and the Internet offer all sorts of options for corresponding with people: hobby forums, computer-related forums, children's forums, professional forums—anything people talk about in person or in print can be found somewhere online.

> Pen pals of all kinds can help, and pen pals these days are by no means limited to the traditional paper-and-pen version.

• • •

America Online and the Internet are a great asset to us in our travels. The friendship and tremendous support we have found online can go with us anywhere we can plug our computer into a phone line, and they are the very best source of information about where we are headed. It's also much easier to stay in contact with our families through e-mail. There are more and more resources available online than we could ever carry with us. We're thrilled with the ever-expanding possibilities. —*Laura,* Texas

. . .

Pen pals, whatever their form, can eventually lead to in-person visits. Instead of frequent overnights with friends, the isolated homeschooler may grow up making extended visits of a week or a month with treasured friends or relatives. And a family's whole collection of pen pals can determine the route for the occasional vacation trip.

Mainly, isolated families learn to plan. They collect catalogs and create wish lists or perhaps become heavy users of interlibrary loan services. They bring their lists with them when they get into town or port, or back to the States, and are prepared to grab items they've been looking or waiting for. Most of all, isolated homeschoolers learn to live with each other and their surroundings, to value each other's company, and to develop their ability to make their own resources.

> Most of all, isolated homeschoolers learn to live with each other and their surroundings, to value each other's company, and to develop their ability to make their own resources.

CHAPTER FOURTEEN

Beyond Homeschooling

THE TYPICAL HIGH school senior is a very busy person. In addition to keeping up with her final high school courses and perhaps a part-time job, she spends most of the autumn taking admissions tests for college, filling out admissions and financial aid forms, gathering letters of recommendation, applying for scholarships, and maybe even squeezing in a bit of a social life. Before she notices, graduation is past, the summer is over, and she's off to college. As she becomes accustomed to living on her own, making her own schedule, and choosing her own courses, she realizes that she never really considered why she is going to college and finds herself wondering what on earth she is going to do with the rest of her life.

It's a pretty familiar scenario to many of us who, despite good grades and test scores and impressive recommendations from our high school years, go off to college with the sneaking suspicion that going off to college is the only thing we're really qualified to do. Most secondary schools simply are not very good at helping students evaluate their strengths and interests and decide what they want to spend their lives working at. And even when schools do try to help, most teens simply have too much scheduled time and too little space to think seriously and realistically about their goals.

For homeschoolers, the picture is a bit prettier. Even the most formal, structured homeschool curriculum leaves teens with plenty of time that they can decide for themselves how to spend. Many homeschoolers end up being just as busy as their schooled counterparts, but they have more control over what they do with their time: They try classes at a local community college; they volunteer in the community; they find mentors to work with and learn from; they try out jobs. They begin to get a feel for the possibilities of life as adults while they still have support from home. With experience doing real, useful work, homeschoolers can be both more realistic and more optimistic about their options than their schooled peers.

> With experience doing real, useful work, homeschoolers can be both more realistic and more optimistic about their options than their schooled peers.

Homeschoolers also have another big advantage as they consider their future. Simply by being homeschoolers, they free themselves from some of those automatic assumptions about college and about jobs. They don't assume that college is their only acceptable option, and they investigate all kinds of possibilities most high school graduates never consider.

What about College?

Homeschoolers are popular people these days in college admissions offices. Homeschoolers have been admitted to hundreds of colleges throughout the country, to Ivy League schools such as Harvard and Yale, state universities large and small, technical institutes such as Rensselaer Polytechnic, small religious colleges, and the military

Homeschoolers are used to making decisions for themselves. They are used to setting priorities, devising schedules, and completing projects on their own.

service academies. On the other hand, a few schools, particularly some state colleges with strict numeric admissions formulas, still aren't quite sure how to deal with homeschooled applicants and might hesitantly suggest applying as a foreign student. But ask most college admissions officers about homeschoolers, and you'll probably hear that homeschoolers are a valued addition to the diverse mix sought for every entering college class, for some of the following reasons:

• Homeschoolers are eager to learn; they do not hesitate to ask questions and actively seek out answers.

• Homeschoolers are focused: They tend to know what they are trying to accomplish and look for the best ways to reach their goals. If they are attending college, they are usually there because they want to be there and expect it to be worth the time and energy they put into it.

• Homeschoolers are used to making decisions for themselves. They are used to setting priorities, devising schedules, and completing projects on their own. Because of their experience with this aspect of living on their own, they are much less prone to the temporary decline in grades typical of college freshmen just getting used to living on their own. (Some homeschoolers report having to watch themselves carefully, though, so that they do not fall into the habit of evaluating what they learn solely on the basis of their test scores and grades.)

So how do homeschoolers apply to colleges when they don't have the traditional transcripts and diplomas? In fact, colleges are seldom much interested in either because most transcripts are very similar and give little information to distinguish one applicant from another, and diplomas are just fancy certificates. The homeschooled applicant normally relies heavily on test scores and on letters of recommendation from parents, mentors, employers, and family friends. In lieu of the formal transcript, most colleges will accept a narrative account of the work done by a homeschooled applicant: what and how he studied, why he took the approach he did, how it fitted him for further study. Recommendation letters should be genuine accounts of the applicant's character and abilities and not just clichéd collections of praise and affection. Admissions committees are interested in how well a candidate is likely to do at their college and in the contribution to the learning atmosphere her presence on campus will make. Letters and essays that make an applicant stand out from five thousand or fifteen thousand other applicants can make the difference between acceptance and rejection.

There are a number of good books on how the admissions process works, including some written especially for homeschoolers. (See Appendix A for specific titles.) Start planning early: Find out whether the colleges your teen is interested in have policies for homeschool applications, learn what information you will need to be able to provide, and give yourself plenty of time to get everything together.

College at Home?

Growing numbers of homeschoolers are beginning to ask the obvious question: If homeschooling works so well for grammar school and high school, why not just keep on learning the same way? Why not homeschool through college?

Admittedly, the word *homeschooling* begins to sound pretty silly to describe independent college-level work, but the principle is sound. The concept especially makes sense for younger teens who are ready for college work but not

> Recommendation letters should be genuine accounts of the applicant's character and abilities and not just clichéd collections of praise and affection.

quite ready for campus life on their own and for those who prefer to learn on their own rather than through a formal college curriculum.

There are several options for college study at home:

- Correspondence courses: Most colleges and universities offer many of their courses by correspondence. Often, correspondence courses use the same texts and assignments as the campus versions of the course, and student work may be evaluated by on-campus faculty, although machine-graded options are also becoming common. Generally, the student has a fixed period of time, usually several months, to complete the coursework. Final exams sometimes must be proctored by an approved individual, such as a local librarian. Credit is equivalent to that given for normal, on-campus classes.

- Credit by examination: Students demonstrate their knowledge by their performance on a test of the material typically covered in a college course. The College Level Examination Program tests are one example of these; tests are available in general areas such as humanities and mathematics and in more specific course topics. Usually, each college makes up its own rules on the minimum scores to receive credit and the amount of credit awarded. Many schools also have their own tests for more specialized courses or will allow professors to create them for particular courses.

- Independent study contracts: Some schools have programs under which the student, in consultation with one or more faculty members, undertakes to complete certain activities (reading texts, performing experiments, writing papers, etc.) to be awarded an agreed-on amount of college credit. Such programs can be created for a single course or for a complete degree program.

- Life experience credit: Some colleges will award college credit for experience that has given the student knowledge equivalent to that required to successfully pass college courses. For such credit, the student must be able to demonstrate or document his knowledge in some way. Few schools will allow an entire degree to be earned in this fashion, but such credit can significantly reduce the amount of more formal work required to complete a degree.

An essential resource for anyone interested in any of these variations of off-campus college work is *Bears' Guide to Earning College Degrees Nontraditionally*. The Bears discuss the advantages of nontraditional degrees, along with the pitfalls involved, and give advice on choosing programs, evaluating accreditation agencies, finding financial aid, and applying for admission. They also list hundreds of colleges with nontraditional programs, complete with brief descriptions of the courses and degrees offered.

Other Options

Many homeschoolers opt to delay college for a while. They may want to wait until they are more sure of their interests and goals, or they'd like to have some work or volunteer experience before they decide on a career direction, or perhaps they want to travel and see other parts of the world before getting serious about more formal education. Other homeschoolers choose to forgo college entirely. A craft or hobby they started years previously may be developing nicely into a full-time business, or they may be interested in a field that does not require college education. Or they may have found an alternate route to meeting a potential employer's requirements.

> Many homeschoolers opt to delay college for a while. . . . Other homeschoolers choose to forgo college entirely. A craft or hobby they started years previously may be developing nicely into a full-time business or they may be interested in a field that does not require college education.

Most homeschoolers will work out some combination of activities—a part-time job, a volunteer position with a local nonprofit organization, some independent reading and study, maybe a few short trips exploring other areas—rather than concentrating solely on one option. The particulars will depend, as always, on each situation: interests, abilities, finances, family support, readiness to try something completely new. Take a look at some examples:

- Mae Shell, of Vermont, volunteered at her local library while taking a few community college classes. She was asked to work as a temporary replacement for an injured librarian and gradually increased to six volunteer and nine paid hours of work. She decided to discontinue the college classes to concentrate on working at the library and developing her own writing.

- Jacob Spicer, after a various jobs helping his father, a theater manager, left his rural home for Chicago at age sixteen. He worked at a copy shop, as a waiter and later as a catering manager in a restaurant, and then in a carpentry shop, where he eventually became foreman. He began taking college classes part-time and is thinking about pursuing a law degree.

- Indira Curry took a computer repair class at fifteen, because of which she was hired for a summer NASA internship. She was asked to continue at NASA during the next year, and NASA eventually awarded her a full scholarship. She attended college studying architectural engineering.

- Raised reading historical fiction, at seventeen Kim Kopel found a volunteer internship at a living history museum. She paid for her expenses with a variety of part-time jobs. In the magazine *Growing Without Schooling* issue 99 she wrote that the experience gave her the confidence that she can do whatever she sets her mind to.

- Britt Barker traveled on her own at age sixteen, working with naturalists in Canada and Europe, and wrote a series of newspaper columns about her travels (since collected into a book, *Letters Home*). Her younger sister Maggie's interest in sled dogs grew into training and racing sled dogs competitively.

- Damian Lester, sixteen, planned a seven-week train trip to visit family and friends along the Pacific coast. During his trip, he developed an interest in sewing and taught himself to make custom clothing without patterns.

- Eleadari Acheson considers her jobs, at a used bookstore and as a gymnastics coach, the most important part of her homeschooling education.

Grace Llewellyn's books, especially *Real Lives*, include detailed stories of teen homeschoolers' experiences. Also, *Growing Without Schooling* frequently features letters from older homeschoolers about the choices they make as they move from home out into the world.

> Most homeschoolers spend much of their teens stepping gradually into adult responsibilities. Rather than being suddenly on their own, they develop their independence bit by bit, rather like infants freeing themselves from dependence on their parents.

Finishing Up

For homeschoolers, the line between youth and adulthood is much fuzzier than for their schooled peers. There are often fewer of the formal milestones to mark the transition—they bypass the cap and gown, the prom, and the commencement exercises. Most homeschoolers spend much of their teens stepping gradually into adult responsibilities. Rather than being suddenly on their own, they develop their independence bit by bit, rather like infants freeing themselves from dependence on their parents. They begin to explore the world on their own wobbly feet, checking occasionally to see that their support is still there but enchanted with the new big world to explore.

In a very real sense, though, homeschooling is never finished. One reason homeschooling parents as well as kids so often identify themselves as homeschoolers is that homeschooling is insidious and infectious. We parents watch our kids become voracious learners, and we find ourselves taking the same approach to life: asking questions, finding new ideas and new projects, looking at how things can be different or better. We realize that homeschooling truly is never finished and that each of us is once a homeschooler, always a homeschooler.

AFTERWORD

By now you've been reading and thinking about homeschooling for some time and you find yourself fascinated by the idea. Perhaps you even know a few homeschoolers or have been to a local support group meeting or park day, and you liked what you saw. Perhaps you've already decided that homeschooling is definitely the choice for you and your family.

And yet . . . when you talk to some of your other friends and family, you find yourself downplaying the idea: "We're thinking seriously about homeschooling, but we're just taking things day by day. We won't decide for sure until the time comes." Or you suffer from the nagging "what ifs?": What if I can't find the right materials for my kids? What if we choose the wrong things? What if I don't like the local school district's homeschooling program? What if we can't find a good support group?

What if I make the wrong decision?

What if you do? One of my tasks as editor of a state homeschooling newsletter a few years back was to write a column called "The New Homeschooler." For one issue I asked experienced homeschoolers what advice they wish they'd had or what one thing they wish they'd known when they first started homeschooling. I asked the question of most homeschoolers I happened to talk to, and I found that the answers fell pretty evenly into two categories: One was "Gee, that's a hard question. I'll have to think about it—there's nothing that turned out to be a major worry." The other response was "Well, I used to worry about (and here came just about anything: socialization, teaching science, adolescence, what the in-laws think, driver training . . .), but it turned out not to be a problem at all."

What we all realized as we thought about this question is that the serious worry we go through when we first start thinking about homeschooling is just like the worry experienced by first-time parents. It's directly related to the novelty of the experience. Didn't you worry about dozens of things that turned out to be silly? Things like folding the diapers the wrong way or giving your baby the wrong first vegetable? Weren't there times you just knew you could permanently warp your baby's personality by burping her the wrong way or that her funny little sneezes were signs of some dreadful incurable disease?

Eventually you calmed down and began to relax a little. You realized that kids are pretty resilient creatures who can handle their new parents' learning curves without much trouble. Lots of those decisions turned out to be pretty unimportant, and you can laugh now at how much you used to worry. Homeschooling works the same way. When you first start, there are indeed decisions to make about such things as legal options and learning styles—you have to learn what your choices are and decide what exactly it is that you're trying to do. But one of the nicest things about homeschooling is that none of your decisions are irrevocable.

Homeschooling is learning by trial and error. If something— scheduling, style, content, whatever—doesn't work, you are not obligated to stick with it until your kids are eighteen. You can dump everything and start again from scratch if you have to, and in the process you learn to trust your own—and your kids'—judgment. You begin to see just what competent and interesting people your kids are turning into, and you develop some perspective as the homeschooling life comes to seem normal and familiar.

After a year or two of homeschooling, most of us get used to it. We expect that there will always be questions and that figuring out the answers and the new questions arising from those answers is a natural part of the whole process. And perhaps surprisingly, as most of those experienced homeschoolers I talked to testified, that process is tremendous fun. Whatever else changes in what our children learn and how they go about learning it, the delicious sense of fun and adventure continues. May you find that fun and adventure with your own children!

APPENDIX A:
HOMESCHOOLING RESOURCES

While homeschooling books can regularly be found in stock in bookstores these days, you may have better luck ordering some of the more specialized titles from one of the suppliers listed in Appendix C.

Books

General Homeschooling

Bell, Debra. *The Ultimate Guide to Home-schooling.* Tommy Nelson/Thomas Nelson, 1997.

This comprehensive volume presents home-schooling from a Christian world view.

Brostrom, David C. *A Guide to Homeschool-ing for Librarians.* Highsmith, 1995.

This guide is for librarians interested in pro-viding library services for their growing numbers of homeschooling patrons; contains much basic information about homeschooling and extensive lists of resources.

Dobson, Linda. *The Homeschooling Book of Answers.* Prima, 1998.

Dobson, longtime columnist for Home Ed-ucation Magazine, *has collected answers from experienced homeschoolers throughout the country to the most commonly asked questions about homeschooling.*

Farenga, Patrick. *The Beginner's Guide to Homeschooling.* GWS Publications/ Holt, 1995.

This little booklet covers the basics of home-schooling, with information about finding resources and support.

Griffith, Mary. *The Unschooling Handbook: How to Use the Whole World as Your Child's Classroom.* Prima, 1998.

This book focuses specifically on unschooling, in the same friendly style as The Home-schooling Handbook.

Guterson, David. *Family Matters: Why Homeschooling Makes Sense.* Harcourt Brace Jovanovich, 1992.

This is a favorite of many homeschoolers for skeptical relatives and friends. Guterson, a homeschooling dad and former high school teacher, talks about why people homeschool and how well it works and addresses some of the most common criticisms.

Hendrikson, Borg. *Home School: Taking the First Step.* Mountain Meadow, 1988.

This is a complete and relatively formal general guide to homeschooling, with especially thorough coverage of planning and record keeping, curriculum development, and teaching techniques.

Holt, John. *Learning All the Time.* Addison-Wesley, 1989.

Holt's last book is about how children learn and how parents can help them without getting in their way.

———. *Teach Your Own: A Hopeful Path for Education.* Dell/Delta, 1988.

Teach Your Own was one of the first books advocating and explaining homeschooling and includes numerous personal accounts from early issues of Growing Without Schooling. *More emphasis on the reasons for trying it than more recent homeschooling guides.* Teach Your Own *is out of print in the United States, although Holt Associates sometimes sells an abridged British edition.*

Home Education Magazine. *The Homeschool Reader.* Home Education, 1995.

A wide-ranging collection of articles from ten years of Home Education Magazine; *this book includes many articles on teaching and learning specific subjects, along with networking and personal experience.*

Hood, Mary. *The Relaxed Home School: A Family Production.* Ambleside Educational, 1994.

This is an excellent book on less formal styles of homeschooling, from a Christian perspective.

Kaseman, Larry and Susan. *Taking Charge through Homeschooling: Personal and Political Empowerment.* Koshkonong, 1990.

This basic guide to homeschooling includes considerable discussion of its social and po-litical implications and is recommended for anyone interested in the politics of homeschooling.

Moore, Raymond and Dorothy. *The Successful Homeschool Family Handbook, Home Spun Schools, Home Style Learning, School Can Wait, Better Late Than Early,* and other titles, all available from the Moore Foundation.

All the Moores' books outline their approach to home education: delayed formal instruction, character building, family health and discipline, and so on.

Pedersen, Anne, and Peggy O'Mara. *Schooling at Home.* John Muir, 1990.

This excellent anthology from Mothering Magazine *covers philosophies, methods, and legal issues from a wide variety of viewpoints.*

Personal Accounts

Barker, Britt. *Letters Home.* Home Education, 1990.

In this little book, a sixteen-year-old homeschooler describes her adventures as she traveled and studied with several naturalists in the United States and Canada, and then on her own through Europe.

Colfax, David and Micki. *Homeschooling for Excellence.* Warner, 1988.

The media fuss about their homeschooled sons going off to Harvard and the ensuing avalanche of requests for information prompted the Colfaxes to write this account of their approach to education, including specific book and equipment recommendations.

———. *Hard Times in Paradise.* Warner, 1992.

Not strictly a homeschooling book, this often-funny account of how the Colfaxes came to homestead in the Mendocino mountains is an interesting look at homeschooling as just a part of everyday life.

Hailey, Kendall. *The Day I Became an Auto-didact.* Dell/Delta, 1988.

This is a fascinating account of a year Hailey spent as an "autodidact"—teaching herself—after leaving high school early.

Lande, Nancy. *Homeschooling: A Patchwork of Days.* Windy Creek, 1996.

These personal accounts from thirty different families give an idea of the range of possibilities homeschooling offers, though the volume is light on the less structured approaches.

Leistico, Agnes. *I Learn Better by Teaching Myself* and *Still Teaching Ourselves.* Holt, 1997.

Leistico's two books, now in one volume, are personal accounts of her family's approach to interest-initiated learning; they are encouraging for those who are nervous about letting their children take the responsibility for their own learning.

Llewellyn, Grace, ed. *Freedom Challenge: African American Homeschoolers.* Lowry House, 1996.

Fifteen black and multiracial families talk about why and how they homeschool and how their experiences compare with those of other homeschoolers; well worth reading for any and all homeschoolers.

Riley, Dan. *The Dan Riley School for a Girl.* Houghton Mifflin, 1994.

This is an unusual account of the author's single year spent homeschooling his teenage

daughter to remedy her lack of interest and her failing grades.

Wallace, Nancy. *Better Than School.* Larson, 1983.

———. *Child's Work.* Holt, 1990.

These are possibly the best personal accounts of how unschooling works. Wallace recounts her children's activities and also the struggle to have their approach to education accepted by doubtful school officials.

Legal and Social Issues

Arons, Stephen. *Compelling Belief: The Culture of American Schooling.* McGraw-Hill, 1983.

This is a provocative look at legal issues in American schooling and some of the seminal court decisions affecting American public and private education.

———. *Short Route to Chaos: Conscience, Community, and the Re-Constitution of American Schooling.* University of Massachusetts Press, 1997.

Arons advocates educational reforms based on the idea that education is a matter of conscience, like religion, with effects on individual liberty and cultural diversity.

Deckard, Steve. *Home Schooling Laws in All Fifty States.* Deckard, biannual.

This includes summaries of laws and regulations concerning compulsory attendance and homeschooling, as well as reproductions of some states' forms. Occasionally somewhat misleading because of frequent gaps between what the law says and how it is actually enforced.

Dobson, Linda. *The Art of Education: Reclaiming Your Family, Community and Self.* Holt, 1997.

Dobson talks about why conventional education no longer works well and how families can change things for the better.

Forer, Lois G. *Unequal Protection: Women, Children, and the Elderly in Court*. Norton, 1991.

Forer describes how legal efforts to "protect" children and others, despite the best intentions, often result in restricting their rights and failing to serve their needs.

Gatto, John T. *Dumbing Us Down: The Invisible Curriculum of Compulsory Schooling*. New Society, 1992.

This is an impassioned, even inflammatory, collection of essays by an award-winning former public school teacher who now recommends independent study, community service, and plenty of opportunity to explore the real world as the best kind of education. Gatto's description of what schools really teach, compared with what they say they teach, is scathing.

Hayes, Charles D. *Beyond the American Dream: Lifelong Learning and the Search for Meaning in a Postmodern World*. Autodidactic, 1998.

Hayes urges lifelong learning and thinking as a means of transforming individuals and society.

Hern, Matt, ed. *Deschooling Our Lives*. New Society, 1996.

If you'd like a solid and readable overview of alternatives to conventional education, this anthology should do the trick: articles by John Holt, John Taylor Gatto, Susannah Sheffer, Ivan Illich, Donna Nichols-White, and many others.

Illich, Ivan. *Deschooling Society*. Harper & Row, 1970.

This classic critique of conventional schooling is somewhat dated, but still interesting and thought-provoking.

Leach, Penelope. *Children First: What Society Must Do—and Is Not Doing—for Children Today*. Vintage, 1994.

Leach, author of the popular Your Baby and Child, *argues that our laws, social policies, and culture ignore children's needs; Leach gives specific recommendations for making our society more humane.*

Louv, Richard. *Childhood's Future*. Anchor/Doubleday, 1990.

A comprehensive look at what children's lives are really like today and at the consequences for the future.

Males, Mike A. *The Scapegoat Generation: America's War on Adolescents*. Common Courage, 1996.

Males examines the huge gulf between the way American society views teenagers and the reality of their lives.

Miller, Ron. *Educational Freedom for a Democratic Society: A Critique of National Goals, Standards, and Curriculum*. Resource Center for Redesigning Education, 1995.

This anthology questions current education reform efforts and offers alternatives.

Nasow, David. *Schooled to Order: A Social History of Public Schooling in the United States*. Oxford University Press, 1979.

Nasow covers the common school movement and the rise of mandatory school attendance laws, the development of the modern high school, and changes in the function and purpose of college education.

Perelman, Lewis J. *School's Out: Hyperlearning, the New Technology, and the End of Education.* Morrow, 1992.

Perelman's look at the possibly drastic changes new computer technology could make in traditional schooling is full of interesting ideas and great fun to read, if a bit far-fetched here and there.

Sommerville, C. John. *The Rise and Fall of Childhood.* Vintage, 1990.

This history of how children have been treated by the societies they live in, from ancient times to the present, makes clear that much of what we "know" about children is determined by where and when we live.

Van Galen, Jane, and Mary Anne Pitman. *Home Schooling: Political, Historical, and Pedagogical Perspectives.* Ablex, 1991.

Much of the material in this anthology of academic research into homeschooling—demographics, legal issues, teaching styles, and so on—will seem fairly irrelevant to readers who are homeschoolers.

Whitehead, John W., and Alexis Irene Crow. *Home Education: Rights and Reasons.* Crossway, 1993.

This is the most comprehensive work now available on legal issues concerning homeschooling; particularly good on constitutional issues. Essential background for anyone interested in homeschooling statutes and case law.

Learning Theory and Philosophy of Education

Armstrong, Thomas. *In Their Own Way: Discovering and Encouraging Your Child's Personal Learning Style.* Tarcher, 1987.

Armstrong includes practical advice for discovering and working with your child's learning styles; concrete suggestions are based on Howard Gardner's theory of multiple intelligences.

Baldwin, Rahima. *You Are Your Child's First Teacher.* Celestial Arts, 1989.

Baldwin's Waldorf-inspired view of child development is one of the more readily available books on Rudolf Steiner's approach to teaching children.

Coles, Gerald. *Reading Lessons: The Debate Over Literacy.* Hill & Wang, 1998.

Coles argues that both phonics and whole-language approaches to teaching reading ignore some crucial basics of the process, most notably that children are not passive recipients of curriculum presented to them.

Deci, Edward L. *Why We Do What We Do: Understanding Self-Motivation.* Penguin, 1995.

Deci offers interesting ideas about intrinsic motivation, and how supporting individual autonomy creates motivated learners and workers more effectively than any system of reward and punishment.

Gardner, Howard. *Frames of Mind: The Theory of Multiple Intelligences.* Basic, 1983.

This book covers scientific evidence for the existence of "multiple intelligences" and the implications of the theory for teaching and learning.

Healy, Jane M. *Endangered Minds: Why Children Don't Think and What We Can Do about It.* Touchstone, 1990.

Arguing that brains are literally shaped by experience, Healy asserts that aspects of our media-based culture drastically affect children's ability to concentrate and to absorb and interpret information.

Kohn, Alfie. *No Contest: The Case against Competition.* Houghton Mifflin, 1986, and *Punished By Rewards: The Trouble with Gold Stars, Incentive Plans, A's, Praise, and Other Bribes.* Houghton Mifflin, 1993.

Kohn's books, especially popular among unschoolers, are thought-provoking critiques of techniques that educators have used unthinkingly for years. Guaranteed to get you to seriously question many of your assumptions about why we do what we do.

Liedloff, Jean. *The Continuum Concept.* Addison-Wesley, 1977.

Liedloff's study of Stone Age child-rearing practices led her to look at how our own practices differ. Basically, she argues that including children in everyday activities allows them to learn about their society by being a natural part of it.

Macaulay, Susan Schaeffer. *For the Children's Sake.* Crossway, 1984.

Macaulay advocates and explains the ideas of nineteenth-century educator Charlotte Mason.

Papert, Seymour. *The Children's Machine: Rethinking School in the Age of the Computer.* Basic, 1993.

Papert, the creator of the LOGO programming language, looks at how children work with computers and the implications for schools and learning in general.

————. *The Connected Family: Bridging the Digital Generation Gap.* Longstreet, 1996.

A friendlier and more basic presentation of ideas from the Children's Machine, *this book also includes Papert's favorable view of homeschooling.*

Resources, Materials, and Curricula

Armstrong, Thomas. *Awakening Your Child's Natural Genius.* Tarcher, 1991.

This is a collection of learning activities and techniques suited to different learning styles.

Beechick, Ruth. *You Can Teach Your Child Successfully.* Arrow, 1992.

Beechick includes specific and practical suggestions for teaching fourth to eighth graders the basics (reading, writing, and arithmetic) and more (science, social studies, music, art, Bible).

Doman, Glenn. *How to Teach Your Baby to Read,* 4th ed. Avery, 1994.

Doman advocates starting lessons early with this method of teaching reading to infants and toddlers.

Duffy, Cathy. *Christian Home Educators' Curriculum Manual.* Home Run Enterprises, 1995.

Two volumes, Elementary Grades *and* Junior/Senior High, *cover learning styles, curriculum planning, and a wealth of recommendations for specific materials, organized by subject area and grade level.*

Hendrickson, Borg. *How to Write a Low Cost/No Cost Curriculum for Your Child.* Mountain Meadow, 1990.

This book can help you figure out your aims and goals for your child's education and translate them into learning objectives and curriculum plans. It is especially useful if you live in a state that requires a formal curricu-

lum; *lots of worksheets lead you through the whole process.*

Hubbs, Don. *Home Education Resource Guide.* Blue Bird, 1994.

This deceptively small resource guide includes listings not found elsewhere.

Kealoha, Anna. *Trust the Children: An Activity Guide for Homeschooling and Alternative Learning.* Celestial Arts, 1995.

This is an impressive collection of activities in music, math, art, language, logic, nature, and more; the author has been a longtime resource teacher for a public school homeschooling program.

Pride, Mary. *The Big Book of Home Learning.* Crossway, 1990.

These huge resource books, lately four volumes but currently being revised, are written from a Christian perspective. Pride is a lively writer, and thoroughly opinionated, but coverage of less structured approaches to homeschooling is a bit spotty, and support group listings omit many long-established nonsectarian homeschool organizations.

Reed, Donn. *The Home School Source Book.* Brook Farm, 1991.

This is one of the best resource guides for homeschoolers; it contains lots of materials, many not officially "educational." You may not always agree with Reed's views, but he's always interesting to read.

Rupp, Rebecca. *Good Stuff: Learning Tools for All Ages.* Holt, 1997.

This Parents Choice Award winner, by Home Education Magazine's *resource columnist, is a terrific collection of recommendations for books, games, tapes, catalogs, and more, all sorted by subject area. There is*

little overlap with other available resource *guides, and it is especially useful to unschoolers and others looking for innovative learning tools.*

Sheffer, Susannah. *Writing Because We Love To: Homeschoolers at Work.* Boynton/Cook Heinemann, 1992.

Sheffer's account of her work helping ten- to fifteen-year-olds improve their writing is a good look at how unschoolers develop their skills.

Stillman, Peter R. *Families Writing.* Writer's Digest, 1989.

Not strictly a resource guide, this is a wonderful collection of ideas for writing within your family: journals, family histories, letters, and dozens of other ideas. The emphasis is on producing writing that is meaningful to family members, not on doing such projects specifically to improve writing skills.

Wade, Theodore E., Jr., ed. *The Home School Manual.* Gazelle, 1995.

My favorite of the Christian resource guides: Wade covers an enormous amount of material, and his appendices (twenty-six of them!) are unequaled in thoroughness.

Teenage Homeschoolers

Llewellyn, Grace. *The Teenage Liberation Handbook: How to Quit School and Get a Real Life and Education.* Lowry House, 1998.

No homeschooling teenager should be without this book, which will get you excited about learning, even if you're long past your teens. Written directly to teens rather than to their parents; terrific advice for teens trying to persuade their parents to give homeschooling a chance. (Make sure you get the complete 1998 second edition—not the abridged version published a few years earlier.)

————. *Real Lives: Eleven Teenagers Who Don't Go to School*. Lowry House, 1993.

A sequel of sorts to the Teenage Liberation Handbook, Real Lives *is a collection of firsthand accounts of homeschooling teens who've taken the initiative for their education. Included are amazing stories of not-so-extraordinary kids leading extraordinary lives.*

Sheffer, Susannah. *A Sense of Self: Listening to Homeschooled Adolescent Girls*. Boynton/Cook Heinemann, 1995.

Sheffer's work with homeschooled teenage girls seems to show that they are significantly more self-confident and independent than their schooled peers and that they avoid the typical loss of self-esteem commonly observed in adolescent girls. An interesting look at one of the potential benefits of homeschooling.

Standardized Testing

Gould, Stephen Jay. *The Mismeasure of Man*. Norton, 1981.

This well-written and thorough historical study of the scientific basis (or lack thereof) for measuring "intelligence" has excursions through scientific racism, the heritability of intelligence, and the difference between cause and correlation. Wonderful for developing a healthy skepticism about testing.

Owen, David. *None of the Above: Behind the Myth of Scholastic Aptitude*. Houghton Mifflin, 1985.

This is a fascinating look at testing as exemplified by the Educational Testing Service's Scholastic Aptitude Test (SAT).

Robinson, Adam, and John Katzman. *The Princeton Review: Cracking the System, the SAT*. Villard, updated annually.

One of the better test preparation books, this book gives rules for understanding what test makers look for and tactics for choosing the "right" answers. Also available for most other major tests.

Standardized Tests and Our Children: A Guide to Testing Reform. FairTest, 1990.

This booklet provides a clear, basic introduction to testing issues, including a brief history of testing, how tests work, problems with tests, and alternative means of evaluation.

Money and Organization

If you have trouble coping with limited time and money or all too many possessions, these books can help. All are usually readily available in bookstores.

Campbell, Jeff. *Speed Cleaning: Cleaning for People Who Have Much Better Things to Do*. Dell, 1991.

————. *Clutter Control: Putting Your Home on a Diet*. Dell, 1992.

Covey, Stephen R. *The 7 Habits of Highly Effective People*. Simon & Schuster, 1989.

Dacyczyn, Amy. *The Tightwad Gazette*. Villard, 1993.

Dominguez, Joe, and Vicki Robin. *Your Money or Your Life*. Penguin, 1992.

Elgin, Duane. *Voluntary Simplicity*. Morrow, 1993.

Moran, Victoria. *Shelter for the Spirit: Create Your Own Haven in a Hectic World*. HarperCollins, 1997.

Tyson, Eric. *Personal Finance for Dummies: A Reference for the Rest of Us*. IDG, 1994.

Special Needs

Armstrong, Thomas. *The Myth of the ADD Child*. Dutton, 1995.

Armstrong is an ADD skeptic and argues his case effectively.

Coles, Gerald. *The Learning Mystique: A Critical Look at "Learning Disabilities."* Fawcett, 1987.

This thorough review of the scientific evidence for learning disabilities is from a skeptic who prefers the concept of learning "differences." If you're doubtful about your child's diagnosis, you may have good reason, according to Coles.

Hallowell, Edward, and John Ratey. *Driven to Distraction*. Pantheon, 1994.

This is one of the most popular of the dozens of ADD books now in print, discussing ADD in both children and adults.

Hartmann, Thom. *Attention Deficit Disorder: A Different Perception*. Underwood, 1993.

Hartmann theorizes that ADD is not a disease but an evolutionary adaptation, and ADD patients are "hunters in a farmers' world."

Sheffer, Susannah, ed. *Everyone Is Able: Exploding the Myth of Learning Disabilities*. Holt, 1987.

This booklet from Growing Without Schooling *includes accounts of dealing with learning disabilities and finding the ways to help kids learn best. Includes information on interpreting and challenging LD jargon.*

College Admissions and Life After Homeschooling

Bear, John B., and Mariah P. Bear. *Bears' Guide to Earning College Degrees Nontraditionally*. C & B, 1995.

This is the basic reference for earning college and graduate (even legal and medical) degrees through correspondence study, life experience credit, examination, and other nontraditional means. It contains good advice on avoiding diploma mills, judging the worth of programs, and a huge listing of institutions offering such programs.

Cohen, Cafi. *And What about College? How Homeschooling Leads to Admissions to the Best Colleges and Universities*. Holt, 1997.

Cohen, whose homeschooled son was accepted to the Air Force Academy, covers documenting a homeschool education, researching and choosing colleges, and preparing the application package.

Fogler, Michael. *Un-Jobbing: The Adult Liberation Handbook*. Free Choice, 1997.

Fogler offers ideas for making a life instead of merely making a living.

Gelner, Judy. *College Admissions: A Guide for Homeschoolers*. Poppyseed, 1988.

Gelner takes you through the admissions process from the homeschooler's viewpoint, covering tests, applications, and finding financial aid.

Gross, Ronald. *The Independent Scholar's Handbook*. Ten Speed, 1982.

This book provides guidance and advice for becoming expert in any field by working independently of classes and institutions.

Hayes, Charles D. *Proving You're Qualified: Strategies for Competent People without Degrees*. Autodidactic, 1995.

Proving You're Qualified *looks at our society's reliance on formal credentials and gives advice on getting your skills and competence recognized even when you don't have an official diploma or degree. It's a terrific companion to* Bears' Guide.

Kohl, Herbert. *The Question Is College: Guiding Your Child to the Right Choices after High School*. Addison-Wesley, 1998.

Kohl's 1989 classic is now back in print.

Robinson, Adam, and John Katzman. *The Princeton Review Student Access Guide to College Admissions: Unique Strategies for Getting into the College of Your Choice.* Villard, 1992.

This describes how the admissions process works and gives advice on making your way through it successfully.

Magazines and Newsletters

At Our Own Pace: A Newsletter for Homeschooling Families with Special Needs, Jean Kulczyk, 102 Willow Drive, Waukegan, IL 60087

F.U.N. News, 1688 Belhaven Woods Court, Pasadena, MD 21122-3727; (888) FUN-7020; http://www.IQCweb.com/fun/funnews.htm

Growing Without Schooling, 2380 Massachusetts Avenue, Suite 104, Cambridge, MA 02140; (617) 864-

3100; HoltGWS@erols.com; http://www.holtgws.com

Home Education Magazine, P.O. Box 1083, Tonasket, WA 98855; information: (509) 486-1351; orders: (800) 236-3278; HEM-Info@home-ed-magazine.com; http://www.home-ed-magazine.com

Home School Digest, Wisdom's Gate, P.O. Box 125, Sawyer, MI 49125

Homeschooling Today, P.O. Box 1425, Melrose, FL 32666; (904) 475-3088

Moore Report International, Box 1, Camas, WA 98607; (360) 835-2736; moorefnd@pacifier.com; http://www.caslink.com/moorefoundation

Practical Homeschooling, Home Life, P.O. Box 1250, Fenton, MO 63026; (800) 346-6322; http://www.home-school.com

Teaching Home, P.O. Box 20219, Portland, OR 97220-0219; (800) 395-7760

Internet Resources

Internet information is volatile: New Web pages appear, old ones vanish, and URLs change frequently, so be prepared to hunt a bit if you can't find these sites immediately. A quick check with your favorite Web search engine will find numerous homeschooling sites for you. (When you type URLs into your browser, be sure to catch all the punctuation and capitalization; Web servers are extremely sensitive to such details.)

Web Pages

American Homeschool Association Web Page
http://www.home-ed-magazine.com/AHA/aha.html

Canadian Homeschooling Resource Page
http://flora.ottawa.on.ca/homeschool-ca/

Heather's Homeschooling Page
http://www.madrone.com/home-ed.htm
Heather Madrone has collected some of her favorite posts from the Home Ed mailing list; good information, all sorted by topic.

Home Education Magazine
http://www.home-ed-magazine.com
Includes articles from recent issues, as well as discussion boards and links to other home-schooling sites.

HomeSchool Association of California
http://www.hsc.org
I've included the HSC Web site here because of its extensive links to Internet homeschooling and general learning resources, compiled by Lillian Jones.

Jon's Homeschool Page
http://www.midnightbeach.com/hs/
One of the oldest and most complete home-schooling sites.

Kaleidoscapes Homeschooling Discussion Board
http://www.kaleidoscapes.com/wwboard
This homeschooling forum is hosted by Kathleen Iuzzolino, Cafi Cohen, and Karl Bunday.

The Mining Company Homeschooling Page
http://homeschooling.miningco.com
Ann Zeise, the Mining Company's home-schooling guide, works hard to keep this varied site up-to-date.

School Is Dead, Learn in Freedom!
http://learninfreedom.org
Karl Bunday maintains an extensive site focusing especially on homeschooling research and publications, the growth of the home-schooling movement, and colleges that have accepted homeschoolers.

Mailing Lists

For information on these and other homeschooling-related mailing lists, check Liszt (http://www.liszt.com/select/Education/ Home_Schooling/) or, especially, Karen Gibson's "Home-schooling e-mail Lists, Newsletters, etc." (http://www.pipeline.com/~wdkmg/ Karen/Lists.htm).

ADD/ADHD HS List: To join, send e-mail to deborahbowman@xc.org with "ADHD HS list" in the subject line.

AHA Networking & Discussion List: To subscribe, send a message with the subject line "subscribe aha-networking-list <your e-mail address>" to major-domo@home-ed-magazine.com

Au-2B-Home List: To join, e-mail tamglsr@sgi.net for information.

Home Ed: To subscribe, send e-mail to home-ed-request@world.std.com with the line "subscribe home-ed <your

e-mail address>." For either of the digest versions (abridged or unedited), e-mail dm@world.std.com and ask for the version you prefer.

Home Ed Politics: To subscribe, e-mail a message with the subject line "subscribe home-ed-politics" to home-ed-politics-request@mainstream.net.

Homeschool Train Up a Child: To subscribe, send a message with the subject line "subscribe HSTUAC" to HSTUAC-request@vms1.cc.uop.edu.

LDS Home Learners: To subscribe, send "subscribe ldslearn" to majordomo@tou.com.

Many Paths Homeschoolers: To subscribe, send "subscribe manypaths" to major-domo@majordomo.net.

Muslim Education Home School E-mail List: To subscribe, send "subscribe madrasah-net <your e-mail address>" to majordomo@muslimsonline.com.

Radical Unschoolers: To subscribe, send "subscribe ru" to majordomo@serv1.ncte.org.

Unschoolers Circle: To subscribe, send "subscribe unschoolers_ circle" to majordomo@mailinglist.net.

Unschooling: To subscribe, send "subscribe unschooling-list" or "subscribe un-schooling-list-digest" to majordomo@ctel.net.

Electronic Newsletters

AHA Online Newsletter: To receive, send e-mail to AHA@home-ed-magazine.com with "a1010" in the subject line for complete information.

Chart and Compass: To receive, e-mail editor@homeschoolersunlimited.org.

Edusource Web Reviews: To receive, e-mail editor@edusource.com.

Newsgroups

misc.education.home-school.christian

misc.education.home-school.misc

APPENDIX B:
HOMESCHOOLING ORGANIZATIONS

Compiling a completely accurate and comprehensive list of home-schooling organizations is nearly impossible. Because of their grass-roots, shoestring nature, many homeschool organizations change officers and mailing addresses with astonishing frequency. Others change names, split into smaller groups, or dissolve entirely, and new groups pop up all the time.

All kinds of groups are included in this list. (Inclusion implies no endorsement of any kind.) If you are interested in a particular type of homeschooling organization (i.e., specifically Christian or specifi-cally secular), be sure to ask when you contact them; often the name of a group is no guide to its nature. Some groups will require mem-bers or officers to sign a statement of religious faith; if this matters to you, it's best to find out up front.

If you're looking for a local support group, and none are listed for your area, try contacting a state-level group. Most maintain current information on local groups and will be happy to refer you to one near you.

National Homeschooling Organizations

Alliance for Parental Involvement in
Education
P.O. Box 59
East Chatham, NY 12060-0059
Seth Rockmuller or Katharine Houk:
(518) 392-6900
allpie@taconic.net
http://www.croton.com/allpie

Alternative Education Resource
Organization
417 Roslyn Road
Roslyn Heights, NY 11577
Jerry Mintz: (516) 621-2195
JMintz@igc.acp.com

American Homeschool Association
P.O. Box 3142
Palmer, AK 99645
AHA@home-ed-magazine.com
http://www.home-ed-
    magazine.com/AHA/aha.html

Canadian Alliance of Homeschoolers
272 Hwy #5, RR 1
St. George, Ontario N0E 1N0
Wendy Priesnitz: (519) 448-4001

The Canadian Homeschool Resource Page
http://www.flora.org/homeschool-ca

Family Unschoolers Network
1688 Belhaven Woods Court
Pasadena, MD 21122-3727
FUN@IQCweb.com
http://www.IQCweb.com/fun

Holt Associates/*Growing Without Schooling*
2380 Massachusetts Avenue, Suite 104
Cambridge, MA 02140
(617) 864-3100
HoltGWS@erols.com
http://www.holtgws.com

Moore Foundation
P.O. Box 1
Camas, WA 98607
(360) 835-2736
moorefnd@pacifier.com
http://www.caslink.com/moorefoundation

National Homeschool Association
P.O. Box 290
Hartland, MI 48353
(513) 772-9580
http://www.n-h-a.org

Religious and Other Special Interest Organizations

Adventist Home Educator
P.O. Box 836
Camino, CA 95709-0836
(916) 647-2110
http://www.adventtech.com/ahe

Home School Legal Defense Association
P.O. Box 3000
Purcellville, VA 20134
(540) 338-5600
http://www.hslda.org

Jewish Home Educator's Network
c/o Koenig
409 North Broad
Carlinville, IL 62626
beithoro@erols.com
http://snj.com/jhen

National Association for Mormon Home
    Educators
2770 South 1000 West
Perry, UT 84302

National Association of Catholic Home
    Educators
P.O. Box 787
Montrose, AL 36559
http://www.nache.com

National Center for Fair and Open Testing
    (FairTest)
342 Broadway
Cambridge, MA 02139
(617) 864-4810

National Center for Home Education
(see Home School Legal Defense
Association)

National Handicapped Homeschoolers
Association,
5383 Alpine Road. SE
Oglalla, WA 98359
Tom and Sherry Bushnell: (206) 857-4257

National Home Education Research Institute
P.O. Box 13939
Salem, OR 97309
(503) 364-1490
http://www.nheri.org

Native American Homeschool Association
P.O. Box 979
Fries, VA 24330
(540) 744-3640
http://www.expage.com/page/nahomeschool

Rutherford Institute
P.O. Box 7482
Charlottesville, VA 22906
(804) 978-3888

State and Regional Support Groups

Alabama

Alabama Home Educators Network
(AHEN)
3015 Thurman Road
Huntsville, AL 35805
Lisa Bugg: (205) 534-6401
KaeKaeB@aol.com
http://members.aol.com/haekaeb/ahen.html

Christian Home Education Fellowship of
Alabama (CHEF)
816 Colonial Drive
Alabaster, AL 35007
(205) 664-2232

Home Educators of Alabama Round Table
(HEART)
http://www.heartofalabama.org

Alaska

Alaska Homeschoolers Association
P.O. Box 230973
Anchorage, AK 99504-3527

Alaska Private Home Educators Association
P.O. Box 141764
Anchorage, AK 99514

Homeschoolers Unlimited
7390 J Street #B
Elmendorf AFB, AK 99506
Sue@homeschoolersunlimited.com
http://www.homeschoolersunlimited.com

Sitka Home Education Association
506 Verstovia Street
Sitka, AK 99835
Molly Jacobson: (907) 747-1483

Arizona

Arizona Families for Home Education
P.O. Box 4661
Scottsdale, AZ 85261-4661
(800) 929-3927

Phoenix Learning Alternatives Network
Nancy Sherr: (602) 483-3381

TELAO Home Educators
4700 North Tonalea Trail
Tucson, AZ 85749
(520) 749-4757

Arkansas

Arkansas Christian Home Education Association (ACHEA)
P.O. Box 4025
North Little Rock, AR 72190
(501) 758-9099

Home Educators of Arkansas (HEAR)
Coalition of Arkansas Parents (CAP)
P.O. Box 192455
Little Rock, AR 72219
http://bucket.ualr.edu/~sort/cap.html

Home Educators of Arkansas Voicing Excellence Now (HEAVEN)
8 Glenbrook Place
Sherwood, AR 72120

California

California Homeschool Network (CHN)
P.O. Box 55485
Hayward, CA 94545
(800) 327-5339
CHNMail@aol.com
http://www.comenius.org/chnpage.htm

Central California Homeschoolers
7600 Marchant
Atascadero, CA 93422
Barbara Alward: (805) 462-0726

Christian Home Educators Association of California
P.O. Box 2009
Norwalk, CA 90651-2009
(800) 564-2432

Homefires: Journal of Homeschooling
180 El Camino Real, Suite 10
Millbrae, CA 94030
(888) 4-HOME-ED
editor@homefires.com
http://www.Homefires.com

HomeSchool Association of California
P.O. Box 2442
Atascadero, CA 93423
(888) 472-4440
info@hsc.org
http://www.hsc.org

Colorado

Boulder County Home Educators
1495 Riverside
Boulder, CO 80304
Valerie Berg: (303) 449-5916

Christian Home Educators of Colorado
3739 East 4th Avenue
Denver, CO 80206
(303) 388-1888
http://www.learnathome.com/chec/index.htm

Colorado Home Educators' Association
3043 South Laredo Circle
Aurora, CO 80013
(303) 441-9938
pinewood@dash.com

Rocky Mountain Education Connection (RMEC)
20774 East Buchanan Drive
Aurora, CO 80011
(303) 341-2242
connect@pcisys.net
http://www.pcisys.net/~dstanley

Connecticut

Connecticut Home Educators Association
80 Coppermine Road
Oxford, CT 06478
Mary Beth Nelson: (203) 732-0102

CT's CURE (CT's Citizens to Uphold the
    Right to Educate)
P.O. Box 597
Sherman, CT 06784
Alison Brion: (203) 355-4724

The Education Association of Christian
    Homeschoolers (TEACH)
25 Field Stone Run
Farmington, CT 06032
(800) 205-8744
http://www.tiac.net/users/bobpers/teach

Unschoolers Support
22 Wildrose Avenue
Guilford, CT 06437
Luz Shosie: (203) 458-7402

Delaware

Delaware Home Education Association
P.O. Box 1003
Dover, DE 19903
(302) 429-0515

Tri-State Home School Network
P.O. Box 7193
Newark, DE 19714-7193
(302) 322-2018

Florida

The Family Learning Exchange
2020 Turpentine Road
Mims, FL 32754
(407) 268-8833

Florida Parent Educators Association
P.O. Box 371
Melbourne, FL 32902-1193
(407) 722-0895
office@fpea.com
http://www.fpea.com

Home Education Resources and Information
711 St. Johns Bluff Road
Jacksonville, FL 32225
(904) 565-9121
herijax@juno.com

Home Educators Assistance League
3343 Shoal Creek Cove
Crestview, FL 32539
Carri Bundy: (904) 682-2422

Home Educators Lending Parents Support
5941 NW 14 Court
Sunrise, FL 33313
Susie Capraro: (954) 791-9733
Scapraro-helps@juno.com

The Homeschool Network
P.O. Box 940402
Maitland, FL 32794
Lyn Milum: (407) 889-4632
gorest5@gdi.net

Georgia

Atlanta Alternative Education Network
1586 Rainier Falls Drive
Atlanta, GA 30329
(404) 636-6348
http://www.mindspring.com/~lei/aaen

Free to Learn at Home
4439 Lake Forest Drive
Oakwood, GA 30566
(770) 536-8077

Georgia Home Education Association
245 Buckeye Lane
Fayetteville, GA 30214
(770) 461-3657

Georgians for Freedom in Education
7180 Cane Leaf Drive
Fairburn, GA 30213
Billie Jean Bryant: (770) 463-1563

LIGHT
P.O. Box 2724
Columbus, GA 31902
(706) 324-3714

Hawaii

Christian Home Educators of Hawaii
91-824 Oama Street
Ewa Beach, HI 96706
(808) 689-6398
CHOHALOHA@aol.com
http://www.maui.net/~madelein/chem-
    news.html

Hawaii Homeschool Association
P.O. Box 3476
Mililani, HI 96789
(808) 944-3339
TGthrngPlc@aol.com

Idaho

Family Unschooling Network
1809 North 7th Street
Boise, ID 83702
(208) 345-2703
NeysaJensen@compuserve.com

Idaho Home Educators
P.O. Box 1324
Meridian, ID 83680
(208) 323-0230

Palouse Home Learning Alternatives
802 White Avenue
Moscow, ID 83843
Peg Harvey: (208) 882-1593

Illinois

Home Oriented Unique Schooling Experi-
    ence (HOUSE)
2508 East 22nd Place
Sauk Village, IL 60411
Teresa Sneade: (708) 758-7374
http://www.geocities.com/athens/acropo-
    lis/7804

Illinois Christian Home Educators
P.O. Box 261
Zion, IL 60099
(847) 328-7129
http://user.aol.com/ilchec

Unschoolers Network
736 North Metchell Avenue
Arlington Heights, IL 60004
PJADK@aol.com

Indiana

Families Learning Together
1714 East 51st Street
Indianapolis, IN 46205
(317) 255-9298
whelan.mullen@juno.com

Homefront
1120 West Whiskey Run Road
New Salisbury, IN 47161-8823
Donnell and Teresa Royer: (812) 347-2931

Indiana Association of Home Educators
1000 North Madison
Greenwood, IN 46142
(317) 638-9633

L.E.A.R.N.
Barbara Benson
9577 East State Road 45
Unionville, IN 47468
(812) 336-8028

Wabash Valley Homeschool Association
P.O. Box 3865
Terre Haute, IN 47803
WVHA@aol.com

Iowa

Network of Iowa Christian Home Educators
P.O. Box 158
Dexter, IA 50070
(800) 723-0438

Rebecca Leach
2301 South Henry Street
Sioux City, IA 51106
(712) 274-0472
Beckyleach@aol.com

Kansas

Circle of Homeschoolers and Unschoolers
in Central Kansas Learning Eclecti-
cally (CHUCKLE)
Rural Route 1, Box 28A
Rush Center, KS 67575
Susan Peach: (913) 372-4457

Christian Home Educators Confederation
of Kansas
P.O. Box 3968
Wichita, KS 66203
(913) 234-2927

Heartland Area Homeschoolers' Association
823 West Street
Emporia, KS 66801
Shiuvaun Sowder: (316) 343-3696

Lawrence Area Unaffiliated Group of
Homeschoolers (LAUGH)
Rural Route 1, Box 496
Perry, KS 66073
Barbara Michener: (913) 597-5579

Kentucky

Bluegrass Home Educators
600 Shake Rag Road
Waynesburg, KY 40489
KyHomeEd@mis.net
http://www.BluegrassHmEd.nvo.com

Christian Home Educators of Kentucky
691 Howardstown Road
Hodgensville, KY 42748
(502) 358-9270

Kentucky Home Education Association
P.O. Box 81
Winchester, KY 40392-0081

Kentucky Independent Learners Network
P.O. Box 275
Somerset, KY 42501
Meg McClory: (606) 678-2527

Louisiana

Christian Home Education Fellowship of
     Louisiana
P.O. Box 74292
Baton Rouge, LA 70874-4292
(504) 775-9709

Homeschoolers Learning from Mother Earth
14189 Ridge Road
Prairieville, LA 70769
Roxann Phillips: (504) 673-8367

Louisiana Home Education Network
     (LAHEN)
http://members.aol.com/LaHomeED/Lah
     en.html

Wild Azalea Homeschoolers
6055 General Meyer Avenue
New Orleans, LA 70131
Tracey Sherry: (504) 392-5647
tws01@gnofn.org

Maine

Homeschool Support Network
P.O. Box 708
Gray, ME 04039
Jane Boswell: (207) 657-2800
hsn@outrig.com
http://www.chfweb.com/hsn

Homeschoolers of Maine
HC 62, Box 24
Hope, ME 04847
(207) 763-4251

Maine Home Education Association
P.O. Box 421
Popsham, ME 04086
(800) 520-0577

Southern Maine Home Education Support
     Network
76 Beech Ridge Road
Scarborough, ME 04074
Eileen Yoder: (207) 883-9621

Maryland

Christian Home Educators Network
P.O. Box 2010
Ellicott City, MD 21043
(410) 744-8919

Maryland Association of Christian Home
     Educators
P.O. Box 247
Point of Rock, MD 21777-0247
(301) 607-4284

Maryland Home Education Association
9085 Flamepool Way
Columbia, MD 21045
Manfred W. Smith: (410) 730-0073

North County Home Educators
1688 Belhaven Woods Court
Pasadena, MD 21122-3727
Billy or Nancy Greer: (410) 437-5109
NCHE@IQCweb.com
http://wwwIQCweb.com/fun/nche.htm

Massachusetts

Massachusetts Home Learning Association
P.O. Box 1558
Marstons Mills, MA 02648
Loretta Heuer: (508) 376-1923
Kathy Smith: (508) 249-9056
http://horthshore.shore.net/~pyghill/mhla.
htm

Massachusetts Homeschool Organization
of Parent Educators (Mass HOPE)
5 Atwood Road
Cherry Valley, MA 01611-3332
(508) 755-4754

Michigan

Christian Home Educators of Michigan
P.O. Box 2357
Farmington Hills, MI 48333
(810) 683-3395

Families Learning and Schooling at Home
(FLASH)
21671 B Drive North
Marshall, MI 49068
Natalie Valle: (616) 781-1069

Heritage Home Educators
2122 Houser
Holly, MI 48442

Hillsdale Area Homeschoolers
5151 Barker Road
Jonesville, MI 49250
Linda Kline: (517) 287-5565

Home Educators Circle
1280 John Hix Street
Westland, MI 48186
(313) 326-5406

Information Network for Christian Homes
(INCH)
4934 Cannonsburg Road
Belmont, MI 49306
(616) 874-5656

Minnesota

Minnesota Association of Christian Home
Educators
P.O. Box 32308
Fridley, MN 55432-0308
(612) 717-9070

Minnesota Homeschoolers Alliance
P.O. Box 23072
Richfield, MN 55423
(612) 491-2828

Mississippi

Coast Military Home Educators
9212A Givens Circle
Biloxi, MS 39531
Lori & John Hudson: (601) 388-4522

Home Educators of Central Mississippi
535 Luling Street
Pearl, MS 39208

Mississippi Home Educators Association
109 Reagan Ranch Road
Laurel, MS 39440
(601) 649-6432

Missouri

Missouri Association of Teaching Christian
    Homes
307 East Ash Street, #146
Columbia, MO 65201
(573) 443-8217

Ozark Lore Society
HC 73, Box 160
Drury, MO 65638
Debra Eisenmann: (417) 679-3391
deb@wiseheart.com

St. Louis Homeschooling Network
4147 East Pine
St. Louis, MO 63108
Karen Karabel: (314)534-1171

Montana

Independent Homeschoolers Network of
    Bozeman
415 South Ninth Avenue
Bozeman, MT 59715
Katie Perry: (406) 586-4564

Mid-Mountain Home Education Network
P.O. Box 2182
Montana City Station
Clancy, MT 59634
Karen Semple: (406) 443-3376

Montana Coalition of Home Educators
P.O. Box 43
Gallatin Gateway, MT 59730
(406) 587-6163

Nebraska

LEARN
7741 East Avon Lane
Lincoln, NE 68505-2043
Rose Yonekura: (402) 488-7741

Nebraska Christian Home Educators As-
    sociation
P.O. Box 57041
Lincoln, NE 68505-7041
(402) 423-4297

Nevada

Home Schools United—Vegas Valley
P.O. Box 93564
Las Vegas, NV 89193
(702) 870-9566
HSU.VEGASVALLEY@juno.com

Northern Nevada Home Schools, Inc.
    (NNHS)
P.O. Box 21323
Reno, NV 89515
(702) 852-6647
NNHS@aol.com

New Hampshire

Christian Home Educators of New
    Hampshire
P.O. Box 961
Manchester, NH 03105-0916
(603) 569-2343

Homeschooling Friends
204 Brackett Road
New Durham, NH 03855
Beverly Behr: (603) 332-4146
nothome@worldpath.net
http://web-enrichment.com/hsf/

New Hampshire Alliance for Home Education
17 Preseve Drive
Nashua, NH 03060
Betsey Westgate: (603) 880-8629

New Hampshire Homeschooling Coalition
P.O. Box 2224
Concord, NH 03304-2224
Abbey Lawrence: (603) 539-7233

New Jersey

Education Network of Christian Home Schoolers of New Jersey
65 Middlesex Road
Matawan, NJ 07747
(908) 583-7128

Homeschoolers of South New Jersey
1239 Whitaker Avenue
Millville, NJ 08332
(865) 327-1224
Tutor@eticomm.net
http://www.eticomm.net/~tutor

Unschooler's Network
2 Smith Street
Farmingdale, NJ 07727
Nancy Plent: (732) 938-2473

Unschooling Families Support Group of Central New Jersey
150 Folwell Station Road
Jobstown, NJ 08041
Karen Mende-Fridkis: (609) 723-1524

New Mexico

Christian Association of Parent Educators
P.O. Box 25046
Albuquerque, NM 87125
(505) 898-8548

New Mexico Family Educators
P.O. Box 92276
Albuquerque, NM 87199-2276
(505) 275-7053

Unschoolers of Albuquerque
8505 Bellrose NE
Albuquerque, NM 87111
Barbara Dawson: (505) 275-0422
Sandra Dodd: (505) 299-2476
SandraDodd@aol.com

New York

Families for Home Education
3219 Coulter Road
Cazenovia, NY 13035
Peg Moore: (315) 655-2574

Fingerlakes Unschoolers Network
201 Elm Street
Ithaca, NY 14850
Clare Grady: (607) 273-6257
Laundress@aol.com

Loving Education at Home (LEAH)
P.O. Box 88
Cato, NY 13033
(716) 346-0939
http://www.leah.org

New York City Home Educators Alliance
8 East 2nd Street
New York, NY 10156
(212) 505-9884
Rtricamo@aol.com

New York State Home Education News
P.O. Box 59
East Chatham, NY 12060
Seth Rockmuller or Katharine Houk:
    (518) 392-6900

Oneida Lake Area Home Educators
P.O. Box 24
Sylvan Beach, NY 13157
Chris Wheeler: (315) 762-5166

Oneonta Area Sharing in Homeschooling
    (OASIS)
P.O. Box 48
Gilbertsville, NY 13776
Darlene Abajian: (607) 783-2271

Tri-County Homeschoolers
P.O. Box 190
Ossining, NY 10562
Chris and Andy Hofer: (914) 941-5607
chofer@croton.com
http://www.croton.com/home-ed

Tri-Lakes Community Home Educators
P.O. Box 270
Raybrook, NY 12977
Lynn Waickman: (518) 891-5657
Royce Cano: (518) 796-4840

North Carolina

Families Learning Together
1670 NC Highway 33W
Chocowinity, NC 27817

North Carolinians for Home Education
419 North Boylan Avenue
Raleigh, NC 27603-1211
Susan Van Dyke: (919) 834-6243

North Dakota

North Dakota Home School Association
4007 North State Street
Bismarck, ND 58501
(701) 223-4080

Ohio

Association of Ohio Homeschoolers
3636 Paris Boulevard
Westerville, OH 43081

Christian Home Educators of Ohio
P.O. Box 262
Columbus, OH 43216-0262
(614) 474-3177
http://www.home-school.com/groups/
    OHIOCHEO.html

Homeschool Network of Greater Cincinnati
3470 Greenfield Court
Maineville, OH 45039
Susan Duncan: (513) 683-1279

Ohio Home Educators Network
P.O. Box 23054
Chagrin Falls, OH 44023-0054
(330) 278-2540

Parents and Children Together (PACT)
8944 Weiss Road
Union City, OH 45390
(927) 692-5680

Oklahoma

Christian Home Educators Fellowship of
    Oklahoma
P.O. Box 471363
Tulsa, OK 74147
(918) 583-7323

Home Educators Resource Organization
    (HERO) of Oklahoma
302 North Coolidge
Enid, OK 73703
Leslie Moyer: (580) 438-2253
mjmiller@pldi.ne
http://www.geocities.com/Athens/Forum/3
    236

Oregon

Oregon Christian Home Education Asso-
    ciation Network
2815 NE 37th
Portland, OR 97212
(508) 288-1285

Oregon Home Education Network
    (OHEN)
4470 SW Hall Boulevard, #286
Beaverton, OR 97005
Jeanne Biggerstaff: (503) 321-5166
sassenak@teleport.com
http://www.teleport.com/~ohen/

Greater Portland Homeschoolers
P.O. Box 82415
Portland, OR 97282
Kathy Schertz: (503) 241-5350
Schertzkat@aol.com

Pennsylvania

Christian Homeschool Association of
    Pennsylvania (CHAP)
P.O. Box 3603
York, PA 17402-0603
(717) 661-2428

Pennsylvania Home Education Network
    (PHEN)
285 Allegheny Street
Meadville, PA 16335
Kathy Terleski: (412) 561-5288

Pennsylvania Home Education News
P.O. Box 305
Summerhill, PA 15958
Karen Leventry: (814) 495-5651
Karenleven@aol.com

Rhode Island

Rhode Island Guild of Home Teachers
    (RIGHT)
P.O. Box 11
Hope, RI 02831
(401) 821-7700
right_right@mailexcite.com
http://www.angelfire.com/ri/RIGHT

South County Homeschoolers
500 Carolina Back Road
Charleston, RI 02813

South Carolina

Home Organization of Parent Educators
1697 Dotterer's Run
Charleston, SC 29414
(803) 763-7833
epeeler@awod.com

South Carolina Association of Independent
    Home Schools (SCAIHS)
P.O. Box 2104
Irmo, SC 29063
(803) 551-1003

South Carolina Homeschool Alliance
1679 Memorial Park Road, Suite 179
Lancaster, SC 29720
ConnectSC@aol.com
http://members.aol.com/connectsc

South Dakota

South Dakota Home School Association
P.O. Box 882
Sioux Falls, SD 57101-0882
Kim Liedtke: (605) 338-9689

Western Dakota Christian Home Schools
P.O. Box 528
Black Hawk, SD 57718
(605) 923-1893

Tennessee

State of Franklin Homeschoolers
494 Mill Creek Road
Kingsport, TN 37664
(423) 349-6125
kramerbg@mounet.com

Tennessee Home Education Association
3677 Richbriar Court
Nashville, TN 37211
(615) 834-3529

Tennessee Homeschooling Families
214 Park Lane
Oliver Springs, TN 37840
Lin Kemper Wallace: (423) 435-9644

Unschoolers of Memphis
Margaret Meyer: (901) 757-9859

Texas

Home-Oriented Private Education
P.O. Box 59876
Dallas, TX 75229
(972) 358-2221

North Texas Self-Educators
150 Forest Lane
Double Oak/Lewisville, TX 75067
Sarah Jordan: (817) 430-4835

South Texas Self-Learners
1005 Delta Drive
Corpus Christi, TX 78412
Becky Davis: (512) 992-7549

Texas Home School Coalition
P.O. Box 6982
Lubbock, TX 79493
(806) 797-4927

Texas Advocates for Freedom in Education
    (TAFFIE)
13635 Greenridge Street
Sugar Land, TX 77478
Beth Jackson: (713) 242-7994

Utah

Latter-Day Saint Home Educators' Associ-
    ation
2770 South 1000 West
Perry, UT 84302
Joyce Kinmont: (801) 723-5355

Utah Christian Home Schoolers
P.O. Box 3942
Salt Lake City, UT 84110
(801) 255-4053

Utah Home Education Association
P.O. Box 167
Roy, UT 84067
(888) 887-UHEA
http://sss.itsnet.com/~uhea

Vermont

Center for Homeschooling
95 North Avenue
Burlington, VT 05401
Deb Shell: (802) 862-9616

Christian Home Education of Vermont
214 North Prospect, #105
Burlington, VT 05401
(802) 658-4561

Vermont Homeschoolers' Association
Rural Route 2, Box 4440
Bristol, VT 05443
(802) 453-5460

Virginia

Community of Independent Learners
P.O. Box 16029
Alexandria, VA 22302

Home Educators Association of Virginia
1900 Byrd Avenue, Suite 201
P.O. Box 6745
Richmond, VA 23230-0745
(804) 288-1608

Virginia Home Education Association
1612 Columbia Road
Gordonsville, VA 22942
(540) 832-3578
vhea@virginia.edu
http://poe.acc.virginia.edu/~pm6f/vhea.html

Washington

Family Learning Organization
P.O. Box 7247
Spokane, WA 99207-0247
Kathleen McCurdy: (509) 467-2552

Homeschoolers' Support Association
P.O. Box 413
Maple Valley, WA 98038
Teresa Sparling: (206) 746-5047

Teaching Parents Association
P.O. Box 1934
Woodinville, WA 98072-1934;
Meriann Roberts: (206) 788-5272
Janice Kugler: (206) 821-2753

Washington Association of Teaching
    Christian Homes
2904 North Dora Road
Spokane, WA 99212
(509) 922-4811

Washington Homeschool Organization
18130 Midvale Avenue North, Suite C
Seattle, WA 98133
(206) 298-8942

West Virginia

Christian Home Educators of West Virginia
P.O. Box 8770
South Charleston, WV 25303-8770
(304) 776-4664

West Virginia Home Educators Association
P.O. Box 3707
Charleston, WV 25337
(800) 736-WVHE
wvhea@bigfoot.com
http://members.tripod.com/~WVHEA

Wisconsin

H.O.M.E.
5745 Bittersweet Place
Madison, WI 53705
Alison McKee: (608) 238-3302

Wisconsin Christian Home Educators Association
2307 Carmel Avenue
Racine, WI 53405
(414) 637-5127

Wisconsin Parents Association
P.O. Box 2502
Madison, WI 53701-2502

Wyoming

Homeschoolers of Wyoming
339 Bicentennial Court
Powell, WY 82435
(307) 754-3271

Unschoolers of Wyoming
Laramie Home Education Network
429 Hwy 230, #20
Laramie, WY 82010

APPENDIX C:
SELECTED LEARNING RESOURCES

This list is a highly arbitrary collection of resources for homeschoolers. Although it barely scratches the surface of what is available, it does include representatives of many different approaches, from the most highly structured to the most free-form. For more complete lists of materials, consult one or more of the resource guides listed in Appendix A.

Correspondence Schools and Curriculum Suppliers

A Beka Correspondence School/Home Video School/Book Publications, Box 18000, Pensacola, FL 32523-9160; (800) 874-BEKA.
Traditional Christian correspondence curriculum through high school.

American School, 850 East 58th Street, Chicago, IL 60637.
Traditional high school correspondence program.

Bob Jones University Press, Greenville, SC 29614.
BJU sells curriculum materials for Christian schools and homeschoolers.

Bridgestone Academy, 300 North McKerny Avenue, Chandler, AZ 65226-2616;

(800) 662-7396; http://www.switched-onschoolhouse.com.
Bridgestone is the correspondence affiliate of Alpha Omega Publications, which produces Christian-based curricular materials.

Calvert School, 105 Tuscany Road, Baltimore, MD 21210; (410) 243-6030; http://www.calvertschool.org.
Traditional K–8 correspondence program.

Clonlara School Home Based Educational Program, 1289 Jewett Street, Ann Arbor, MI 48104; (313)769-4515; Clonlara@delphi.com; http:/www.clonlara.org.
Supports individualized learning with complete private school services; also offers high school program over the Internet.

CyberSchool, 200 North Monroe, Eugene, OR 97402; (541) 687-6939; http://CyberSchool.4j.lane.edu.

CyberSchool, operated by Eugene Public Schools, offers high school credit courses worldwide over the Internet.

HCL Boston School, P.O. Box 2920, Big Bear City, CA 92314; (909) 585-7188.
Private homeschool services from interest-initiated approach.

Konos Curriculum, P.O. Box 1524, Richardson, TX 75083; (214) 669-8337.
Unit study curriculum based on character traits.

Oak Meadow School, P.O. Box 740, Putney, VT 05346; (802) 387-2021; oms@oakmeadow.com; http://www.oakmeadow.com.
Waldorf-based homeschooling program.

Rod and Staff Publishers, Highway 172, Crockett, KY 41413.
Rod and Staff supplies biblically based materials across the curriculum.

Seton Home Study School, 1350 Progress Drive, Front Royal, VA 22630.
Catholic home study program.

Sonlight Curriculum, Ltd., 8185 South Grant Way, Littleton, CO 80127.
Complete unit study–style curriculum from a Christian perspective.

Sycamore Tree, 2179 Meyer Place, Costa Mesa, CA 92627.
Catalog of books and resources; also curriculum guidelines and homeschool record-keeping services; high school diploma available.

University of Nebraska Independent Study High School Program, Continuing Ed-

ucation Center, Room 269, Lincoln, NE 68583

West River Academy, 2420 North First Street, Grand Junction, CO 81501; (970) 241-4137; wru2420@aol.com

General Homeschooling Materials

Animal Town, P.O. Box 485, Healdsburg, CA 95448; (800) 445-8642.
Cooperative board games.

Aristoplay, Ltd., P.O. Box 7529, Ann Arbor, MI 48107; (800) 634-7738.
All kinds of educational and cooperative games.

Charlotte Mason Research and Supply Company, P.O. Box 936, Elkton, MD 21922-0936.
Books and materials based on Mason's educational philosophy.

Cobblestone Publishing, 7 School Street, Peterborough, NH 03458.
Publishes children's magazines: Cobblestone *(American history),* Calliope *(world history),* Faces *(anthopology), and* Odyssey *(science and technology). Also sells topical packs of back issues.*

Dover Publications, 31 East 2nd Street, Mineola, NY 11501.
Huge selection of paperback books, on all topics. Children's and other specialized catalogs available in addition to their main catalog.

The Drinking Gourd Book Company, P.O. Box 2557, Redmond, WA 98073; (800) TDG-5487.

Amazing catalog full of tempting books, including Joy Hakim's American history series, A History of US. *Especially strong in multicultural resources, science, and math.*

Elijah Company, Route 2, Box 100B, Crossville, TN 38555; (615) 456-6384.

Wide variety of curricular materials from a Christian perspective. Catalog thoroughly explains different approaches to homeschooling.

FUN Books, 1688 Belhaven Woods Court, Pasadena, MD 21122-3727; (888) FUN-7020; FUN@IQCweb.com; www.IQCweb.com/fun/funbooks.htm.

Bill and Nancy Greer's catalog is full of interesting materials and especially appealing to unschoolers.

Genius Tribe, P.O. Box 1014, Eugene, OR 97440-1014.

Intriguing catalog "for unschoolers and other free people" from the author of the Teenage Liberation Handbook. *Aimed at older children, teenagers, and adult learners.*

John Holt's Bookstore, P.O. Box 8006, Walled Lake, MI 48391-8006; (617)864-3100; fax: (617) 864-9235.

From the folks who publish Growing Without Schooling, *books by John Holt and other educators, books and other materials on specific areas of learning.*

Lifetime Books and Gifts, 3900 Chalet Suzanne Drive, Lake Wales, FL 33853-7763; (813) 676-6311.

Materials from a Charlotte Mason approach; also special needs materials.

Michael Olaf's Essential Montessori, P.O. Box 1162, Arcata, CA 95518.

Extensive collection of Montessori-based materials for children from birth to adolescence, plus Montessori literature for parents and teachers.

Moore Foundation, Box 1, Camas, WA 98607.

Homeschooling books by Raymond and Dorothy Moore and curricular materials they recommend.

Zephyr Press, P.O. Box 13448, Tucson, AZ 85732.

Books, games, tapes, and other materials.

Science and Mathematics

Cuisenaire Company of America, P.O. Box 5026, White Plains, NY 10602-5026; (800) 237-3142.

Books, games, manipulatives for math and science.

Edmund Scientific Company, 101 East Gloucester Pike, Barrington, NJ 08007-1380.

This catalog of science goodies still has kids poring over it covetously.

Garlic Press, 100 Hillview 2, Eugene, OR 97408.

Garlic publishes the Straight Forward Math Series.

Key Curriculum Press, P.O. Box 2304, Berkeley, CA 94702; (800) 995-MATH.

Publishes Key to . . . series of math workbooks on fractions, decimals, geometry, measurement, and so on. Also Miquon Math manipulatives for younger children. Good, clear, and to-the-point materials used by many homeschoolers.

Macmillan/McGraw-Hill School Division, 4635 Hilton Corporate Drive, Columbus, OH 43232; (614) 759-6600.

Among the available texts is the Spotlight on Math series.

Saxon Math, Saxon Publishers, Inc., 1300 McGee, Suite 100, Norman, OK 73072.

Math textbooks popular with many homeschoolers.

Science-by-Mail, Museum of Science, Science Park, Boston, MA 02114; (800) 729-3300.

Science packets for exploring and experimenting on various topics, usually two or three per year, with opportunity to correspond with working scientists about the projects.

TOPS Learning Systems, 10970 South Mulino Road, Canby, OR 97013; tops@integrityonline.com; http://topscience.org.

Hands-on science using everyday household materials. Lots of open-ended activities rather than fill-in-the-blanks experiments.

Humanities and Arts

Audio Forum, 96 Broad Street, Guilford, CT 06437-2636; (800) 345-8501.

Extensive selection of foreign language audiotapes; also includes several native American languages.

Boomerang! The Children's Audio Magazine about Big Ideas, 13366 Pescadero Road, La Honda, CA 94020; (800) 333-7858.

Something like a monthly seventy minutes of National Public Radio for kids: news, features, stories, jokes, and more on each tape. Apparently irresistible to kids.

Chinaberry Book Service, 2780 Via Orange Way, Suite B, Spring Valley, CA 91978.

One of the best children's book catalogs. Titles are grouped roughly by age level, and their descriptions are guaranteed to hook any avid reader. An easy catalog to spend a lot of time with.

Cricket Magazine Group, Box 300, Peru, IL 61354-9969; (800) 827-0227.

*Great literary magazines (*Cricket, Spider, Ladybug, Babybug, *and others) for kids at various reading levels, with stories, games, and other activities.*

Greenleaf Press, 1570 Old Laguardo Road, Lebanon, TN 37087.

History resources, including biographies and historical fiction.

Hands on History, 201 Constance Drive, New Lenox, IL 60451.

Kits with books, toys, costume pieces, and so forth, focusing on specific historical periods.

Hearthsong, P.O. Box B, Sebastopol, CA 95473; (800) 325-2502.

Gorgeous crafts, games, and toys, selected from a Waldorf perspective.

Homespun Music Tapes, Box 694, Woodstock, NY 12498.

Incredible collection of instructional tapes (both audio and video) for guitar, banjo, fiddle, and other folk instruments.

International Learning Systems, P.O. Box 16032, Chesapeake, VA 23328; (800) 321-8322.

Markets Sing, Spell, Read and Write, *a phonics program.*

Italic Handwriting Series, Portland State University, Division of Continuing Education, Box 1394, Portland, OR 97207.

Special prices for homeschoolers.

Lark in the Morning, P.O. Box 1176, Mendocino, CA 95460; (707)964-5569; larkinam@larkinam.com; http://www.larkinam.com.

Incredible collection of musical instruments from all over the world, plus music books and recordings.

Music for Little People, P.O. Box 757, Greenland, NH 03840; (800) 409-2457.

Terrific assortment of music for kids: audio and video recordings, musical instruments, related items.

The Paradigm Co., P.O. Box 45161, Boise, ID 83711.

This company supplies Samuel L. Blumenfeld's Alpha-Phonics: A Primer for Beginning Readers, *a phonics program popular with some homeschoolers.*

Teachers and Writers Collaborative, 5 Union Square West, New York, NY 10003; (212) 691-6590.

Resources for learning to write.

Curriculum Guides/Scope and Sequence Materials

Comprehensive Curriculum of Basic Skills, American Education Publishing.

One volume per grade through eighth grade. These are available in most general bookstores.

E.D. Hirsch, *What Your First Grader Needs to Know,* and so on, Core Knowledge Series, Dell/Delta.

Currently available for kindergarten through eighth grade; curriculum guides with eurocentric approach to history and literature.

Unschoolers Network, 2 Smith Street, Farmingdale, NJ 07727.

Offers course of study guides with advice on individualizing your curriculum.

World Book Educational Products, 101 Northwest Point Boulevard, Elk Grove Village, IL 60007.

The publishers of the World Book Encyclopedia *also sell a "Typical Course of Study" booklet useful for curriculum planning.*

Educational Resources Information Center (ERIC): http://ericir.syr.edu

Internet Learning Resources

Bad Astronomy: http://smart.net/~badastro/bad.html

Bizarre Stuff You Can Make in Your Kitchen:
    http://freeweb.pdq.net/headstrong

Cornell Theory Center K–12 Gateways:
    http://www.tc.cornell.edu/Edu/MathSciGateway/about.html

Digital Librarian: http://www.servtech.com/~mvail/home.html

Exploratorium: http://www.exploratorium.edu

Great Writers and Poets:
    http://www.xs4all.nl/~pwessel/writers.html

Halls of Academia: http://www.tenet.edu/academia/main.html

Human Languages Page: http://www.jun.29.com/HLP

Library of Congress: http://www.loc.gov

My Virtual Reference Desk: http://www.refdesk.com

Natural Math: http://www.naturalmath.com

Quotations Page: http://www.stalingtech.com/quotes

Smithsonian Institution Home Page: http://www.si.edu

United States Civil War Center:
    http://www.cwc.lsu.edu/cwlink.htm

Virtual Renaissance: http://www.district125.k12.il.us/
    Renaissance/GeneralFiles/Introduction.html

VolcanoWorld Home Page: http://volcano.und.nodak.edu

World Wide Arts Resources: http://wwar.com

APPENDIX D: COLLEGES THAT HAVE ACCEPTED HOMESCHOOLERS

Since 1993, Karl Bunday has maintained his "Colleges That Have Accepted Homeschoolers" page (http://learninfreedom.org/colleges_4_hmsc.html) on his School Is Dead, Learn in Freedom Web site (http://learninfreedom.org). Anyone interested in college admissions for homeschoolers will find a visit to Bunday's Web site well worth the effort. In addition to the college list, Bunday includes information and links to a wide assortment of resources on college admissions and financial aid.

While the list was originally based on versions compiled by Dan Endsley of the Home Education League of Parents and HSLDA, Bunday has worked correcting, confirming, and updating it since 1993. The version printed here was current as of August 1998. (For the latest update, be sure to visit Bunday's Web site.)

All of these nearly 750 accredited institutions are reported to have offered admission to at least one homeschooled applicant (who may or may not have chosen to enroll there). Bunday has been able to confirm that those marked with an asterisk (*) have definitely made a firm offer of admission to a homeschooled applicant. Colleges known to recruit homeschoolers, those that describe admission procedures for homeschooled applicants in their application materials, or those whose admission officers indicate that they would admit homeschooled applicants are marked with a dagger (†). Undoubtedly, other colleges recruit and admit homeschoolers as well; do not assume that any institution missing from this list has not or will not admit homeschooled applicants. (And if you know of some of those schools, Karl Bunday would be pleased to hear from you at his Web site.)

Abilene Christian University, (Texas)

Adams State College, CO

Adrian College, MI

Agnes Scott College, GA*

Alabama Agricultural and Mechanical University, AL

Albertson College, ID*

Albion College, MI*

Allegheny College, PA*

Allentown College, of St. Francis de Sales, PA*

Alverno College, WI*

American Institute of Business, IA

American University, DC*

Amherst College, MA*

Anderson University, IN*

Andrew College, GA

Angelo State University, TX

Anne Arundel Community College, MD

Anoka-Hennepin Technical College, MN

Antioch College, OH*

Appalachian Bible College, WV*

Aquinas College, MI

Arizona State University, AZ*

Arkansas State University, AR

Asbury College, KY*

Ashland University, OH*

Assumption College, MA*

Atlanta College of Art, GA

Atlantic Union College, MA*

Auburn University, AL*

Augsburg College, MN†

Augustana College, IL*

Austin College, TX*

Australian National University, Australian Capital Territory, Australia

Averett College, VA

Azusa Pacific University, CA*

Ball State University, IN*

Baptist Bible College of Pennsylvania, PA

Barat College, IL*

Bartlesville Wesleyan College, OK*

Bates College, ME

Bay Path College, MA

Baylor University, TX

Beaver College, PA*

Becker College, Worcester Campus, MA

Belhaven College, MS*

Bellevue University, NE*

Belmont University, TN

Beloit College, WI*

Bemidji State University, MN*

Benedictine College, KS

Bennington College, VT*

Berea College, KY

Berklee College of Music, MA*

Berry College, GA*

Bethany College, WV*

Bethany Lutheran College, MN

Bethel College, IN

Bethel College, MN*

Biola University, CA*

Birmingham-Southern College, AL*

Blackburn College, IL

Bob Jones University, SC*

Boise State University, ID*

Boston College, MA*

Boston Conservatory, MA*

Boston University, MA*

Bowdoin College, ME*

Bowling Green State University, OH*

Bradley University, IL*

Brandeis University, MA*

Bridgewater State College, MA*

Brigham Young University, UT*

Brown University, RI*

Bryan College, TN*

Bryant College, RI*

Bryn Mawr College, PA*

Buena Vista University, IA*

Butler University, IN*

California Institute of Technology, CA*

California Polytechnic State University, CA*

California State University, Dominguez Hills, CA*

California State University, Fullerton, CA*

California State University, Los Angeles, CA*

California State University, Monterey Bay, CA*

California State University, Sacramento, CA

California State University, Stanislaus, CA*

Calvin College, MI*

Cambridge University, U.K.*

Canadian Bible College, Saskatchewan, Canada†

Capital University, OH*

Cardinal Stritch College, WI*

Carleton College, MN*

Carlow College, PA*

Carnegie Mellon University, PA*

Carroll College, MT*

Carroll College, WI*

Carson-Newman College, TN†

Carthage College, WI*

Case Western Reserve University, OH*

Casper College, WY

Catholic University of America, D.C.*

Cedarville College, OH*

Central College, IA*

Central Methodist College, MO*

Central Michigan University, MI

Central Missouri State University, MO*

Central Washington University, WA†

Centre College, KY

Champlain College, VT*

Chapman University, CA

Chatham College, PA*

Chowan College, NC

Christendom College, VA

Christian Brothers University, TN*

Christian Heritage College, CA

Cincinnati Bible College and Seminary, OH*

Circleville Bible College, OH

The Citadel, SC

Claremont McKenna College, CA*

Clark University, MA

Clearwater Christian College, FL

Coastal Carolina University, SC*

Coe College, IA*

Colby College, ME*

College of Charleston, SC

College of Notre Dame of Maryland, MD

College of St. Benedict, MN*

College of St. Catherine, MN*

College of St. Mary, NE

College of St. Scholastica, MN*

College of St. Thomas More, TX*

College of the Atlantic, ME*

College of William and Mary, VA*

College of Wooster, OH*

Colorado Christian University, CO*

Colorado College, CO*

Colorado Mountain College, CO

Colorado School of Mines, CO*

Colorado State University, CO*

Columbia International University, SC

Columbia University, NY

Columbia Union College, MD*

Concord College, WV

Concordia College, MN*

Concordia University, IL†

Concordia University, MN*

Concordia University, WI*

Cornell College, IA*

Cornell University, NY*

Cornerstone College and Grand Rapids Baptist Seminary, MI

Covenant College, GA*

Creighton University, NE*

Crichton College, TN

Criswell College, TX*

Crown College, MN*

Cumberland College, KY†

Dakota County Technical College, MN

Dalhousie University, Nova Scotia, Canada

Dallas Christian College, TX

Dartmouth College, NH*

Davidson College, NC*

Davis and Elkins College, WV†

Dekalb College, GA

Delaware Valley College, PA

Delta State University, MS

Denison University, OH*

DePaul University, IL*

DePauw University, IN*

Dickinson College, PA*

Dickinson State University, ND

Dordt College, IA*

Drake University IA*

Drew University, NJ*

Drexel University, PA*

Duke University, NC*

Dundalk Community College, MD

Dunwoody Institute, MN

Duquesne University, PA*

East Carolina University, NC

East Central College, MO

East Texas Baptist University, TX

Eastern Connecticut State University, CT*

Eastern Mennonite University, VA

Eastern New Mexico University, NM*

Eastern Oregon University, OR†

Eckerd College, FL*

Edgewood College, WI*

Edinboro University of Pennsylvania, PA*

Elizabethtown College, PA*

Elon College, NC

Embry-Riddle Aeronautical University, FL*

Emmanuel College, GA*

Emmaus Bible College, IA

Emory University, GA*

Emory and Henry College, VA

Eugene Bible College, OR†

Evangel College, MO

Evergreen State College, WA*

Fairleigh Dickinson University, NJ*

Faith Baptist Bible College and Theological Seminary, IA

Faulkner University, AL*

Ferrum College, VA

Fitchburg State College, MA

Flagler College, FL*

Florida Institute of Technology, FL*

Framingham State College, MA*

Franciscan University of Steubenville, OH*

Franklin and Marshall College, PA*

Franklin College, Switzerland*

Freed-Hardeman University, TN*

Fresno Pacific University, CA*

Frostburg State University, MD

Gannon University, PA*

Gardner-Webb University, NC*

Geneva College, PA*

George Fox University, OR*

George Mason University, VA*

George Washington University, D.C.*

Georgetown College, KY

Georgia Institute of Technology, GA

Georgia State University, GA

Gettysburg College, PA*

GMI Engineering & Management Institute, MI*

Goddard College, VT*

Gonzaga University, WA

Gordon College, MA*

Goshen College, IN

Goucher College, MD*

Grace College, IN*

Grace University, NE*

Grand Canyon University, AZ

Grand Valley State University, MI

Grayson County College, TX†

Grinnell College, IA*

Grove City College, PA*

Guilford College, NC*

Gustavus Adolphus College, MN*

Hampshire College, MA*

Hanover College, IN*

Harding University, AR

Hartnell College, CA*

Harvard University, MA*

Harvey Mudd College, CA*

Hastings College, NE*

Haverford College, PA

Hawaii Pacific University, HI*

Henderson State University, AR*

Hendrix College, AR*

Hillsdale College, MI*

Hobart and William Smith Colleges, NY*

Hollins College, VA

Hood College, MD*

Hope College, MI*

Houghton College, NY*

Houston Baptist University, TX*

Howard Payne University, TX*

Humboldt State University, CA*

Huntingdon College, AL

Huntington College, IN*

Idaho State University, ID†

Illinois Institute of Technology, IL*

Illinois Wesleyan University, IL*

Indiana State University, IN*

Indiana University, Bloomington, IN*

Indiana University of Pennsylvania, PA*

Indiana Wesleyan University, IN

Iowa State University, IA*

Ithaca College, NY

Jacksonville College, TX†

Jacksonville State University, AL*

James Madison University, VA*

Jan Ganmencuri College, IN

John Brown University, AR*

Johns Hopkins University, MD*

Johnson & Wales University, RI*

Johnson Bible College, TN†

Johnson State College, VT*

Judson College, IL*

Juniata College, PA*

Kalamazoo College, MI*

Kansas City Art Institute, MO*

Kansas State University, KS*

Kennesaw State University, GA*

Kent State University, OH

Kentucky Mountain Bible College, KY

Kenyon College, OH

Keystone College, PA

King College, TN*

The King's University College, Alberta, Canada

Knox College, IL*

Kutztown University of Pennsylvania, PA*

Lafayette College, PA*

Lake Forest College, IL*

Lamar University, TX*

Lancaster Bible College, PA*

Lawrence Technological University, MI

Lawrence University, WI*

Lebanon Valley College of Pennsylvania, PA†

Lee University, TN*

Lesley College, MA

LeTourneau University, TX*

Lewis and Clark College, OR*

Lewis University, IL*

Liberty University, VA*

Lincoln College, IL*

Linfield College, OR*

Lipscomb University, TN*

Loma Linda Unversity, CA*

Longwood College, VA

Louisburg College, NC†

Louisiana College, LA†

Louisiana State University and Agricultural and Mechanical College, LA*

Louisiana Tech University, LA*

Loyola College, MD*

Loyola University of Chicago, IL*

Lubbock Christian University, TX*

Luther College, IA*

Lutheran Bible Institute of Seattle, WA

Lyon College, AR

Macalaster College, MN*

Malone College, OH*

Manchester College, IN

Mansfield University of Pennsylvania, PA*

Maranatha Baptist Bible College, WI

Marian College, WI*

Marietta College, OH*

Marlboro College, VT*

Marquette University, WI*

Marshall University, WV*

Mary Baldwin College, VA

Maryland Institute College of Art, MD*

Maryville College, TN

Massachusetts College of Art, MA

Massachusetts Institute of Technology, MA*

The Master's College, CA*

McNeese State University, LA

Mesa State College, CO*

Messiah College, PA*

Miami University, OH*

Michigan State University, MI

Michigan Technological University, MI*

Middle Tennessee State University, TN*

Middlebury College, VT*

Midwestern State University, TX

Milligan College, TN*

Mills College, CA*

Millsaps College, MS

Minneapolis College of Art and Design, MN*

Mississippi College, MS*

Mississippi State University, MS*

Mississippi University for Women, MS*

Missouri Western State College, MO*

Monmouth University, NJ*

Montana State University, Billings, MT*

Montana State University, Bozeman, MT*

Montana Tech of the University of Montana, MT*

Monterey Peninsula College, CA*

Montreat College, NC

Moody Bible Institute, IL*

Moraine Park Technical College, WI

Morgan State University, MD

Mount Holyoke College, MA*

Mount Mary College, WI

Mount Vernon Nazarene College, OH*

Muhlenberg College, PA*

Murray State University, KY†

Nazareth College of Rochester, NY

Nebraska College of Technical Agriculture, NE

New College of the University of South Florida, FL*

New Mexico State University, NM*

New Mexico Institute of Mining and Technology (New Mexico Tech), NM*

New York University, NY*

Newbury College, MA

Niagara University, NY

North Carolina State University, NC*

North Central Bible College, MN†

North Central College, IL*

North Central Texas College, TX

North Georgia College, GA*

Northern Kentucky University, KY*

Northern Michigan University, MI

Northwest Christian College, OR*

Northwest College, WA*

Northwest Nazarene College, ID

Northwestern College, IA*

Northwestern College, MN*

Northwestern Michigan College, MI*

Northwestern University, IL*

Northwood University, MI*

Nyack College, NY*

Oakland University, MI

Oberlin College, OH*

Occidental College, CA*

Oglethorpe University, GA*

Ohio Northern University, OH*

Ohio State University, OH*

Ohio State University, Agricultural Technical Institute, OH

Ohio University, OH*

Ohio Wesleyan University, OH*

Oklahoma Baptist University, OK†

Oklahoma Christian University of Science and Arts, OK

Oklahoma City University, OK*

Oklahoma State University, OK

Old Dominion University, VA

Olivet Nazarene University, IL*

Oral Roberts University, OK*

Oregon Institute of Technology, OR*

Oregon State University, OR*

Otterbein College, OH*

Ouachita Baptist University, AR*

Oxford University, U.K.*

Pacific Christian College, CA†

Pacific Lutheran University, WA*

Pacific Union College, CA

Pacific University, OR†

Paul Smith's College, NY

Peace College, NC

Pennsylvania College of Technology, PA*

Pennsylvania State University, McKeesport, PA

Pennsylvania State University, University Park, PA*

Pennsylvania State University, York, PA

Pepperdine University, CA*

Philadelphia College of Bible, PA*

Philadelphia College, of Pharmacy and Science, PA*

Piedmont Bible College, NC

Polytechnic University, NY†

Pomona College, CA*

Portland State University, OR*

Potomac State College of West Virginia, WV

Pratt Institute, NY*

Prescott College, AZ

Princeton University, NJ*

Purdue University, IN*

Radford University, VA*

Randolph-Macon Woman's College, VA

Rasmussen College, Mankato, MN*

Reed College, OR*

Regis University, CO*

Reinhardt College, GA*

Rensselaer Polytechnic Institute, NY*

Rhode Island School of Design, RI*

Rhodes College, TN*

Rice University, TX*

Richard Stockton College of New Jersey, NJ*

Ricks College, ID*

Rider University, NJ

Ripon College, WI*

Roanoke College, VA

Roberts Wesleyan College, NY

Rock Valley College, IL*

Roger Williams University, RI*

Rosary Dominican University, IL*

Rose-Hulman Institute of Technology, IN*

Rutgers, State University of New Jersey, Rutgers College, NJ*

St. Andrews University, Scotland

St. Bonaventure University, NY

St. Edward's University, TX

St. Francis College, IN

St. Francis College, PA

St. John's College, MD*

St. John's College, NM*

St. John's University, MN*

St. Joseph's College, ME

St. Joseph's Hospital Health Center School of Nursing, NY

St. Joseph's University, PA*

St. Leo College, FL*

St. Louis Christian College, MO

St. Louis University, MO

St. Mary College, KS*

Saint Mary's College, IN*

St. Mary's College of Maryland, MD*

St. Mary's University, TX

St. Mary's University of Minnesota, MN

St. Norbert College, WI*

St. Olaf College, MN*

St. Philip's College, TX

St. Vincent College, PA*

Salem-Teikyo University, WV

Salisbury State University, MD

Salve Regina College, RI*

Sam Houston State University, TX

Samford University, AL*

Sarah Lawrence College, NY*

Seattle University, WA*

Seton Hall University, NJ*

Sheldon Jackson College, AK

Shelton State Community College, AL

Shepherd College, WV†

Shimer College, IL*

Shippensburg University of Pennsylvania, PA

Shorter College, GA*

Siena Heights College, MI

Simmons College, MA*

Simon's Rock College of Bard, MA*

Simpson College, CA

Smith College, MA*

Snow College, UT†

Southeastern Louisiana University, LA

Southern Adventist University, TN*

Southern Arkansas University, AR

Southern Illinois University, IL*

Southern Methodist University, TX*

Southern Nazarene University, OK*

Southwest Baptist University, MO

Southwest Texas State University, TX

Southwestern College, KS*

Southwestern Oklahoma State University, OK

Southwestern University, TX

Spring Arbor College, MI*

Spring Hill College, AL

Springfield College, MA

Stanford University, CA*

State University of New York at Binghamton, NY*

State University of New York at Buffalo, NY

State University of New York College of Agriculture and Technology, Morrisville, NY

State University of New York College of Technology, Alfred (Alfred State College), NY*

Stephen F. Austin State University, TX*

Stephens College, MO*

Sterling College, VT*

Stetson University, FL*

Stillman College, AL

Suffolk University, MA

Sul Ross State University, TX

Swarthmore College, PA*

Sweet Briar College, VA*

Syracuse University, NY*

Tarleton State University, TX*

Taylor University, IN*

Temple College, TX*

Tennessee State University, TN*

Tennessee Temple University, TN

Texas A & M University, College Station, TX*

Texas A & M University, Commerce, TX*

Texas A & M University, Corpus Christi, TX

Texas A & M University, Kingsville, TX*

Texas Christian University, TX*

Texas Tech University, TX*

Texas Woman's University, TX

Thomas Aquinas College, CA*

Thomas More College of Liberal Arts, NH*

Toccoa Falls College, GA*

Towson State University, MD*

Trevecca Nazarene University, TN

Trinity Christian College, IL†

Trinity College, CT

Trinity College of Vermont, VT

Trinity University, TX*

Trinity Western University, British Columbia, Canada*

Troy State University, AL*

Truman State University, MO

Tulane University, LA*

Union College, NE*

Union University, TN*

United States Air Force Academy, CO*

United States Coast Guard Academy, CT*

United States Military Academy, NY*

United States Naval Academy, MD*

Unity College, ME*

University of Akron, OH*

University of Alabama, Tuscaloosa, AL*

University of Alabama, Birmingham, AL

University of Alabama, Huntsville, AL

University of Alaska, Fairbanks, AK*

University of Alaska, Southeast, AK

University of Arizona, AZ

University of Arkansas, AR

University of Bridgeport, CT†

University of California, Berkeley, CA*

University of California, Davis, CA*

University of California, Los Angeles, CA

University of California, Riverside, CA*

University of California, Santa Barbara, CA

University of California, Santa Cruz, CA*

University of Charleston, WV†

University of Chicago, IL*

University of Cincinnati, OH*

University of Colorado, Boulder, CO*

University of Colorado, Colorado Springs, CO*

University of Connecticut, CT*

University of Dallas, TX*

University of Dayton, OH*

University of Delaware, DE*

University of Denver, CO*

University of Dubuque, IA*

University of Evansville, IN

University of Florida, FL*

University of Georgia, GA*

University of Hawaii, Hilo, HI*

University of Hawaii, Manoa, HI

University of Houston, TX

University of Idaho, ID*

University of Illinois, Urbana-Champaign, IL*

University of Iowa, IA*

University of Judaism, CA†

University of Kansas, KS*

University of Kentucky, KY*

University of London, U.K.

University of Louisville, KY*

University of Maine, Farmington, ME*

University of Maine, Orono, ME*

University of Mary Hardin-Baylor, TX*

University of Maryland, Baltimore, MD*

University of Maryland, College Park, MD*

University of Maryland, Eastern Shore, MD

University of Massachusetts, Amherst, MA*

University of Melbourne, Victoria, Australia

University of Memphis, TN*

University of Miami, FL*

University of Michigan, MI*

University of Minnesota, Crookston, MN

University of Minnesota, Duluth, MN*

University of Minnesota, Morris, MN*

University of Minnesota, Twin Cities, MN*

University of Mississippi, MS*

University of Missouri, Columbia, MO*

University of Missouri, Kansas City, MO*

University of Missouri, Rolla, MO*

University of Mobile, AL*

University of Montana, MT*

University of Montevallo, AL

University of Nebraska, Lincoln, NE*

University of Nevada, Reno, NV*

University of New England, ME*

University of New Hampshire, NH*

University of North Carolina, Chapel Hill, NC*

University of North Carolina, Greensboro, NC

University of North Carolina, Wilmington, NC†

University of North Dakota, ND*

University of North Texas, TX*

University of Northern Colorado, CO*

University of Notre Dame, IN*

University of Oklahoma, OK*

University of Oregon, OR*

University of Otago, Dunedin, NZ*

University of Ottawa, Ontario, Canada*

University of Pennsylvania, PA*

University of Pittsburgh, PA*

University of Portland, OR

University of Prince Edward Island, Prince Edward Island, Canada

University of Puget Sound, WA*

University of Redlands, CA*

University of Rhode Island, RI*

University of Richmond, VA

University of Rochester, NY*

University of St. Thomas, MN*

University of St. Thomas, TX

University of San Francisco, CA*

University of Saskatchewan, Saskatchewan, Canada

University of South Carolina, SC

University of South Dakota, SD*

University of Southern California, CA*

University of Southern Indiana, IN

University of Southern Maine, ME*

University of Tennessee, TN*

University of Texas, Arlington, TX*

University of Texas, Austin, TX*

University of Texas, El Paso, TX

University of Texas, San Antonio, TX

University of the Arts, PA

University of the Incarnate Word, TX

University of the South, TN

University of Toledo, OH

University of Utah, UT*

University of Vermont, VT*

University of Virginia, VA*

University of Washington, WA*

University of West Alabama, AL

University of West Florida, FL†

University of Wisconsin, Eau Claire, WI

University of Wisconsin, Green Bay, WI

University of Wisconsin, Madison, WI*

University of Wisconsin, Milwaukee, WI*

University of Wisconsin, Parkside, WI*

University of Wisconsin, Platteville, WI

University of Wisconsin, Stevens Point, WI

University of Wisconsin, Stout, WI

University of Wisconsin, Superior, WI

University of Wyoming, WY*

Ursinus College, PA*

Valdosta State University, GA*

Valley Forge Christian College, PA†

Valparaiso University, IN*

Vanderbilt University, TN*

Vassar College, NY*

Vermont Technical College, VT

Villanova University, PA*

Virginia Commonwealth University, VA*

Virginia Military Institute, VA

Virginia Polytechnic Institute and State University, VA*

Virginia Wesleyan College, VA

Viterbo College, WI*

Wabash College, IN*

Walsh University, OH

Warren Wilson College, NC*

Wartburg College, IA*

Washington and Lee University, VA

Washington Bible College, MD

Washington College, MD*

Washington University, MO*

Wayne State College, NE*

Webster University, MO*

Wellesley College, MA*

Wells College, NY*

Wesleyan University, CT*

West Chester University of Pennsylvania, PA*

West Liberty State College, WV†

West Virginia University, Parkersburg, WV*

West Virginia University, WV

West Virginia Wesleyan College, WV†

Western Baptist College, OR*

Western Maryland College, MD

Western Michigan University, MI

Western New England College, MA

Western Texas College, TX

Western Washington University, WA

Westfield State College, MA*

Westminster Choir College, of Rider University, NJ*

Westminster College of Salt Lake City, UT*

Westmont College, CA*

Wharton County Junior College, TX

Wheaton College, IL*

Wheaton College, MA*

Wheelock College, MA*

Whitman College, WA*

Whittier College, CA*

Whitworth College, WA*

Willamette University, OR*

William Jewell College, MO†

Williams College, MA*

Wilson College, PA*

Wingate University, NC*

Winona State University, MN*

Wisconsin Lutheran College, WI*

Wittenberg University, OH*

Wofford College, SC*

Worcester Polytechnic Institute, MA

Wright State University, OH*

Xavier University, OH*

Yale University, CT*

York College, NE

York College of Pennsylvania, PA

York University, Ontario, Canada*

WORKS CITED

Calvery, Robert, et al. *The Difference between Home Schooled and Public Schooled Students for Grades 4, 7, & 10 in Arkansas.* Paper presented in the Annual Meeting of the Mid-South Educational Research Association, Knoxville, Tennessee, 1992.

Chatham, April D. *Home vs. Public Schooling: What about Relationships in Adolescence?* Unpublished doctoral dissertation, University of Oklahoma, 1991.

Knowles, J. Gary. "Homeschooling and Socialization." University of Michigan Education School of Education Study press release, 1993.

Mayberry, Maralee. "Effective Learning Environments in Action: The Case of Home Schools." *School Community Journal* 3, no. 1 (1993): 61–68.

Medlin, R. G. "Predictors of Academic Achievement in Home Educated Children: Aptitude, Self-Concept, and Pedagogical Practices." *Home School Researcher* 10, no. 3 (1994): 1–7.

Rakestraw, J. *An Analysis of Home Schooling for Elementary School-Age Children in Alabama.* Unpublished doctoral dissertation, University of Alabama, Tuscaloosa, 1987.

Ray, Brian D., and John Wartes. "The Academic Achievement and Affective Development of Home-schooled Children," in *Home Schooling: Political, Historical, and Pedagogical Perspectives.* Norwood, NJ: Ablex, 1992.

Shyers, L. Edward. *Comparison of Social Adjustment between Home and Traditionally Schooled Students.* Unpublished doctoral dissertation, University of Florida, Gainesville, 1992.

Tipton, Mark. *An Analysis of Home Schooled Children's CTBS Results and Demographic Characteristics of Their Families.* Unpublished master's thesis, Antioch University, Yellow Springs, Ohio, 1990.

Wartes, J. *The Relationship of Selected Input Variables to Academic Achievement among Washington's Homeschoolers.* Woodinville, Washington: Washington Homeschool Project, 1990.

INDEX

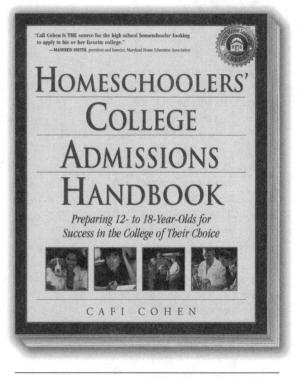

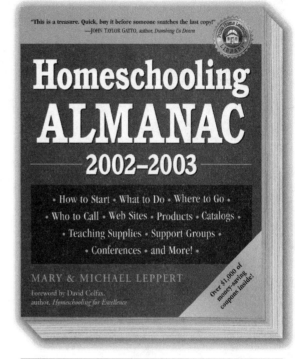